Family Tree

...on **m** Anne Young
(b.1759. Widowed twice. In 1822, Anne Young
with 5 children immigrated to Van Diemen's Land)

...e Thomson **m** William McRobie   Jeremiah Ware **m** Mary
(immigrated to Van Diemen's Land in 1822)

Anne Young McRobie **m** Jeremiah Ware
(settled in Victoria's Western District in 1838)

Fanny Govett **m** William Greene
(immigrated to Australia 1853)

Jack   May

Elisabeth MURDOCH

Two Lives

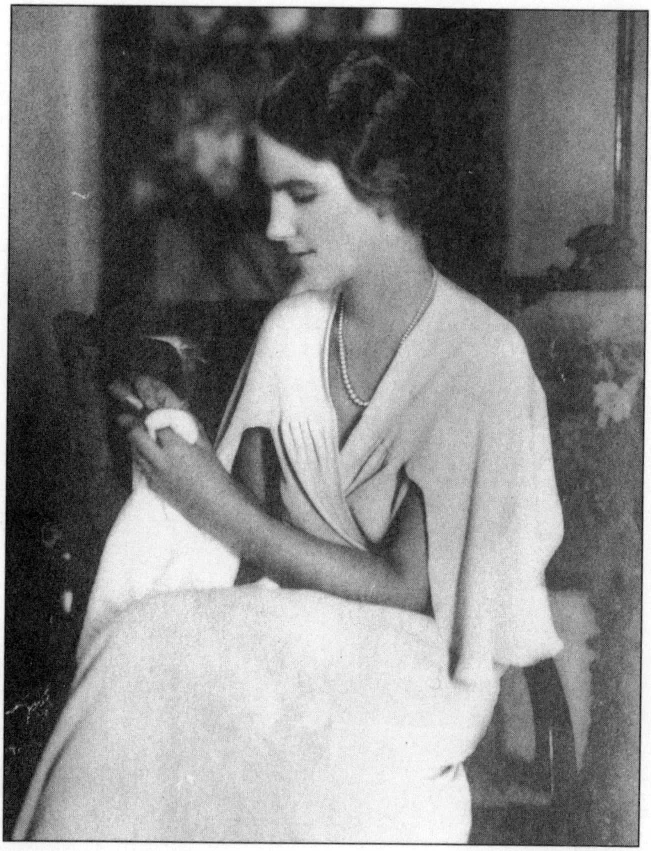

Elisabeth Murdoch

Two Lives

JOHN MONKS

MACMILLAN
AUSTRALIA

Elisabeth Joy Murdoch is donating all royalties from the sale of this book to the Royal Children's Hospital.

First published 1994 in Macmillan by Pan Macmillan Australia Pty Limited
63–71 Balfour Street, Chippendale, Sydney

Copyright © Elisabeth Joy Murdoch 1994

All rights reserved. No part of this book may be reproduced or transmitted in any form or by any means, electronic or mechanical, including photocopying, recording or by any information storage and retrieval system, without prior permission in writing from the publisher.

National Library of Australia cataloguing-in-publication data:
Monks, John, 1929– .
Elisabeth Murdoch: two lives.

ISBN 0 7329 0797 7.

1. Murdoch, Elisabeth, Dame, 1909– . 2. Women in charitable work – Victoria – Melbourne – Biography. 3. Women – Victoria – Melbourne – Biography. 4. Melbourne (Vic.) – Biography. I. Title.
361.92

Designed by Mary Callahan
Typeset in 11/16 pt Stempel Garamond by Bookset
Printed in Australia by Griffin Paperbacks

CONTENTS

List of Illustrations VII
Preface XI
Author's Note XIII

1 *The Forth Heritage* 1
2 *A Childhood in Toorak* 18
3 *Sago, Prunes and Junket* 33
4 *Waiting at the Gate* 41
5 *Carefree at Clyde* 47
6 *Coming Out* 58
7 *The Meeting* 65
8 *The Murdoch Connection* 74
9 *'I'd rather have twenty years with Keith . . .'* 89
10 *New Horizons* 99
11 *A Most Eventful Year* 107
12 *Weathering the Storm* 122
13 *The Travelling Murdochs* 129
14 *At the 'Country Seat'* 136
15 *The War Years* 146

16　*The Great Fire* 159
17　*'I think he's got it.'* 165
18　*A New Life Begins* 181
19　*In the Beginning* 190
20　*The Hospital Years* 202
21　*The Dame at Delphi* 220
22　*The National Gallery Years* 228
23　*Vintage Years* 236
24　*A Rich Tapestry* 244
25　*Well-Used Opportunities* 251
26　*Cap and Gown* 257
27　*The Murdoch Institute* 262
28　*The Garden that Grew* 267
29　*'Mothers are always right...'* 279
30　*Visions of Splendour* 287
31　*That Wedding* 296

Life with Elisabeth 301
HELEN HANDBURY 301
RUPERT MURDOCH 310
ANNE KANTOR 317
JANET CALVERT-JONES 324

Acknowledgements 332
Index 335

Endpapers: Family Tree

LIST OF ILLUSTRATIONS

Frontispiece: Elisabeth Murdoch in the 1930s.
1. Mrs Rupert Greene, in 1909, with her daughters, Marie, nine, Sylvia, six, and Elisabeth, nine months.
2. Keith, at twenty-three, just before his departure for London on 14 April 1908.
3. Elisabeth, aged eighteen months, at Pemberley.
4. Nathaniel Parker Forth, Elisabeth's great-great-grandfather, c. 1770.
5. Great-grandparents Jeremiah George Ware and wife, Anne McRobie, c. 1840–50, of Koort-Koort-Nong, near Camperdown in the Western District of Victoria.
6. The Forth Family.
7. Elisabeth's uncle, Nowell de Lancey Forth, c. 1900.
8. Elisabeth's grandfather, William Greene, as a young man, c. 1860.
9. Elisabeth's grandmother, Fanny Govett (Mrs William Greene), c. 1880.
10. The future gardener. Toddler Elisabeth at Pemberley, c. 1911.
11. Pemberley in the early 1900s – Elisabeth's childhood home.

12. Pemberley pirates.
13. A very proud father, c. 1914.
14. Elisabeth's parents, Rupert and Bairnie Greene.
15. Elisabeth's grandmother, Anne de Lancey Forth.
16. Elisabeth at Clyde, aged thirteen.
17. 'One of the nicest photographs ever taken of me.' Elisabeth at seventeen before she met Keith.
18. Eighteen-year-old Elisabeth Greene.
19. The *Table Talk* photograph of eighteen-year-old Elisabeth which attracted Keith's attention.
20. Keith Murdoch in the 1930s.
21. Keith and Elisabeth at a wedding in the 1930s follow her parents 'at a respectful distance'.
22. Keith's parents, the Rev. and Mrs Patrick Murdoch.
23. Keith – war correspondent, Gallipoli.
24. War correspondent Keith Murdoch, with map in France, 4 September, 1918.
25. Elisabeth's wedding day with sister, Marie, as bridesmaid.
26. Cruden Farm cottage before the architect's renovations in 1929.
27. Cruden Farm cottage after the architect's renovations.
28. Elisabeth holding Anne, with Rupert, 4, and Helen, 6, at Heathfield.
29. Rupert and Helen at Cruden Farm in the mid-1930s.
30. In the garden at Cruden Farm in 1932.
31. Elisabeth ready for a ride at Cruden Farm in the mid-1930s.
32. Keith and Elisabeth on their tour of inspection of Tasmanian forests in 1935.
33. Keith and Rupert Murdoch in the mid-1930s.
34. Elisabeth with Helen and Rupert at Pompeii in 1936.
35. All day picnic in the early 1930s.
36. Elisabeth, holding Anne, with Keith, Rupert and Helen in the mid-1930s.
37. Lady Gullett and Rupert in the mid-1930s.
38. Rupert – Wantabadgery holiday in the 1940s.
39. Anne recuperating in the garden at Heathfield in 1939.

List of Illustrations

40. Davey's Bay, Mt Eliza. Nanny with Anne and Helen in the late 1930s.
41. Elisabeth, with Helen and Rupert, in his Adwalton school uniform, at Heathfield in the late 1930s.
42. Albany Road, Toorak, the Murdochs' home from 1946 to 1952.
43. Helen's wedding day – with her parents at Albany Road in 1949.
44. Ready for school, Rupert, in Geelong Grammar uniform, with his father in the early 1940s.
45. A favourite photo – Sir Keith and Lady Murdoch on the steps at Cruden Farm in the late 1940s.
46. Keith Murdoch and Winston Churchill at the Empire Press Union in the late 1940s.
47. Elisabeth coming home from her overseas trip with Keith Murdoch in 1950 to a 'lovely welcome from my daughters'.
48. Rupert as a young man with Elisabeth in the early 1950s.
49. Elisabeth says 'thank you' to 3DB listeners for their donations to the Royal Children's Hospital Good Friday Appeal in the 1950s.
50. Rupert Murdoch, now 29, holds the first edition of his recently purchased Sydney *Daily Mirror* in June, 1960.
51. Elisabeth meets the Queen at the Royal Children's Hospital, 1963, with the Premier, Sir Henry Bolte and Prince Philip.
52. Dame Elisabeth watches the proceedings at the 1963 Royal opening ceremony of the Children's Hospital with Prince Philip and Henry Bolte.
53. The Queen bestowing upon Lady Murdoch the order of Dame Commander of the Most Excellent Order of the British Empire in 1963.
54. A galaxy of Dames at Dame Merlyn Myer's eightieth birthday at the National Gallery of Victoria: Dame Elisabeth, Dame Hilda Stevenson, Dame Merlyn Myer, Dame Peggy van Praagh and Dame Margaret Scott.
55. A critical eye. Elisabeth at an art exhibition.
56. Dame Elisabeth at the Victorian Tapestry Workshop.
57. A recent photograph of Dame Elisabeth and Rupert Murdoch.
58. The new honorary Doctor of Laws in 1982.
59. Walking along the Great Wall of China with Alison Leslie in 1984.

60. Elisabeth and Michael Morrison with Douglas Stephen's sculpture, *Pisces*, at Cruden Farm.
61. Dame Elisabeth, her golf buggy and Lily the dog.
62. Cruden Farm's driveway with the beautiful lemon-scented gums.
63. The lake at Cruden Farm.
64. Cruden Farm in bloom.
65. The picking garden at Cruden Farm.
66. Rupert Murdoch outside the Herald and Weekly Times in Flinders Street, Melbourne, in the late 1980s.
67. A face in the crowd – Elisabeth beams her approval at the press conference as the Herald and Weekly Times returns to the family in 1987.
68. The Governor-General, Bill Hayden, bestowing upon Dame Elisabeth the Companion of the Order of Australia in 1991.
69. Elisabeth and Inge King supervise the placement of the sculptor's work beside the lake at McClelland Gallery in the early 1990s.
70. Dame Elisabeth at home in the sitting room, the 'soul' of Cruden Farm, in 1993.
71. Dame Elisabeth and her son, Rupert, in the 1990s.
72. Rupert Murdoch and his daughter, Elisabeth, at her wedding in 1993.
73. Elisabeth Murdoch's marriage to Elkin Pianim in Los Angeles.
74. Family photo taken in 1989 on Dame Elisabeth's eightieth birthday.
75. Helen Handbury.
76. Rupert Murdoch.
77. Anne Kantor.
78. Janet Calvert-Jones.

PREFACE

My life has been truly a most fortunate and happy one and I do want to finally express my warm appreciation of the wonderful support of my parents over my long life, and also of my family, friends and all the splendid people who made it possible for me to be of some use within the community.

Of course, my husband is at the top of the list. In himself he was an inspiration and largely responsible for the best qualities in our precious children. And then there were those unforgettable men and women who were so loyal in the background of our home and garden. Our beloved Nanny, Sarah Russell, and dedicated governess, Kimpo; two devoted maids, English sisters who were the ongoing strength of a large and loyal household, alas, all no longer alive; a succession of devoted gardeners and farm managers who have also been a great comfort.

When still very young, I had the opportunity to work for the

Royal Children's Hospital. Several notable women, Lady Latham, Mrs H. B. Higgins, and Mrs J. J. Fogarty, were my early mentors and a great example to me. And through my long years of working for the hospital, my life has been enhanced by a multitude of friendships.

In later years, a host of colleagues, friends and relations have encouraged and supported me in the various involvements which still hold my interest, among whom Mr Jack Kennedy, my friend and financial adviser, has been outstanding.

I am deeply grateful for the warmth of affection which has always flowed around me.

I want to thank John Monks most sincerely for his gallant effort to portray accurately and interestingly this overall picture of my antecedents, my descendants and my life.

When we began, I intended to simply make an account for my family of what has passed, before records and memories were lost forever. Since then it has all grown.

Now I dedicate this book to my children and grandchildren and all those who will follow them.

Elisabeth Murdoch

AUTHOR'S NOTE

A WEEK or so into my cadetship with *The Herald* in 1948, I was carrying race results from the fourth floor radio room to the sub-editors a floor below.

With youthful enthusiasm, I by-passed the lift, bounded down the stairs and launched myself into the air five or six steps from the bottom. Unfortunately, the man who had just given me my first job was turning the corner when I landed, sending us both sprawling over the editorial floor lobby. 'I'm sorry,' was all I could gasp as I helped him to his feet.

'You're in a hurry, young man,' was the reply as I tried to explain about the urgent race results needed for Saturday's late edition stop press. 'Well, you had better be on your way then,' said the smiling Sir Keith Murdoch, proprietor of *The Herald*, as he went up the stairs to the compositors room.

A week or so later as I sat trying to type some small paragraph with two fingers, I looked up to see Sir Keith standing by my desk. 'This is John Monks, one of our keen new cadets,' he told Lady Murdoch, then making one of her regular after-deadline visits to the reporters room.

It was Sir Keith who encouraged and assisted many young reporters, including myself, to make our first foray into London's Fleet Street, so when, more than forty years later, I was asked to help Dame Elisabeth prepare her memoirs 'for the family', I was delighted to begin what became a fascinating project.

JOHN MONKS

CHAPTER ONE

The Forth Heritage

THE CLOUDS OF WAR were already gathering over the fragmented kingdoms and dictatorships of old Europe as, in London in the early spring of 1909, a tall twenty-two-year-old Australian watched with Calvinistic disapproval the glittering pomp and circumstance surrounding the State opening of Parliament by King Edward VII and Queen Alexandra. 'It was all a beastly humbug...', the unimpressed young Australian, who frequently expressed dismay at the starkly contrasting poverty he saw in London, wrote home to his father, the Reverend Patrick Murdoch, a Scottish-born Presbyterian minister who twenty-five years earlier had migrated to Australia with his family.

Keith Murdoch was a typical God-fearing son of the manse and like Max Aitken, the future Lord Beaverbrook, and many others of similar colonial birth and stern Scots upbringing, he had the inborn genius and drive to make him a formidable force in the world of publishing. But he was sadly already planning to return home to Melbourne after his first failed bid to break into journalism in London's mecca of newspapermen, Fleet Street. This was a dream that had been frustrated by a severe speech impediment, a stammer which, try as he may, he could not control. Despite Murdoch's undoubted intellect and impressive presence, that stammer, always made worse when the shy Australian confronted prospective employers, seemed forever to preclude a career in the fast-talking profession of journalism.

With the Royal opening and the King's speech from the throne disposed of, the British House of Commons sanctioned the building of six more dreadnoughts for the Royal Navy to counter the threat posed by the German Kaiser's growing naval might. In Melbourne, a loyal outpost of Empire whose citizens still spoke of Britain as 'home', the fledgling Australian Government dutifully ordered two new-fangled steam torpedo boats, and a school was opened to train Light Horse troopers. But for the most part on Monday 8 February 1909, the day on which Elisabeth Greene was born in Melbourne to a family steeped in the traditions of the Anglo-Irish 'Ascendency', the staid, church-going people of that city were expressing outrage that a Miss Freda Cuthbert was that night preparing to perform her daring Salome Dance, with seven veils, at the popular Wax Works.

Half a world apart on that day, Keith Murdoch and his Elisabeth Greene were not even destined to meet for another eighteen years. They were to be eighteen momentous years. Years in which the young Murdoch was to fight and overcome that stammer, help change the course of the First World War and quickly rise to spectacular international fame and fortune in journalism – the profession that had spurned him in London in 1909.

* * *

Elisabeth Greene was the third daughter of Rupert Greene, a popular and astute first generation Australian who had already won respect in Britain and Australia as an expert valuer in the booming Empire wool trade. A devil-may-care horseman and sports all-rounder, Rupert Greene's batting skills would have won him a place in the Australian Cricket Team had the demands of the wool trade allowed. Unfortunately, young Rupert Greene's skills were less obvious when applied to the sport of kings.

Elisabeth's mother was the beautiful, dignified Marie de Lancey Forth, Australian-born daughter of a distinguished Anglo-Irish family with a long and exciting history of service to Crown and community and a proud ancient family motto upheld by generation after generation of her forebears: 'A Forth Never Yields'. There are even earlier historic references to members of the family Forth whose seat was at the Manor of Ballymacormack in County Longford in the Irish province of Leinster, but at the first major clash of the Civil War, the 1642 battle of Edgehill, in the beech woods and green fields near Stratford-upon-Avon, Lieutenant General Nathaniel Forth dramatically changed the course of the battle.

More than five thousand Englishmen were left dead on that Civil War field, but Forth, unwillingly impressed into the Parliamentary army, is reported as having taken his regiment of cavalry from the Roundhead ranks and crossed over to the Royalist Cavaliers. This loyal act at a critical point of the battle was later credited with temporarily saving the doomed King Charles II, and leaving the way to London open for him and his forces. Forth was grievously wounded but, by the time the Monarchy was restored, he had recovered sufficiently to be made Secretary of War by a grateful Charles II.

Just forty-eight years later, in the same province as the Forths' Longford estates which were well beyond what was then known as the English Pale, or safe enclave, Colonel Samuel Forth prepared for the critical Battle of the Boyne. Forth, who lived at Ballymacormack Manor – now sadly almost swallowed up beneath the ancient bogs – was High Sheriff of County Longford and a Colonel in Wolseley's Regiment of Horse. At the historic battle, Forth was aide-de-camp to the seventy-year-old Marshal Friedrich Schomberg, a veteran German mercenary soldier who was the favourite general of William of Orange.

Two Kings of England, Protestant William III with his army of English, Dutch and Huguenot troops, and Catholic James II with a much smaller force of Irish soldiers led by French and English Catholic officers, faced each other across the River Boyne that tragic day. Neither could have imagined that the outcome of the next few hours of furious fighting would still be a bitter, burning issue in Ireland and beyond more than three hundred years later. In fact, William's force easily won the day, storming across the river fords and fighting on the banks until James was forced to retreat to Dublin and then flee to France, his hopes of restoration to the British throne ended forever. But in the clash of mounted men and foot soldiers, Schomberg was fatally wounded and Forth, fighting near his commander's side, received wounds that nearly cost him his life. It was that gallant Colonel Forth's son, the remarkable Nathaniel Parker Forth, later a Court Chamberlain to King George III, who really gave this most loyal of British families, 'The Fighting Forths', their place in history.

Nathaniel, Elisabeth's great-great-grandfather, ran a brilliant secret British intelligence network on the Continent during both the French and American Revolutions to frustrate French efforts to help their American allies oust the British. Britain's Lord Chief Justice, Lord Mansfield, had dubbed the tireless Forth 'Mercury' and was soon telling King George that the messenger of the gods was 'a sluggard

The Forth Heritage

compared to Forth'. As a trusted British Royal agent, with instructions to remain as close as possible to the threatened French Royal Family, Forth found time to outwit a London-based plot to blackmail Marie Antoinette and, later, recover the stolen jewels of the vulgar Royal mistress Comtesse Du Barry, before both ladies went to the guillotine. To this day, Nathaniel Forth is also credited with introducing English-style horseracing – and racehorses – to France. By the 1770s, during one of his longest periods of productive sanity, King George was heaping praise and promises of honours on Nathaniel, now also his Ambassador, or Minister Plenipotentiary, at the Court of Versailles. After one particular Forth triumph of diplomatic espionage over the French, King George proclaimed: 'Forth does wonders. He is like a light sent from Heaven.'

Soon the King's Prime Minister, William Pitt, had dispatched Forth on another perilous mission to Paris, this time to try to negotiate the cession of Canada as a price for peace with France. Instead, Forth returned to Britain with proof that the French Committee of Public Safety was plotting to assassinate both King George and Pitt, and had actually sent a squad of hired murderers to Windsor – a disclosure which probably saved the King's life and strengthened the Royal resolve to stand firm against Britain's old enemy. Later, while still on secret Royal service on the Continent recovering financial documents on which it was said – probably with some accuracy – the honour and credit of the Prince of Wales depended, Forth was stabbed by French agents but still managed to carry out his sensitive mission, to the delight and relief of the future King.

But perhaps the activity that most endeared Nathaniel Forth to the Royal Family was his unwilling role as a fundraiser for the profligate Prince of Wales and his brothers. Asked to assemble the then astronomical sum of £300,000 to meet some pressing Royal debts, Forth soon presented the princes with £350,000. Then for good measure, Forth renounced his own cast-iron claim to the riches of the Duchy of Cornwall, heavily pledged to him by the near-bankrupt Prince Regent and his brother princes. He was never fully repaid.

A contemporary French description of Nathaniel Forth survives in which he is said to be 'a most adept master of the Machiavellian arts'. He was also said to be a man who 'beneath a scatter-brained appearance concealed an infinity of understanding'. Scornfully the French went on to label Forth as: 'A thorough-going royalist nursed in the lap of despotism. The most dangerous man on French soil, and the first to be got rid of.' Many not as fleet of foot and mind as Forth lost their heads for far less in those terrible times. Still in the Forth family archives are letters from the kings, emperors, statesmen and generals of Europe applauding the abilities, integrity, fidelity and discretion of Nathaniel Forth, clearly a latter-day man for all seasons, with more than a touch of the Scarlet Pimpernel's dashing fictional style.

While steadfastly loyal to Britain and its monarchs to the end, Nathaniel Forth chose Paris as his final home and in April, 1804, at the age of fifty-nine, he married the strikingly beautiful nineteen-year-old Eliza Petrie, daughter of a business partner, John Petrie, who was a member of the British Parliament and a wealthy East India trader. By now Forth's health was declining, but nevertheless, in 1808, Eliza presented him with their first son, Frederick. However, the Royal agent extraordinaire died before their second son, Alexandre, was born a year later. Left in poor circumstances, Eliza quickly re-married, this time into the noble French family of Rouen. Frederick carried on the surviving British line of Forths, while Alexandre was adopted by his stepfather, Baron Rouen, and continued the French connection which still flourishes and bears the Forth name to this day.

The Forth Heritage

Frederick joined the British army and served in the 75th Foot – later the Gordon Highlanders – and then the Royal Scots Fusiliers. Dispatched on some typically Forth undercover mission to Paris during the Three Day Revolution in 1830, the twenty-five-year-old officer was contacted by the wily French statesman, Prince Talleyrand. Clearly remembering the unique and troublesome talents of Frederick's father, Nathaniel, Talleyrand tried to persuade Frederick to leave the British army and take a senior appointment with the government of France. It was an offer that Forth had no difficulty in rejecting. Then, in 1833 while still a young captain, Frederick sailed with a detachment of his regiment aboard the fetid convict transport ship, *Atlas*, bound for the distant penal colony of Van Diemen's Land. Also with him on that grim four-month journey were two hundred male convicts, his young, pregnant wife Caroline Jemima, née Sherson, and their eleven-month-old daughter Minnie.

Three years before the Forths arrived in Hobart Town the Lieutenant Governor, Colonel George Arthur, had founded the notorious British prison at Port Arthur and had sought to provide the final solution to the problem of the Tasmanian Aboriginals by forming a line of three thousand soldiers and settlers and driving the remnants of the tribes onto a small peninsula. A year later he shipped all the surviving Aboriginals off to Flinders Island in storm-tossed Bass Strait.

Undoubtedly Arthur was a martinet, hated by many free settlers – although considered by others to be reasonably humane by the standards of that age. After establishing the tragic Port Arthur prison complex he maintained stern, but some would say fair, discipline on the unfortunate convicts in his charge. History shows that Arthur, who as Sir George Arthur later became Lieutenant Governor of Upper Canada, and then Governor of Bombay, India, was a fine colonial administrator. Certainly he spotted the talents of the keen young Captain Forth soon after he reported to his regimental headquarters and was posted to the Government House staff in Hobart.

Before long, Forth had become Tasmania's first visiting magistrate, and, two years later, he was appointed aide-de-camp to Arthur and given command of the Colonial Mounted Police, beginning a very early and important Australian connection for the family Forth. By 1834, Captain Forth and his family were well established in Hobart Town, that mellow gem of British colonial cities, where convict chain gangs daily shuffled past the shops and houses as they built the roads and drainage system. Deeply troubled by the treatment of the prisoners, Forth prepared Arthur's firm but just code of standing regulations for the management of convicts which brought some comfort to their miserable and hopeless lives. Although often in disagreement with Arthur's authoritarian style of government and ruthless press censorship, Forth was publicly loyal to him. Later, after resigning his commission, Frederick Forth became the convict colony's Coroner and Director-General of the road network then being painfully cut by convict chain gangs over the craggy mountains and through the dense rainforests of what is known today as Tasmania.

Under Forth's instructions, prudent means were to be used by overseers to restrain the chain gang members from using profane language. At the same time Forth ordered: 'Their food must be wholesome and well-cooked and no pains must be omitted to secure every convict his full ration ... Harsh and abusive language on the part of superintendents and overseers is at all times interdicted and a kind anxiety is to be manifested to secure to the convicts as much comfort as is consistent with their conditions under the regulations of the Government.' In this day and age in Australia Frederick Forth, who served for fifteen years in the Empire's principle penal colony, would probably have been called 'a bleeding heart liberal'.

The Forth Heritage

With reports from Arthur and succeeding governors, including Arctic explorer Sir John Franklin, singing his praises and acclaiming his ability, zeal, integrity and singleness of purpose, Forth was not forgotten back in London. In 1848, after his long stay in what was certainly regarded as the hardship post of Tasmania, Forth, Caroline and a family which had by now grown to nine, began the voyage back to England. Before they left, a gifted convict artist, possibly Thomas Griffiths Wainewright, transported for the term of his natural life to Tasmania for forgery, executed a charming portrait of Alfred Charles Forth, thirteen, and his brother, Robert de Lancey Forth, then twelve and later destined to be Elisabeth's grandfather. Robert was given the name 'de Lancey', in honour of Frederick's godfather, Sir William de Lancey, the Duke of Wellington's trusted Quartermaster-General and lifelong friend.

Back in London, Frederick Forth was soon appointed President and Lieutenant-Governor of the Turks and Caicos Islands when those West Indies islands were separated from the Bahamas. During his term in office, Forth built schools, superior lighthouses and canals, and even managed to rapidly liquidate a hefty public debt. Senior colonial service in Hong Kong and China followed.

The fame of generation after generation of Forths in British ruling and military circles continued to spread when Frederick Forth's eldest son, Alfred, joined the British Army. His second son, Robert, never forgetting his boyhood days in Tasmania, returned with another brother, Henry, to Australia in 1860 – a country which he believed had a great and prosperous future. After travelling around Australia and returning briefly to Tasmania, now free of convicts and their British army guards, Robert became interested in sheep farming. He had inherited the family love of horses and was an accomplished horseman long before he arrived in Warrnambool, on the coast of Victoria's Western District.

ELISABETH MURDOCH

In the hot, dry summer of 1877, the illustrious Forth family became linked with another pioneering British family. The Ware family, Jeremiah, Mary and their four children from Chesham, Buckinghamshire, had migrated to Van Diemen's Land in 1822, accompanied by a nurse and two male servants. Jeremiah was a young artillery expert, probably a civilian with army experience, appointed to be officer-in-charge of the island's ordnance store at a time when there were still fears about both French and Russian intentions in the Pacific. Although no record remains, during their years in Tasmania there is no doubt that the paths of the Wares and Forths crossed in the small Hobart Town community where the people were always anxious to seek out new arrivals and learn of the latest happenings 'at home'.

In 1838, brothers Jeremiah (Junior), and Joseph Ware crossed treacherous Bass Strait for mainland Australia where they landed with their flock of sheep and headed for the rich grazing land of the Western District near Camperdown where they became squatters. By the time their brother, John, the first of four more Ware children born in Hobart, had turned seventeen and joined them in 1844, the brothers were running big flocks of sheep on their first vast holdings near Colac. In 1851 Jeremiah, now a prosperous grazier, married a beautiful Hobart girl, Anne Young McRobie, granddaughter of Anne Young and John Thomson.

Anne Young was born in Edinburgh in 1759. In 1780, she married an Edinburgh merchant, Hugh Murray. Later, widowed with a grown family, she married Edinburgh lawyer John Thomson. In 1822, again widowed and now a sprightly sixty-three, she began the greatest adventure of her life.

The combined Murray and Thomson families, including Anne's three sons and two daughters, set sail in a small ship, the *Urania*, chartered by the family, a rare arrangement in those days. After a tedious voyage, with land sighted at Madeira, then a long delay at Cape Town, the family arrived in Hobart Town in January 1823 with all the merchandise necessary for a new settlement, and accompanied by a carpenter, blacksmith, ploughman, shepherd and servant. Family members took up land under the Grant of Land system, which allotted them land free of rates and taxes and guaranteed them more land as the original holding was improved. Until she died at the age of seventy-three, Anne lived with her son, Hugh Murray, on their property at St Leonards in Tasmania.

A daughter from Anne's second marriage, Anne Thomson, married William McRobie, a young Scot, and it was their daughter, christened Anne Young McRobie, who was to later marry Jeremiah Ware in Hobart. The Wares' daughter, yet another Anne, was born in 1855 on her parents' 32,000 acre property, Koort-Koort-Nong, sprawling over volcanic hills and plains near Camperdown, 150 miles west of Melbourne. It was Anne Ware who was to marry Tasmanian-born Robert de Lancey Forth, now a renowned horseman and manager of Dwaroon sheep station near Warrnambool, not far on the vast Australian scale of distances, from the splendid bluestone residence the Wares had built on their land. In what appears to have become a family marriage tradition, Robert was much older, forty-two, while his bride was just twenty-one.

Their daughter, Marie – Bairnie – de Lancey Forth, future mother of Dame Elisabeth Murdoch, was born and brought up in the Forth tradition as an English gentlewoman at Dwaroon, and attended a small private boarding school called Shipley, in Melbourne's fashionable South Yarra. Bairnie's eldest brother, Nowell de Lancey Forth, born at Dwaroon in 1879 and educated at Geelong Grammar School, was destined to become an officer hailed by his military peers as being of the calibre of Lawrence of Arabia – without the controversy and tragedy that surrounded Lawrence's well-publicised and remarkably parallel career. Forth, known to his fellow officers as de Lancey, loved the desert and its people and was said to be 'a man apart – exalted – almost spiritual'.

At eighteen, Nowell had left school and travelled north to Queensland to work as a jackeroo on the three-million-acre Sesbania sheep station on the head-waters of the Diamantina River. But then the Boer War broke out and Nowell, a member of a family which had produced a line of soldiers from father to son with only one break since 1670, rode off on a journey of several hundred miles to Brisbane. There he joined the 4th (Queensland Imperial Bushmen) Contingent, a regiment of skilled rough-riding horsemen. Promoted to Sergeant after action on the Orange River and in the Transvaal, Nowell was in fierce fighting against the Boers at Zilikats Nek and was invalided back to Australia.

At the end of the Boer War, Nowell was offered a commission in Kitchener's Imperial forces and joined the Manchester Regiment in Britain before being posted to the Sudan and other Middle East trouble spots as a Bimbashi – Battalion Commander – in the Camel Corps. At the age of twenty-one he had already been mentioned in dispatches and awarded the Military Cross. In 1914 he was in command of the British forces on the Abyssinian frontier when he volunteered to join his old unit, the Manchester Regiment, then being decimated under fire on the Western Front. Emerging unscathed from the trenches in France, he was sent to Palestine as Commander of the 3rd Battalion of the crack Imperial Camel Corps, made up of Australians, New Zealanders, Britons and Sikhs.

Leading a camel charge against the Turks at Gaza, Colonel Forth rode relentlessly on despite a bullet in the shoulder and bullet holes in his helmet which he laughed off by saying: 'That bullet scorched the hair on my head. I fear those blighters over there have spoiled a

The Forth Heritage

brand new helmet.' Four weeks later, he was playing a leading role in the successful advance on Jerusalem.

Back in Australia in 1917, Elisabeth Greene, then eight, was proud to learn that her dashing uncle had been awarded the Distinguished Service Order and bar for his courage and leadership in these engagements. These new honours went with his MC and chest full of decorations and service medals including ribbons for the Order of the Nile and the Order of the Mejidieh. Nowell de Lancey Forth also found time to be made a fellow of the Royal Geographic Society for his explorations in search of the legendary oasis of Zehzura, still lost beneath the shifting dunes in the middle of the scorching Libyan desert. Finally appointed Commander of British Forces in the whole of Northern Egypt, Nowell ended his distinguished army career with his body weakened by wounds and years of hardship while serving in the Empire's harshest climes. He returned briefly to Australia to see Bairnie and her family but died, unmarried, in Alexandria, Egypt, in 1933, surrounded by friends with whom he was still planning to mount another search for his lost oasis.

Elisabeth's great-grandfather, Jeremiah Ware, had died at the early age of forty-one as the result of a horse and buggy accident. He had made a name for himself in his adopted state of Victoria as a great horseman and owned thousands of acres of rich sheep and cattle grazing land. He was also elected as a member of Victoria's first parliament and, when he died, a newspaper obituary said this of the much-loved pioneer grazier: 'Had all been like him, the country would surely have been Australia Felix.' Sadly Jeremiah died intestate and much litigation was to be required before his affairs were finally settled. His widow Anne lived for another eight years and married James Aitkin. When she died, the Ware children were brought to Melbourne as wards of state while a famous legal battle was fought over the estate.

Finally, after a less than happy childhood, Anne did finally inherit a substantial interest in her father's large estate, which was just as well for Robert had inherited grandfather Nathaniel Forth's passionate interest in gambling, horses and horseracing. At Dwaroon, Robert became an expert 'whip' who delighted in driving the state governor's four-in-hand whenever he visited the Western District. Like many Australians, Robert's love of the turf was almost obsessive. He even established a private racecourse on his flat land near Mt Emu Creek. Sadly, his gambling debts mounted, with Anne Forth forced to use her inheritance to meet the constant demands. Then, with their four children still at school, there was more tragedy for Anne when Robert died. He had been out riding when he got caught in a deluge of rain. His clothes dried out on him and he caught a cold that proved fatal when it turned into pneumonia.

In the normal progression of the harsh Australian climate, bushfire followed flood and, not long after Robert's death, the extensive Dwaroon stables were completely destroyed. Country friends rallied around but life was clearly difficult for Robert Forth's widow. Frequently, food for the growing family was sparse. Somehow they managed and admiring locals called Anne the 'Little Trojan' as she moved to a small farm on the banks of the Hopkins River near Warrnambool and scraped up the money to send Nowell, his brother Jack, and sister Bairnie, to good schools. Sadly May missed out, but cleverly educated herself by reading all the books in the Forth library. Elisabeth believes that early undernourishment affected the health of Bairnie and the other Forth children in later life.

No one knows now where Bairnie and Rupert Greene first met at the turn of the century, although Elisabeth believes it could have been at one of those country race meetings – perhaps even the Mt Emu Creek picnic races – that brought the scattered families of the Western District together every few months. Certainly Rupert

The Forth Heritage

Greene, already a daring, pipe-smoking horseman with an infectious smile and all the charm of his Anglo-Irish forebears, did meet the beautiful Bairnie de Lancey Forth when they were both in their early twenties. He immediately fell in love with the graceful young girl with the trim waist and soft, cultured English accent.

Rupert's father, William Greene, was born in Drogheda, site of the Battle of the Boyne and within a short distance of the old Forth estates in Longford, in the same province of Leinster in Ireland. If the adventurous Forths had lived beyond the Pale, the Greenes were brought up well within that social and religious Anglo-Irish enclave. Before he was twenty-five, William was a skilled railway engineer with Spanish railway experience and an impressive engineering degree from Trinity College, Dublin. He migrated to Australia in 1853. Rupert's mother was an English beauty who, before her marriage to William Greene, was Fanny Govett. She was admired for her wisdom and charm in the professional engineering circles in which her husband moved. The migrant Govetts owned big tracts of fine land in Eastern Australia before eight years of drought in Queensland caused them to lose much of what they had worked so hard to secure.

However, William and Fanny Greene managed to live in some style at Avington, an early mansion in St Kilda Road, Melbourne's wide, tree-lined avenue leading to the city. William Greene soon rose to be a Commissioner in the rapidly expanding Victorian state railway system. It was William Greene who planned and constructed the long railway viaduct leading along the Yarra River to Melbourne's central railway station – now the Flinders Street Railway Station and still one of the world's busiest city rail terminals. At the time, David Syme, the crusty, opinionated proprietor of Melbourne's *Age* newspaper, attacked the new viaduct as 'Greene's Folly', but it is still in constant use nearly one hundred years later carrying the trains servicing Melbourne's vast suburban network.

Rupert Greene was educated at fashionable Toorak College and Elisabeth still has the handsome silver cup he won there for being the best sports all-rounder in 1890. While his mother and father were away on a business trip to Japan, Rupert Greene was left in the charge of an aunt and his older sisters, Ethel and Olive. Soon the irrepressible Rupert was on crutches after breaking a leg, but that didn't stop him climbing onto the roof of his parents' two-storey house. Balanced precariously on his crutches, Rupert refused to heed the pleas for him to come down – unless he was promised more pocket money. There is no family record of the outcome of that impasse, but Elisabeth suspects that her father won the day.

Sadly, both Rupert Greene's parents died before Elisabeth was born, but Bairnie and her mother, Grannie Forth, would recount details of the courtship to Elisabeth and her sisters and laugh at the remarkable proviso that had been laid down when she was taken to meet Fanny. Enchanted by the innocent beauty of Bairnie de Lancey Forth and being only too aware of her son's wild ways, the wise Fanny Greene had welcomed the couple's engagement but insisted that before the wedding Bairnie must move into the Greene home for three months: 'So that she would know what she was taking on.'

As Elisabeth says today: 'My father must have been on his best behaviour because after those three months my mother took him on with love and optimism.' In 1900, Bairnie de Lancey Forth married Rupert Greene, uniting two Anglo-Irish families from the same Leinster Province. Two daughters, Marie and Sylvia, were born at Karuah, the first Greene home in Kooyong Road, Malvern. The births were difficult. Newborn baby Marie was left for some time safely swaddled in the empty fireplace while anxious doctors fought to save her mother's life.

Bairnie and Rupert journeyed to England when Sylvia was six months old and her sister Marie just three, so that Rupert, employed by the prosperous New Zealand Loan and Mercantile Agency with good future prospects, could learn more about the highly specialised wool trade in Bradford. The indomitable Grannie Forth and Bairnie's sister May, moved in to look after the two young girls while their parents were away. Soon after their return to Australia, the Greenes were shown Pemberley, a modest but comfortable and solid villa, ideally situated on Toorak Road then, as now, Melbourne's most fashionable suburban thoroughfare. Here the Greenes were still living in February, 1909, when Elisabeth was born at Windarra Hospital just around the corner from Pemberley – as a precaution, in view of Bairnie's past difficulties.

This then was the multifaceted family heritage of Elisabeth Greene – a coming together of brave Anglo-Irish, English, Scottish and Australian military men, strong, beautiful women, diplomats, pioneers, migrants and farmers, all brought up to believe in the twin ethics of hard work and adventurous loyal service.

CHAPTER TWO

A Childhood in Toorak

RUPERT GREENE, although clearly yearning for a son and heir, doted on his new daughter and wanted to name her Joy. Bairnie preferred Elisabeth. So Elisabeth Joy Greene she was christened ... and from the start Rupert established almost a father–son relationship with his lively little daughter. To this day Elisabeth remembers her indulgent father allowing her to puff his pipe – as he would later secretly allow his grandchildren to do – and Elisabeth shudders as she recalls accepting her father's early dare to chew a small plug of pipe tobacco. 'I was terribly ill and mother was furious with us,' Elisabeth laughs more than seventy years later.

Toorak, the leafy suburb where land now ranks among the world's most expensive residential real estate, was where the Greene family lived, just five miles from the heart of Melbourne. Then Toorak was still largely divided into paddocks, market gardens and big estates dominated by the mansions funded by pioneer land-dealing and lucky strikes on the rich Victorian gold fields. A 1909 map shows that Pemberley, the Greenes' single-storey brick home built on solid bluestone foundations, was next door to a large market garden later to be divided up into residential lots. The purchase turned out to be a very sound family investment. 'Often, over the years, it was the means by which we survived as, on a number of occasions when my father's finances were in dire straits, we were able to let the house for a very good rent and move into less expensive lodgings,' says Elisabeth. She recalls that in the back garden of Pemberley there was a laundry converted from a rough bush cottage with a bluestone clinker floor, which had been the first shepherd's cottage erected in early colonial times when Toorak was one vast sheep and cattle run. Pemberley also had a small stable which would one day be converted to a garage.

Before the gold rush caused Melbourne to burst at its seams and sprawl towards the blue Dandenong Ranges in the north-east, the lush land of Toorak was known as 'the finest farm in Australia'. Homesick Britons planted English trees and cypress hedges along the wide roadways and laid out rose gardens and shrubberies in the fertile black soil. Every grand mansion had stables for the horses that still, at the turn of the century, drew the carriages.

While her earliest memories are of the cable trams rattling past her front gate in Toorak Road, Elisabeth recalls that in those days horse-drawn carriages and vans still outnumbered puttering Edwardian motor cars. Until a few years before Elisabeth was born, wattle bark would be spread over the roadway outside the mansions in times of family illness to deaden the sound of horses' hooves in the night. Como, the gracious colonial mansion owned by the Armytage family and now preserved by the National Trust, was only a short distance from Pemberley, and the Greenes' nanny would often wheel Elisabeth in her pram down the track towards the Yarra River while her two elder sisters scampered alongside.

Those carefree outings ended – as did the employment of that nanny – when a bull charged the walkers as they were crossing a paddock near what is now the Como Park cricket oval. Terrified, the nanny ran off leaving Elisabeth and her pram in the path of the angry bull. Fortunately, the animal lost interest as Nanny, Marie and Sylvia Greene fled.

Elisabeth had another adventure in her pram, too. This time she was being pushed up Toorak Road by a nurse, with Sylvia and Marie holding on to either side of the pram, when a dog catcher lassoed the family dog 'Scamp', an Australian terrier. Sylvia can still remember the children 'setting up a tremendous bellow, as the whole of Toorak Village rushed to our defence and tried to make the man release Scamp – which he wouldn't. Much to his rage, Dad had to come and pay him ten shillings before he'd give Scamp back.'

Later, at the age of three or four, Elisabeth remembers being regularly taken by her sisters for a walk of a few hundred yards up Toorak Road to the exciting shopping centre, even then known as 'The Village', to buy snowballs – two for a halfpenny – at Miss Kane's sweet shop and admire the horses being led in and out of Patrick's Livery Stables and the Williams bakery. Elisabeth can, to this day, point out the location of the shops once occupied by Crotty the greengrocer, Mrs White the Draper, Hall's shoe store – where Elisabeth's first shoes cost two shillings and sixpence a pair – and the house where Dr Reginald Morrison, the handsome Scottish family physician and friend, lived.

Early photographs of those carefree days show the Greene sisters manning a 'boat' fashioned from an upturned wheelbarrow, bricks, planks and a wicker chair in the garden. Young David Morrison, toy gun held threateningly, is the captain and already there is a mischievous glint in Elisabeth's eye not covered by unruly blonde locks. In rumpled smock, socks down around her ankles and straw hat at a jaunty angle, she is clearly the tomboy who brought so much joy to Rupert Greene and encouraged him to spend less time with his hard-drinking sporting friends at the Bohemian Club and Melbourne Club.

In the days before television or computer games, the pretty Greene girls and their friends would play happily and dare each other to climb the fence into the spacious garden of Aroona and attempt to run around the oak tree in the middle of the lawns and return to the safety of Pemberley without being caught by the frustrated Aroona gardener. But Elisabeth also remembers making her own fun while her sisters were studying with their governess in the schoolroom. At first the three girls shared a room with their governess, sleeping together in the night nursery. But when she was not learning to read Elisabeth often amused herself in the garden and, almost as soon as she could walk, she learnt to scramble up the trees growing in the Pemberley garden. Soon she was able to perch up in the branches, and wave to the grip-men and conductors on the passing cable trams. Elisabeth knew them all and in those friendly days they would ring their bells and wave to the little girl high up in the leafy branches.

Elisabeth's sister, today Mrs Sylvia Ritchie, still stands by her early recollections that the youngest Greene was spoilt outrageously by their father and was quite capable of lying on the floor, kicking her legs and screaming if she didn't always get her way. This is a charge Elisabeth laughingly denies. However, Sylvia insists: 'You can understand that one could feel a little left out when everything Elisabeth said and looked and did was absolutely marvellous in Dad's eyes.'

Uppermost in Elisabeth's earliest memories are recollections of her father coming home from work at his wool firm and encouraging her to perform all kinds of gymnastic feats. She even learnt a party trick as she grew older and stronger which enabled her to climb up an open door frame with arms and legs stretched out in a human '*X*' – 'Like a crab, I remember. I quite thought when I was little that I was going to be an acrobat in a circus. In fact, I probably did prove to be one in the end, didn't I?' Elisabeth was taught other party tricks too. 'In those days I was really very agile and supple and I could stand on my head for longer than any other child I knew, and as for scrambling up the tallest of trees...'

Elisabeth still retains the happy memories of life with her sporting father but she also recalls Bairnie telling her of the year she dreamt that a horse called The Parisian won the 1911 Melbourne Cup. 'The Parisian did win by two lengths and, thanks to Mother's dream, Dad won an awful lot of money, but by the time he got home he didn't have a penny left. All his racing friends came up and said "Did you put that fiver on for me?" and being Dad he paid out without question while my mother was sitting at home waiting for this lovely largesse. People loved Dad, but he was a poor provider for his family – although he was very generous with everyone else,' says Elisabeth, who was a babe in arms in 1911.

Certainly, the Greenes lived in a genteel Edwardian style and had a governess or nanny, a maid, a cook–laundry-woman and a visiting gardener, all well-trained in the formal British traditions of the time. Bairnie Greene had a copy of *The 20th Century Cooking Book* at the start of her housekeeping days. 'I came across it years later and the secret of Mother's success was revealed in a whole chapter aptly titled "On how to train a green maid",' says Elisabeth. 'That is where the detailed list of duties, and what time they were to be performed, came from. I can still see them hanging in the Pemberley pantry and kitchen. When, much later, I married Keith and took on quite a large household at nineteen years of age, I organised it much the same way as suggested in Mother's old cookbook.'

But by the standards of gold-rich 'Marvellous Melbourne' towards the end of the long, secure reign of Queen Victoria, the Greenes of Pemberley were far from prosperous and there were inevitably tensions between the loving parents. Bairnie and Rupert did share an Anglo-Irish heritage yet their backgrounds were really very different – although the Greene and the Forth families did share a distinct lack of prosperity at the time of Rupert's marriage to Bairnie. These disagreements, often triggered by money problems, particularly upset Elisabeth, the youngest Greene. 'Our mother was a remarkable woman. Somehow, she always managed to appear serene however difficult my father was. I remember one occasion when he was being particularly trying – probably as a result of mother insisting that she must have money to pay the bills.

'He worked himself into a rage, called for his bags to be packed and announced that he was leaving never to darken the door again. I put on a brave face, although I turned to pulp inside and was really terrified that perhaps this time he would not come back – but after a night or two at the Melbourne Club he always did. I still laugh when I remember how after one of these performances, while the atmosphere was crackling and he was about to depart, I heard mother's quiet but firm voice calling from her bedroom: "Rupert, Rupert please don't forget to post my letter."

'Mother was a very remarkable character. She was always so impeccably dignified no matter how imminent disaster appeared to be. We girls have often agreed that if it hadn't been for Mother and her wonderful grit we would not have survived and would probably have had to turn out and earn our living on a very low plane of existence – or, as Sylvia says, "Living behind a privet hedge near the Flemington Racecourse."

'I remember Dad, when he was raging, saying "I'm going to cut your mother up and put her in a little black box in the garden under the gardenia." We did go through it, yet when Dad died, Mother was amazing. She forgot so much of those awful times. She really was very fond of him.' Elisabeth can still remember the tension as she lay in her bed sobbing while Sylvia sat up reading a book and enjoying tea and Thin Captain biscuits. 'Sylvia would say: "Stop snivelling you miserable little brute, stop snivelling and feeling sorry for yourself." And I'd feel so ashamed because I was feeling so dreadfully anxious about Dad not coming back.'

More than seventy years later, hearing of her sister's secret childhood traumas, Sylvia Ritchie says: 'I never thought you were anxious. I thought you sailed through life.' Elisabeth shakes her head: 'It's extraordinary, you see. I think that although we went through the hoops as children we survived. We couldn't have survived if it wasn't for Mother. I once dreamt of living in a little cottage with lemon trees and selling lemons.'

But Elisabeth Murdoch, while admiring the strengths of the de Lancey Forths and, through her grandmother, the Wares, does not underestimate the gifts passed on by the Greenes and other members of her widespread family. 'We certainly inherited very valuable traits from Dad,' she insists. With her only son, Rupert Murdoch, clearly in mind she says: 'Dad's enthusiasm, zest for life and adaptability greatly enhanced our lives and, I hope, the lives of others.'

By no standards of the day could Pemberley be described as a mansion. It was a comfortable Toorak villa and, though rare for the times, the house boasted an internal water closet. This modern luxury was strictly for the use of Rupert and Bairnie Greene. Except on nights when there was a frost or heavy rain, Elisabeth, her sisters and the governess, were expected to use the outside toilet then common to most of the established houses in Toorak. Fortunately for the maids, they had their own inside toilet.

Despite the occasional domestic upheaval, the Greenes' home was run impeccably by the benevolently imperious Bairnie. 'Mother was wonderful with our maids and governesses who always stayed for many years. They were beautifully trained, though they must have had to work pretty hard, and they loved and respected my mother. I know her example helped me when I was very young and suddenly had to manage a large staff.'

The happy memories by far outbalance the sad as Elisabeth recalls her childhood, but she says: 'One of my most vivid and painful memories was when I was five years old and a tricycle was delivered by the Mutual Store for me. In my ecstasy of delight of such an unexpected and joyful event, I seized it and rode in pride and triumph down the path and out the front gate into Toorak Road. Almost as swiftly my mother swooped on me declaring that this treasure must be returned to the store immediately. "We cannot afford it and your father was very wrong to buy it for you," she told me. It was a very bitter and efficacious lesson for me which served me well through my childhood. Dad loved to be generous, but he had an inbuilt dislike for meeting obligations of domestic finance.'

There were many nights when, at her mother's bidding, she had to dial 921, the phone number of the Bohemian Club, and ask the head porter if Mr Greene was still at the club. Always the tactful reply would be that Mr Greene was no longer there. Still, the message would have been delivered!

At the Bohemian Club stakes were high as members played cards until early in the morning, and wagers of one hundred pounds to a bottle of port were often laid on the outcome of a horserace. More akin to an army officers' mess than a gentlemen's club, Bohemian members often displayed feats of strength and acrobatic daring in the bar, and there were regular weekend fox hunts, polo and cricket matches to entertain Rupert Greene and his sporting fellow members. Rupert and many of his friends were also members of the rather more sedate Melbourne Club at the other end of Collins Street, but even there younger members were said to have climbed around the grand dining room without touching the carpet – by clinging to the panelling and scaling the tall ornate mantlepieces. At times, in his younger days, the clubs were a home away from home for Elisabeth's father.

Elisabeth can't remember her elder sister, Marie, very clearly when they were children. 'I do remember though that my father was often very impatient with her,' she says. 'She wasn't very strong, and stooped rather badly, and this seemed to irritate Dad. He was certainly sometimes very unkind to her verbally too. I've often thought, rather sadly, that he was almost sadistic in the way he treated Marie when she was young and very sensitive – although she had many of Dad's more attractive qualities, intelligence and warm personality. As she got older she became very amusing and they did get on so much better in later life.'

Elisabeth's sister Sylvia was, she says, 'A bird of another feather. She never allowed Dad to get the better of her, though, no doubt, she suffered inside, as we all did, from his rather uncertain temper and scathing disapproval of our perfectly natural weaknesses and small misdemeanors. They maddened him and he would explode declaiming: "Why did God Almighty inflict me with such daughters?"'

Today, at eighty-nine, Sylvia Ritchie remembers her father saying to her: '"What have I done to be cursed with a daughter with legs like that?" Awfully encouraging wasn't it? If I had known what I know now, I would have said plenty,' she laughs as the two sisters, in the garden of Delatite, the beautiful Ritchie vineyard and property in the foothills of the majestic Victorian Alps, recall their childhood.

'However,' says Elisabeth, 'I believe he really did love us all, including our remarkable mother whom he sorely tried and to whom he sometimes behaved very badly. Undoubtedly Mother's character was of a superior quality to our father's. He knew it and on occasions this must have rankled with him and perhaps caused him to try and take it out on her – a very unattractive trait. It was to her great credit that she coped with him as well as she did. She supported him, stuck to him through thick and thin and enabled him to build up and maintain his position in business and sporting life. He was really very endearingly enthusiastic about people, and anything he was interested in, and he is still remembered with the warmest affection by the family and the few remaining people still alive whom he trained in the wool trade and racing world.'

Rupert Greene was also, at times, very unlucky. On countless occasions Bairnie had to use her charm and gentle persuasion to keep creditors at bay, preventing a crisis by letting Pemberley and moving the family out to stay with Elisabeth's redoubtable Grannie Forth, the former Anne Ware. Often the many friends and admirers of the Greene family would come to their aid too, but finally when Rupert overstepped the mark with a string of severe gambling losses, his rich and powerful club and sporting friends decided to step in.

Knowing that the position of starter for the Victoria Racing Club was about to become vacant and that by strict racing tradition, probably going back as far as the days of Nathaniel Forth, starters were not allowed to place bets on the horses they sent on their way, Rupert Greene was made official starter in 1914 . . . a role he fulfilled with skill and distinction, starting every Melbourne and Caulfield Cup for the next thirty-one years. On his first day as starter Rupert Greene fined all the jockeys a hefty five pounds for tardy reactions and earned their respect and attention from that day on – although in one official history of the Melbourne Cup race he is described as a 'martinet'.

Although the Greene lifestyle began to improve, Elisabeth still has an early impression that her father seemed to resent paying for his daughters' education: 'He considered that he had done very well without very much conventional schooling.' He played the wag a great deal from Toorak College – although his more dutiful brothers were working towards academic distinction when the eight-year Queensland drought eroded the fortunes of the Governments and, with them, the William Greenes.

As the youngest member of the family, Elisabeth could have been a lonely child often left to her own devices, but there was her own private fairyland in the trees, and a friendly gardener who encouraged her love of gardening and flowers. At five, Elisabeth's life was clearly focused on the Pemberley garden and Robbie, the gardener the little girl adored. 'I used to follow him around as he cut the wide lawns with a hand mower. I simply loved the smell of him – cut grass and a flannel shirt heavily impregnated with sweat. It was a marvellous smell for a child.'

Robbie came on Wednesdays and Saturday mornings, making the trip by pony and gig from Richmond, then a noisome inner-city industrial suburb of narrow streets and workers' cottages, light-years away from the sweet-smelling rose gardens of spacious Toorak. For this he was paid a total of twenty-one shillings and sixpence for the one-and-a-half days. Elisabeth can still see her mother writing out the National Bank cheque in her superb copperplate hand.

The Pemberley garden was always immaculate and covered in blooms when Bairnie held her Sunday afternoon tea parties for overseas visitors and the friends she had made in Toorak. On those occasions, Rupert Greene would usually be out with his sporting friends, but there were times when he came home in a 'low'. 'Although my father did at times drink too much he really held his liquor very well, but it was a great worry for us all when he was "low" and mother would tell us: "Your father isn't quite himself." I never heard Mother use the word "drunk" and she never mentioned "class" in her life.

'The remarkable thing was that Dad always managed to be in excellent form when he had to face the great responsibility which both his jobs incurred – being the VRC, and later VATC, starter, as well as the chief wool expert of New Zealand Loan. He had a great eye which was essential for a starter before the starting gate was invented and the same quality was necessary when it came to his judgment of wool. He started thirty-one consecutive Melbourne Cups and countless other races,' says Elisabeth proudly.

But at home, Rupert Greene did continue to make a great deal of his youngest daughter, encouraging her to 'show off' to guests by walking on her hands or doing a series of double somersaults. Fearing that Elisabeth was being outrageously spoilt, her sisters joined their mother in trying to restore the balance. 'Poor dears, they were probably doing that entirely for my own sake, but I was five years younger and I think I had a slight inferiority complex – which they wouldn't for one moment accept today. However, the fact is that at first I didn't really have a very close relationship with my mother, definitely not as close as my two older sisters. They always thought I was my father's girl.

'Fortunately, as I grew older I became devoted to Mother and realised what wonderful qualities she had, but as a small child Dad was always the one. I now catch myself looking just as Mother looked, and it gives me quite a turn. She was dark, with beautiful dark eyes, and I am a very poor, wan edition of her. I think I am really more like her than I was the Greenes. She was a good-looking woman, there's no doubt about that.

'My earliest memories are of Mother with her beautiful small waist in a long skirt and something elegant around her neck. Goodness knows, she wasn't an expensive dresser, but she was always elegant. She was very dignified, and had an air of authority, but I can never remember mother laughing hilariously about anything. She was always rather restrained, almost stern.' Today, Elisabeth's daughters, who only really remember their grandmother in her advanced years, say that Bairnie Greene gave them the impression of being cold. This is not a view shared by Elisabeth or Sylvia.

'Of course, my father was always so much fun, but at the same time he could be difficult and annoying. There is no doubt that Mother was slightly disapproving of my father and I do remember that, very often, she would frown when she thought he was showing off or being unrestrained in his behaviour. I think we were very lucky. My mother might have dug her toes in and said that life was impossible with Rupert Greene and sped off, but that didn't happen.

'We were very fond of our father but we were also rather disapproving when he played up, and we were always very anxious if he was sarcastic or unkind to mother, or bullied any of us but, thanks to his charm and endearing ways, we came through and I believe we were stronger for it. Today children can be just as sensitive as we were, but unfortunately they are conditioned to all sorts of situations by what they see on television or what they read. Children today haven't known the gentleness of the age in which we were brought up. That is the sad thing that television has done to a lot of semi-educated homes. It has done away with so much conversation – any sort of dialogue.

'Mother was always very good and kind to everybody, friends, relatives, our wonderful maids, governesses and nannies. She was a very thoughtful, caring person, my mother. She read a great deal and wrote essays and had quite a leaning towards literary pursuits – she even organised a class of gentlewomen to discuss matters of literary interest with a learned Professor, Archibald Strong. She could have been, I think, quite an intellect. She wrote with such a beautiful hand and read aloud to us and gave a lot of thought to our education. I think we owe a great deal to our mother but I think the joie de vivre we got from Pa. I hope Mother passed on solid good characteristics to me and my children, but of course my father had very interesting parents too. Very fine, intelligent parents, so it's an odd, interesting mix.'

Elisabeth was just five when war broke out and loyal Melbourne men joined long queues outside the recruiting depots in Melbourne to fight for 'King and Country'. Elisabeth was told of the fighting in the trenches of France and quickly took to digging practice trenches in corners of the garden. At the same time she was earning pennies for those favourite snowballs, as a bounty for collecting small flowerpots full of snails from Robbie's neat flowerbeds. 'We were obviously going through a difficult period with father's finances and Mother would let the house for a short time and we would go and live with Grandmother Forth down near the beach in Sandringham,' is Elisabeth's memory of those days.

At the time that Keith Murdoch was achieving international fame by exposing the folly of the Gallipoli campaign, young Elisabeth was busy knitting cotton washers for the troops while her sisters were trying to knit the far more difficult army socks. Elisabeth can remember still Toorak nights with the sound of reveille being played at an army camp in an inner suburb. But the most exciting wartime memory is of the hunt for the escaped German POW. 'He came to hide for the night in our garden and my sister saw him and went and told Dad, who chased this poor unfortunate man down Toorak Road and, I think probably purposely, lost him.'

Rupert Greene, still a fit young man, was not called up during the war – although Elisabeth says he was a 'very belligerent person with lots of physical courage'. No record remains but it seems clear that Rupert's skill and expertise in the vital Australian wool trade, and the fact that he had three young daughters, prevented him joining Australia's young volunteer army. With Bairnie's brother, Nowell, and other Forth family members serving with such distinction in the armed forces, Elisabeth remembers being told of their exploits: 'Mother was very attached to the English part of her heritage and had great respect for everything English and she had great respect for the establishment.'

But if Elisabeth was aware of the landing of British, Australian and New Zealand troops in Gallipoli, she knew nothing of the prolonged and costly struggle, and certainly nothing of the furore, caused by Keith Murdoch's revelations to the British and Australian Cabinets. The first meeting of Keith and Elisabeth was still many years ahead. However, Elisabeth does recall that as a five- or six-year-old she was taken by her mother and grandmother to see a re-enactment of the historic ANZAC landing on the sand dunes at Black Rock.

With Marie and Sylvia at school, Elisabeth's life was still centred on the trees and garden. But one day as the cable tram stopped at the front gate and Elisabeth waved to the crew she heard the grip-man say to the conductor: 'Our little girl is growing up.'

CHAPTER THREE

Sago, Prunes and Junket

FORMAL EDUCATION for the Greene girls was a long time coming. Before Marie and Sylvia finally went off to school, Elisabeth sat with them, and a succession of governesses, in the Pemberley schoolroom, and learnt how to read and write while Sylvia and Marie took part in more advanced studies. Eventually Marie and Sylvia were both sent off as boarders to the Hermitage School in Geelong. Sylvia was fourteen when she first went off to school. 'It was a pretty difficult time and I think we were in reduced circumstances. Mother was always hard-pressed to pay the housekeeping bills, although she would make arrangements with the grocer and the butcher in the most dignified way. They would respect her enormously and give her a fortnight or a month to pay and they knew she would always somehow meet this,' says Elisabeth now.

'But it must have been hard for her, because my father's friends were all much better off than he was and Mother had to make quite an effort to maintain her position and dignity, and I remember her as quiet and thoughtful in those days. We sisters owed an awful lot to her. Dad was fun, fascinating and everything else, but few women could have managed him the way Mother did.'

At the time, although Bairnie was thought to be 'delicate', Elisabeth suspects she may really have been 'as strong as a horse'. Still, on one day of each week she would take to her bed and read, 'on doctor's orders'. But she was always ready when the handsome Dr Reggie Morrison would come to take her for a therapeutic ride in his sporty de Dion Bouton tourer with its big brass motor horn. Bairnie would rug up in a holland coat and hat with gossamer veil and motoring gloves before she was helped into the little French car. 'Looking back it was a very gentle life – for the men. You should have seen the lives they led, while the women . . . well, I do get cross with today's militant feminism, but I do think it was necessary to change from the days of my childhood,' says Dame Elisabeth Murdoch all these years later.

During the war, Miss Dennis, daughter of the head pilot at the port of Williamstown, came to Pemberley as governess and won the devotion of the Greene girls, partly for her determination to stand up to the head of the household. 'I remember Den outside the bathroom door – I don't know, but Dad must have been horrid to me in some way. Perhaps he ordered me out of the bath or something – anyway Den said: "Mr Greene how dare you! Don't be so unjust to Elisabeth." We all adored her,' says Elisabeth.

When a Greene family friend, Sam McCulloch, was widowed with two little boys, Rupert Greene suggested Miss Dennis should take over in the McCulloch household. 'She became a surrogate mother and did a wonderful job, but over the years I lost sight of darling Miss Dennis,' says Elisabeth. Many years later, Helen, Dame

Elisabeth's eldest daughter, while working with the elderly in Anglican Church homes, spotted Miss Dennis, then a frail ninety-two. There was a joyous reunion at Cruden Farm where the former governess revealed for the first time that she had actually spent her childhood in the 1890s living in the farm's original orchard cottage and walking each week the three miles to Frankston with a sugar bag and a single one pound note to buy the family provisions. 'She knew Keith had bought it for me, but never told us it used to be her home,' says Elisabeth.

But at the end of the First World War, Miss King, 'Kingo', was the highly respected governess who was happy to live in and help with the Greene housekeeping. Today, Elisabeth shakes her head sadly as she recalls that on her one day off each week, Kingo was expected to take young Elisabeth off to lunch with her when she visited her married sister. 'Kingo thought it would be nice if we could have hens – and eggs – and, as we had plenty of land and an old fowlyard tucked away at the back of the garden, we set out to get a clucky hen. Kingo had been governess to the family of old Dr Plowman, the original Frankston doctor, so off I went with her by steam train from South Yarra to Frankston,' Elisabeth recalls as if it were today, instead of 1917. 'I was carrying a basket of lemons picked from the Pemberley gardens for Mrs Plowman and at the station I upset the basket and scattered the lemons all over the railway line. Ghastly! Ghastly!'

From Frankston railway station where they left the train, Kingo and Elisabeth walked up hill over ploughed fields to get to the doctor's home, just a few miles from the land which Elisabeth and Keith Murdoch were one day to make famous as Cruden Farm. For lunch with Mrs Plowman there was pumpkin which, for fear of letting Kingo down, a reluctant Elisabeth forced herself to swallow. Then there was the trip back with Elisabeth carrying the basket, now with a plump clucky hen inside. 'I was so mortified because the hen clucked all the way home and I was so ashamed. I don't remember if that hen ever did its stuff, but in the mind of a child my first visit to Frankston was a terribly embarrassing experience.'

Later, Elisabeth remembers her father walking up Toorak Road – 'he couldn't have been on the way to church' – while her mother was away, and hearing of this exchange between Rupert and the very proper Village chemist, Mr Wallis, who was dressed in his morning suit and on the way to take the collection plate around the congregation of St John's Church:

'Morning, Wallis,' said Rupert.

'Good morning Mr Greene. You must be missing Mrs Greene very much,' said the chemist doffing his top hat.

'Not half as much as you, Wallis,' said Rupert tipping his far less formal headgear as he continued on his way.

'Well mother did set great store on her tonic and other necessities and our chemist bill must always have been very high and this greatly irritated my father,' Elisabeth explains.

Twice a year, Bairnie would gather her daughters and catch the cable tram with them to the city, a rocking bell-clanging thirty-minute ride from peaceful Toorak, with the grip man calling out 'Hang on round the corners!' to Elisabeth's delight. The family would go to Stainer's, the ribbon and button shop in Swanston Street, then on to the grand stores of Buckley and Nunn's or Robertson and Moffatt's in Bourke Street. 'I remember they had revolving stools and I had great joy in swinging around and kicking the counters,' says Elisabeth, who was at that stage scornfully called 'Baby' by her disapproving elder sisters.

'I was always very resentful when Mother bought blue material for me, because I wanted to have pink like my sisters, but Mother thought that blue was the colour that suited my blue eyes. I was very young and intolerant and all I wanted was pink. Poor Mother never minded her children being dressed differently to everyone else but, of course, we were bitterly conscious of it,' says Elisabeth who, with her sisters, would help Bairnie home with lengths of material so that a visiting dressmaker could come in and run up winter and summer dresses for the Greene girls on the family's sewing machine.

Meanwhile, life at Pemberley had its ups and downs. The sisters recall the 'awful' nursery meals they shared with their governesses. 'Poor mother always had trouble to make ends meet. That's why we had endless stewed prunes and junket,' Elisabeth remembers. But Sylvia remembers the tapioca and sago puddings although she is quick to point out that her mother went to extraordinary lengths to make certain that her children were properly educated. 'Mother insisted on letting the house and making some money while she took us off to live in some rather awful boarding houses,' Sylvia says.

During those difficult periods, Bairnie would take up the role of governess herself and read to her daughters. Elisabeth can still remember her mother reading *The Song of Hiawatha* to them. 'She had beautiful diction and quite a gift for English.' But Elisabeth is still at a loss to understand how her sisters were so successful when they were finally sent to school. 'I always excused myself for non-performance academically, but Mother somehow saw to it that Sylvia and Marie had wonderful early training – but really I had nothing, not a class at all until I was eleven. I just used to sit with my sisters at the schoolroom table and listen and listen,' says Elisabeth. But Sylvia insists that in fact she had not gone to boarding school until she was nearly fifteen. 'I just had governesses. I was supposed to be delicate and I was sent to the country a lot and then Mother used to send me up history books and English literature to read.'

But there were happy times spent at Pemberley too and Sylvia says that Elisabeth was a 'very outgoing child'. She says she was 'absolutely covered in shame' on a tram one day when, on the way to a party, Elisabeth hitched up her party dress and said to a friendly conductor 'Look, I've got my party pants on.' The sisters laugh together as Elisabeth protests: 'What a terrible story!'

Elisabeth has almost total recall and can reel off the well-remembered past and present phone numbers of friends and family – even the registration number 7766 on her father's Buick. 'I don't know how father managed to acquire his car, but we weren't allowed to touch it. Mother, who had no car sense at all, was very keen to learn to drive though, and there were some very painful occasions with Dad becoming absolutely enraged, and the lessons ended. The extraordinary thing is that years later when my son Rupert gave me a fax machine at Cruden Farm, I was able to use one of those old car numbers again as my personal fax number.'

Unknown to her husband, Bairnie took driving lessons although she was never allowed to drive Rupert's office car, by now a French Delage. 'The first time I went out with Mother in a borrowed car she lost her nerve going down Toorak Road hill towards Chapel Street and, although a novice myself, I had to help by grabbing the wheel and steering the car into the kerb to stop it,' says Elisabeth, who today remains a keen driver. 'It is so interesting to contrast our lives with today's family structure. There was simply no question of Dad's young family having access to his big grey Buick, or his cream and brown Delage. We didn't go on many trips with Dad,' she says.

But there were some memorable holidays on the New South Wales property of her Aunt Ernestine, a Govett who had been brought up by 'Granny Greene' before she married Reggie Clarke. Ernestine's husband died at a young age leaving her with three children but 'very well-provided for' by the standards of the times. 'I loved those holidays. The country always went to my head and the trip from Melbourne was such a glorious adventure. We left at daybreak in two cars, Aunt Ernestine proudly driving her Rolls Royce and Robbie, the chauffeur, driving the Straker Squire – two cars that would be highly treasured today by vintage car enthusiasts.

'We would have a lovely picnic on the way up and then there would be the excitement of crossing the Murray River. We would finally reach Holbrook and drive on to Woomargama station just before dark – a drive that would take about four hours today. Those days were precious and memorable for me and one of the highlights of the holiday were the picnics we went on in the bullock waggon. The team of six bullocks was driven by a wonderful old bullocky whose name was Bob. To our young, unsullied ears Bob the Bullocky's language was livid and shocking, but today I can really only remember him using the word "bloody".'

Aunt Ernestine, who was very fond of young Elisabeth, loved to shoot and, as Australia was then in the grips of one of its early rabbit plagues, Elisabeth and Ernestine's children were taken out to retrieve the wounded pests. 'Her children were very timid and she was always hoping that the example of my toughness would be a good influence,' says Elisabeth, who quickly learnt to snap a rabbit's neck – a skill she passed on to her children Helen, Rupert, Anne and Janet when the family grew up at Cruden Farm. Feeling she had to maintain her reputation of fearlessness, Elisabeth once clambered onto a large station horse which was clearly beyond her control. The horse bolted and Elisabeth ended up being dragged with her foot in the stirrup – leaving her with a badly crushed foot which gave her pain for many years to come.

'Though I was very attached to Aunt Ernestine for some reason I don't think I was so deeply attached to her children, possibly because she always overemphasised their temerity and was always holding up "Joy" – she always called me by my second name – as an example of courage,' Elisabeth confesses. But overall the days at

Woomargama left many happy memories, particularly of the hours Elisabeth spent picking wonderful violets from her aunt's thick garden borders.

Another cherished childhood memory of Elisabeth's is of Granny Forth's musical talent. The sprightly old lady could play the piano and the harp and sing beautifully. Sylvia had learnt to play simple pieces on the piano, so Elisabeth was determined to be musical too. 'I was quite certain I would be able to play well if only given the chance, but it always seemed to me that Sylvia hogged the piano,' says Elisabeth, who was in later years to become a proficient pianist. 'On one shameful occasion I was so desperate to be given a turn on the piano, that I jumped up on it and stamped my foot on the inside of our grand, breaking a string. Sylvia would deny this, but for the next two years whenever I gave her any trouble, she would simply have to say "Note, Note," intimating that she was going to tell mother, and I would feel very miserable and ashamed. Is it any wonder that I longed to get away to school?' Elisabeth laughs today.

CHAPTER FOUR

Waiting at the Gate

ELISABETH GREENE was eleven before she was finally sent to St Catherine's, a school for the daughters of Toorak's prosperous gentry. St Catherine's was then in Williams Road, just around the corner from Pemberley, and Elisabeth had often stood at the school gates looking longingly at the young ladies in their neat uniforms going off to classes or heading for the hockey field. Athletic, and bursting with pent-up energy, Elisabeth had long wanted to escape the restraints of the Pemberley schoolroom but, as she says now, the Greene fortunes were not looking up at the time and it must have been a struggle for Rupert to find the fees for Elisabeth as well as his two elder daughters, now at boarding school.

The Greenes had just returned to Pemberley, which had been let once again to rescue them from financial difficulties. While boarding with her dispossessed family in South Yarra, Elisabeth had become seriously ill after badly gashing her leg during an unauthorised cycle ride. After keeping the extent of the injury secret and failing to have necessary stitches, Elisabeth's ugly wound had turned septic and Bairnie had paid a great deal of money to secure a newly available drug developed to treat wounds during the war. But then Elisabeth caught pneumonic influenza and nearly died as doctors battled to bring down her soaring temperature.

Bairnie, too, caught influenza as she nursed her critically ill daughter, and so did the dedicated governess, Miss Dennis. But they recovered and it was decided that, at last, Elisabeth must begin school. 'At first I was a day girl and I was so eager to get there in the mornings that I arrived before the boarders had finished their breakfast. Looking back, it was amazing how they got all those pupils in – how we managed to have some room to play games on that small playing field and tennis court. I was forced to get there early to have first "bags" – turn – on the tennis court apart from anything else. We didn't have a court at home and tennis soon became one of the great things in my life – along with the piano.

'Anyway, I just loved school and, like my father, I seemed to be good at sport. Before long I was begging to be allowed to board. I don't know if it suited the family or how they paid the fees but I suppose they thought that if I was going there at cockcrow I may as well live there. Well finally, in second term, off I went to board. And I was thrilled, although now I know how ill-equipped I was sartorially compared with the other boarders. My remarkable mother imagined, I am sure, that despite the financial difficulties she dressed us very nicely. I know my sisters remembered the agony of being dressed in dark blue serge with the most wonderful covered buttons and white pique collars.

'Yet I marvel that I suffered so little from the awful blue woollen stockings which my dear mother had found somewhere as a bargain. They were quite unique. No one else wore them except me. My dress for the evening, black velveteen with Irish crochet collar was, of course, handed down from my sisters and like most of my very few clothes, was quite unlike anyone else's. According to my mother, our clothes were in rather better taste than other people's and I don't think we felt embarrassed. I cannot remember really resenting this state of affairs.'

At St Catherine's, Elisabeth Greene forgot her fears and sleepless nights at Pemberley just around the corner and simply revelled in life as a boarder at school ... even though she came close to revolt on the occasion she was served roast parsnips for lunch: 'I had never had roast parsnips at home and I simply couldn't stomach them. However, I was told to eat them – and stay there in the dining room until I had done so. One Sunday three o'clock came and I was still sitting there in a defiant and solitary state, until I decided to stuff those parsnips in my bloomers. Then I went onto the upstairs verandah and threw them down into Williams Road. How disgraceful! If my children had done that I would have thought it was TERRIBLE of them, so deceitful. But then it was a question of survival. I had to do it.'

At about this time Elisabeth was attending dancing classes conducted by the famous Miss Jenny Brennan. 'I suffered from an extraordinary delusion for a time because I imagined I would become a rather good ballet dancer. Of course, I didn't! I was tremendously acrobatic – but completely wrongly built.

'The companionship and competition in the classroom and at games was so exciting. I topped my classes in just about all subjects – a feat that I didn't manage again in my five years at Clyde School,' she laughs now. 'I think I did well at St Catherine's because I had been wanting to go to school for so long – and I suppose those early days in the Pemberley schoolroom helped.

'Years later, Sir James Darling, the famous headmaster at Geelong

Grammar, told me that the three most intelligent women he had met in Australia had not been educated in the traditional way – they had all received a good deal of their education from governesses at home. I am quite sure I was not included in that trio. In fact, I think he may have been referring to Lady Casey, my sister Sylvia, who was brilliant, and someone else.'

Although Elisabeth now spent far less time climbing the trees in the garden, life went on as before at Pemberley with the milkman coming down the drive each day to ladle out the family milk supply. 'We had no refrigerators, no fly wire on the windows. No one did then. We had an ice chest that was always giving trouble as the ice melted and the pan underneath overflowed. I can see the iceman delivering blocks of ice wrapped in a sack on his shoulder. The butcher delivered, the grocer delivered and the chemist delivered – constantly. We often joked about the chemist because mother was always taking delivery of the tonic Dr Morrison prescribed for her. Well, I suppose she was very harassed. Her children took a lot out of her and so did my poor father. I well remember the frequent visits by the chemist's boy who would appear about three o'clock after school in the afternoon.

'I rather think that there was a crisis in my parents' life when I was first at St Catherine's, because I spent two miserable holidays with the headmistress, Miss Langley, one in a little boarding house in the Dandenong Ranges and the other at Beaumaris. Apparently there was nowhere else for me to go. I believe my mother had gone off to Port Moresby in Papua New Guinea to stay with Sir Hubert Murray, taking Marie with her. Sylvia was probably staying at Delatite and goodness knows where my father was – possibly temporarily in disgrace. That was probably the most miserable period of my young life. Miss Langley wasn't fond of me and I had very bad whooping cough at Beaumaris. Of course, it must have been miserable for her too, to be landed with me,' says Elisabeth.

Sir Hubert Murray, the great Australian colonial administrator, was just one of Bairnie's good and admiring friends. As Elisabeth says now: 'He was devoted to my mother, and she to him. They had a deep friendship which was totally platonic. Because Lady Murray couldn't stand the tropical climate, Mother went twice to New Guinea on holidays, each time taking Sylvia or Marie with her.' The Greenes were even taken right into the PNG hinterland with Sir Hubert on his tours of inspection. 'This friendship was a great solace to my mother, and my father didn't seem to take exception to it, which was fortunate, because she was worthy of that kind of nourishment – and she did get it from her wonderful men and women friends.

'She was twice president of the Alexandra Club and once President of the Victoria League, and that was very much my mother's milieu. She really was so very much attached to the English part of her heritage and did have so much respect for the establishment ... and really that was the climate I was brought up in.' At the same time, Elisabeth's upbringing taught her to pay scant heed to material possessions. 'Usually, we didn't have a car and we never thought that was odd. I can honestly say that we never felt any resentment or self-consciousness that we wore each other's clothes. Clothes were handed down and there never was quite enough money to go round. There was always an anxiety about money,' says Elisabeth.

Meanwhile, around the corner at St Catherine's, Elisabeth was making up for lost time with her music lessons and delighting in the time she could spend at the school piano. 'I fell in love with my music mistress, Miss Winifred Pillars, who encouraged me, rightly or wrongly, that I was very musical, and for the next two years music was a very important part of my enjoyment of St Catherine's,' says Elisabeth.

Today, St Catherine's is one of Australia's best-equipped and most prestigious girls' schools, but in Elisabeth's day conditions were spartan. The school buildings were old and ramshackle, but she was so overjoyed at belonging to an institution that provided competition, companionship and piano lessons, that she made no complaint. 'Conditions at St Catherine's in those days were really quite appalling. The school building where we boarders lived was draughty and very sub-standard. They would certainly not be accepted these days by parents or health authorities,' Elisabeth says.

After weekends and holidays spent at home, she was always anxious to get back to school, but any unruly behaviour at Pemberley now resulted in the warning: 'Behave or you'll be sent to The Hermitage.' Elisabeth had already been regaled with her sisters' tales of cold nights and harsh discipline at the Geelong school and had no wish to join them there.

But already Elisabeth's days at St Catherine's were numbered. Perhaps her unhappy holiday spent with Miss Langley led to the headmistress expressing criticism of the Greenes' failure to make other arrangements for their daughter, perhaps the Greenes were not satisfied with standards at the school, but certainly Bairnie was not impressed by Miss Langley. Soon a decision was made that Elisabeth should be moved to another school.

Clyde, a girls' school on the slopes of Mt Macedon, one hundred kilometres north of Melbourne, was recommended by several of Bairnie and Rupert's friends as the ideal school for the energetic and clearly intelligent young Elisabeth.

CHAPTER FIVE

Carefree at Clyde

CLYDE, SADLY, is no more. The unique mountain-side school that produced so many outstanding Australians was shut in 1985 and amalgamated with Geelong Grammar School.

In 1919, Clyde, whose motto was *Spectamur Agendo* (We are Judged by our Acts), had moved from St Kilda to 'Braemar', formerly a mountain guesthouse which, early pictures show, was constructed of weatherboard fashioned into a Victorian country house with impressive entrance hall and fancy friezes topped off by a tall tower. Braemar was surrounded by dense mountain bushland inhabited by koalas, kangaroos and other topsy-turvy Australian marsupials. It was to be one of Australia's first 'boarders only' schools for girls.

On the seventy-fifth anniversary of the school in 1985, Elisabeth wrote her 'Recollections of Clyde' alongside a schoolgirl 'snap' of herself taken out in the bush wearing a sunhat and loosely belted cotton smock – made, Elisabeth says, out of some of Bairnie's spare curtain material. Except for the long pigtails tied in bows with two large ribbons, she still has the looks of the mischievous tomboy beloved by Rupert Greene.

In 1985, Elisabeth wrote: 'Distance lends enchantment. Perhaps sixty years is a long time for one's recall to be accurate but I remember my five years (1922–6) at Clyde with warm affection and gratitude. I have never forgotten my first journey to Woodend in a railway carriage packed with excited and happy girls all out to convince me that I was on the way to "The Best School of All". The trip up the mountain in old Mr South's wagonette was a thrilling experience. The track was appalling and quite perilous and the challenge to the driver, horses and girls was the forerunner of many endurance tests ahead of us at Clyde. Life was rugged during the long, cold winters, but I believe we were the healthier for those spartan conditions which today would be considered unbearable – as indeed would be the isolation.'

There were six bathrooms with showers for the ninety girls, but there never was enough hot water, so Elisabeth would hop out of bed at 5.15 a.m. to have the first hot shower. 'We had pretty primitive hygiene, but getting up early meant that I could always have first turn at the school's best piano to practise on.'

'Parents visited very rarely, if at all, and telephoning was allowed only in real emergencies. We became self reliant and had to take the hard knocks, disappointments and the discipline, without which I consider we would have been less secure. We soon learned, living together for long periods, that concern and consideration for others were the best ingredients for happiness and satisfaction. Of all my treasured memories of my school days, the most precious would be that of the beauty and enchantment of our glorious bush and country surroundings. They were at the heart of my happiness in being at Clyde.'

Carefree at Clyde

But Elisabeth has not forgotten the challenging side of life at Clyde either. 'There was no heating in that huge barn of a place except for the wood fires in the hall, drawing room and dining room and the room in which we met for assembly and morning tea when we were given slabs of bread with terrible jam spread on thickly. That repast was repeated after school. The passages and bedrooms upstairs were absolutely freezing; in fact, the long passage was known as "Iceberg Alley".

'At one stage I slept on the verandah with very inadequate flapping blinds which were supposed to protect one but, without a word of exaggeration, the weather penetrated, well, not actually the rain, but the mist and cold. We thought nothing of it, but sometimes the bedclothes actually iced over. Of course, we used to grumble and try to hog a good possy near one of the fires whenever possible ... To this day it is said that you can always tell a Clyde girl because she instinctively stands with her backside as near as possible to a fire.'

Life in the Clyde classrooms in the winter was little better although there were pipes through which hot water was run. 'Quite honestly they were quite ineffective except for the few who could bag a seat beside the heaters. Yet, in my mind, we were none-the-worse – in fact the better – for conditions which today would simply not be supported by modern parents.

'Certainly the active sporting type, such as myself, fared the best on that cold mountainside. To reach our hockey field, our tennis courts, or the baseball field, we had to tear down the mountainside. The ball fields were half a mile away and if you were in all the teams, as I was, one raced back, perhaps to play basketball on the terrace, and then one raced further up the hill to the cottage arriving panting to be scolded by my music teacher. It seems to me now that I have always lived my life at a very fast tempo,' says Elisabeth – an observation to which today all members of her family would attest.

For three years, Elisabeth was the centre-half-back in the school hockey team and, while lacking pitching talents, she was captain of the baseball team and a member of every other school team from tennis to basketball. She even played golf, with borrowed clubs, on the school's hillside nine-hole course. 'I loved anything to do with a ball game and I suppose I was fortunate to be at a small school that allowed me to be in all the teams. There was great excitement about once a term when we came down to Melbourne to play St Catherine's, Toorak College or Lauriston.

'In the winter you started off in the morning with hockey, played basketball after lunch and then finished with tennis. It was a big day when you had to play in the three teams as I did. In the summer we played baseball instead of hockey.

'About once a year at Clyde we'd get a heavy fall of snow and that was heavenly. We'd be given a half day's holiday and, in great excitement, we would scramble up another of those rocky outcrops called the Camel's Hump. But at other times we'd be excited when bushfires came close to the forests around us. Once we were all taken out into the centre of the playing fields in the middle of the night. The most wonderful drama, fire blazing all around us and the headmistress, Miss Tucker, assuring us all that we were safe, that the wind would ensure that Clyde – and us – did not burn. We sometimes were told to get ready to evacuate the school, but somehow we survived snow and fire.'

One of the school activities that so fascinated Elisabeth was music and, again at Clyde, Elisabeth had a teacher who believed in encouraging her young pupils. 'She was Mrs Noall, a much more rugged character than Winifred Pillars at St Catherine's, but also very gifted with a capacity to encourage the students' belief in themselves.

'For five years at Clyde I was always awarded the music prize but, unfortunately, was always very nervous and suffered agony

1 Mrs Rupert Greene, in 1909, with her daughters, Marie, nine, Sylvia, six, and Elisabeth, nine months

2 Keith, at twenty-three, just before his departure for London on 14 April 1908

3 Elisabeth, aged eighteen months, at Pemberley

4 Nathaniel Parker Forth, Elisabeth's great-great-grandfather, c. 1770

5 Great-grandparents Jeremiah George Ware and wife, Anne McRobie, c. 1840-50, of Koort-Koort-Nong, near Camperdown in the Western District of Victoria

6 The Forth Family — 'Granny' (Anne de Lancey Forth), centre, with Bairnie (Elisabeth's mother) and Nowell on her right; Jack and May on her left, c. 1890s

7 Elisabeth's uncle, Nowell de Lancey Forth c. 1900

8 Elisabeth's grandfather, William Greene, as a young man, c. 1860

9 Elisabeth's grandmother, Fanny Govett (Mrs William Greene), c. 1880

10 The future gardener. Toddler Elisabeth at Pemberley, c. 1911

11 Pemberley in the early 1900s - Elisabeth's childhood home

12 Pemberley pirates: David Morrison, with toy pistol, urges the Greene girls - Marie, with plaits, Sylvia, and the three-year-old Elisabeth - to row faster in their make-believe boat using clothes props for oars, 1912

13 A very proud father. Rupert Greene and daughters, Marie, Sylvia and Elisabeth, far right, c. 1914

14 Elisabeth's parents, Rupert and Bairnie Greene

15 Elisabeth's grandmother, Anne de Lancey Forth

16 Elisabeth at Clyde, aged thirteen

17 'One of the nicest photographs ever taken of me.' Elisabeth at seventeen before she met Keith

18 Eighteen-year-old Elisabeth Greene

19 This is the *Table Talk* photograph of eighteen-year-old Elisabeth which attracted Keith's attention

when I had to play one or two solos at school speech nights. I have always loved music and had a lot of enjoyment from playing the piano, but have regretted that I was not quite up to giving others real pleasure when they listened to me play,' says Elisabeth.

Elisabeth owed her happy days at Clyde to her godfather, the shy John Riddoch, for it was he who had insisted that he be allowed to pay Elisabeth's school fees – an offer gratefully accepted by Rupert Greene. 'It must have been a godsend for him,' Elisabeth says with a smile now.

Mr Riddoch and his wife were a childless couple who befriended the Greenes not long after they moved into Pemberley. They lived in a graceful mansion off Toorak's Heyington Place and made a great fuss of Elisabeth whenever they visited. Sadly Mrs Riddoch died leaving John an ageing man alone except for the servants in his big house. Soon after his wife's death, John Riddoch gave some of her beautiful jewellery to the Greene sisters.

Elisabeth says now that the attention her godfather paid to her was excessive. On school holidays he would invite her around to Sunday lunch and sit with her as the parlour maid served a roast dinner and beautiful desserts. After each such formal luncheon, John Riddoch would present his goddaughter with a lovely bunch of flowers and a gold sovereign which, as she says now, 'unfortunately I did not keep for long'. At the same time, John Riddoch opened a cheque account for Elisabeth at the National Bank in Collins Street, and paid a generous fifty pounds to her credit every year. It is an account which Elisabeth has kept open to this day. Although the Greenes accepted John Riddoch's generosity with no qualms, Elisabeth was right in thinking that her benefactor's attitude to her was at times bordering on the obsessive – a fact that was sadly to be confirmed a few years later.

However, future difficulties were the last thing on Elisabeth's mind as she submerged herself in the joys of life in the Australian bush surrounded by splendid new friends at a school she loved from the day she arrived. From the start she made wonderful friends. There was Peggy Macfarlan, daughter of a judge, Bobbie Hay, daughter of a Moonee Ponds doctor, and June Whitehead of Goodwood, Minhamite.

Elisabeth's first holiday from Clyde was spent at the Macfarlans' home in Alma Road, East St Kilda. Elisabeth remembers that Mrs Macfarlan was very kind to her but says that the atmosphere in the family, which included four good-looking sons then at Melbourne Grammar, was 'stressful ... none of the boys got on with their father and the stress told on Peggy and her mother.' They had a difficult life with the judge who, after the family had finished breakfast, rang a bell and descended to sit alone at a table in solitary state while his wife danced attendance upon him with the best breakfast fare.

Then there were the charming Ramsay girls, Betty, Catherine and Paddy, who were later to invite Elisabeth to spend wonderful school holidays with them at their enchanting old property, Turkeith. Seeing how the other half lived made an impression on Elisabeth who appreciated even more her holidays in the very different atmosphere. 'They were all absolute dears,' she says now. 'A great deal of unpunctuality existed in that regime, but they were always so interesting and charming. Mr and Mrs Ramsay were always so kind to me and many other young visitors.'

But there was a problem or two at school. Elisabeth has gone through life with her admirers saying: 'Oh, but you were so clever at school.' Today she says firmly: 'But I wasn't! I may have topped my class at St Catherine's but perhaps the competition wasn't so very great there. At Clyde I soon found I wasn't very well grounded. There were quite a few gaps in my education, particularly algebra and trigonometry. They were a ghastly problem for me in my second year. The headmistress, Miss Dorothea Tucker, tried very hard to teach me, but it was to no avail.' Still Elisabeth says she 'adored' Clyde, as did most of that select band of hardy girls isolated out in the Australian bush. 'I loved the country and I loved the games and music. There wasn't the same pressure that there was at home in Toorak.

'It may sound ridiculous now, but on Sundays when the morning service was over, my friends and I would lay out rugs in the crisp mountain air and I would write letters and sketch the beautiful towering mountain ash trees. I was no artist, although my sisters were rather good, but I enjoyed it. I was expressing myself. You know, when you are an adolescent you get carried away by the beauty of it all and you want to express your appreciation of it. We were so lucky. We had the space and we had the beauty and I think it did something for us all.'

In later years, one Clyde 'old girl', Lady (Joan) Lindsay who preceded Elisabeth at Clyde, was to write an enchanting book called *Picnic at Hanging Rock*. Later, long after the Lindsays had become close neighbours of the Murdochs, the book became a hauntingly beautiful Australian movie of the same name, capturing a somewhat mystical feeling of the ancient rocks not shared by any of the other girls from Clyde who frequently visited the volcanic rock pile not far from their school and climbed all over it – without ever vanishing.

'Our parents rarely came to visit us in those days. People weren't so mobile and we were up in the mountains. I don't think my father ever visited the school,' says Elisabeth. Nor did he write letters – 'Well, perhaps, three, and I hardly had any letters at all from my mother. I wasn't aggrieved although some girls seemed to get letters from their parents three or four times a week. My mother did write marvellous letters. She carried on a wonderful correspondence with some people, but my sisters and I seldom got any. So there I was at boarding school and only getting away for a weekend at half-term.'

Despite her joy at being a boarder at Clyde, Elisabeth did have one setback in her first year. One of the close friends she had made, after meeting her on the train on the way to Woodend, was Phil Windeyer from Sydney. Tragically, the unfortunate young girl contracted pneumonia at Easter and died almost overnight, greatly distressing Miss Henderson and all her young friends.

Not long after this, the senior girls arranged a midnight feast in the prefects' bush cottage up the hill from the school and Elisabeth, already a new girl admired for her sporting prowess, was invited. But as a junior member of the group, Elisabeth was told to stand guard outside the school where she was caught, shivering in the cold night air, by an alert Miss Henderson. 'Poor Miss Henderson, still overwrought by Phil's death decided, rather unfairly, to make an example of me and I was locked up in the music room and forbidden to leave until I had learnt a long, difficult passage of Shakespeare. Then, on top of that, although I was the only one punished, I was forced to sit in silence at the headmistress's table in the huge dining hall at Clyde for two and a half days – until I just couldn't stand it any longer.

'It was a very cruel thing to do to a child in her first term at school, but it did teach me that life wasn't always fair and that was a very, very good lesson for me. I got over it, and now believe that Miss Henderson was a marvellous woman. I still have great admiration for her character and personality ... although I can still remember the cold of that music room on the mountainside,' says the always forgiving Elisabeth nearly seventy years later.

Elisabeth did not become a prefect at Clyde. She says: 'I was not in any way undisciplined or difficult. I was very happy and had lots of friends and I got on very well with all the mistresses ... but there were ninety pupils at Clyde and only six girls were elected as prefects each year. I was the best all-rounder at sport and took an active role in everything, but I was never a prefect. I was captain of baseball and I was in all the other sporting teams – a most zealous competitor.'

Years later the daughters of Elisabeth and Keith Murdoch were to follow their mother to Clyde where they distinguished themselves at their studies and sport.

As they grew together at Clyde, Elisabeth and her classmates forged friendships which have carried through their lives. During their holidays they visited each other's homes and properties, met brothers and other boys and attended carefully supervised dances and parties. Elisabeth became a keen rider during the holidays riding along Alexandra Avenue and around the Botanical Gardens on the 'tan' and trotting through the marshlands, which have long since become Albert Park, under the kindly eye of Edward Fitzgerald. At the time, the Greenes couldn't afford proper riding gear for Elisabeth, but she looked smart in a school tunic and well-polished leggings, and during one of the enforced Greene family spells at St Ives guesthouse in South Yarra she was encouraged to ride by 'Ted' Fitzgerald, a keen horseman who also lived at the guesthouse.

During one of the Greenes' enforced stays at St Ives, General Sir Harry and Lady Chauvel also lived there and that was the beginning of a lifelong friendship with the family of the heroic former commander of the Australian Light Horse, who were also keen equestrians.

At home at Pemberley, Bairnie had always instilled into her daughters the Forth family ideals of service. Clyde had remarkably similar goals for its girls too. 'It was the one thing Clyde really did for us. We were put firmly on the track at school of believing that we were very fortunate and that there were many other people who, through no fault of their own, were suffering or were underprivileged, and because we had this opportunity to be educated, we must go out into the world and do what we could. It was quite a thing. I was there for five years and I am sure that this urge to help was encouraged at Clyde. A large proportion of the girls who went to school with me have done very worthwhile and useful things,' Elisabeth says.

One project that captured Elisabeth's imagination was knitting woollen singlets for the tiny babies at Melbourne's Children's Hospital. Told that the girl who knitted the most garments would be given an escorted tour of the hospital in Melbourne, Elisabeth began knitting furiously, under the desk during lessons, and after lights out at night. 'I may not have been the best knitter, but I knitted more of those grubby little singlets than anyone else in the three years I sat at the back of the class in the sixth form.'

Her visit to the hospital in the days before the Great Depression made a great impact on Elisabeth. She was shown the wards, met doctors and nurses and asked questions. Then she saw the tiny babies coming out of the theatres red-faced and screaming. In those days before great strides were made in surgery, many were doomed to a short, sickly life and Elisabeth was devastated by what she saw – too upset to go back to Clyde the next day.

When she did arrive back at school, there were thoughts implanted in her mind that would one day lead her to take on her great work in hospital administration and, later, the Murdoch family to help fund the great institution pioneering research into the genetic causes of complaints that shorten and damage the lives of the world's children. But, until her schooling ended, there were tennis, hockey, baseball, basketball and bushland hikes – along with the study. Elisabeth thrived, toughened up in the cold mountain air blowing through the open dormitories. With unlimited access to tuition, and a piano to practise on, she also became one of the school's better pianists, playing the hymns at assembly and at school speech nights and events, but always dreading the moment when, with all eyes upon her, she sat at the keyboard and began to play.

Back in Toorak, the cable trams were still running past Pemberley's front gate, but the conductors and grip-men would never have recognised the poised young lady who finally came home from the mountain school as 'our little girl' who once waved to them from the tree branches. No longer 'Baby' to Marie and Sylvia, Elisabeth Joy Greene had grown up while away in the Australian bush.

CHAPTER SIX

Coming Out

MEMORIES OF her senior years at Clyde are still precious to Dame Elisabeth Murdoch. She had thrived as she matured in the closely knit school community on the mountainside and, although she had no aspirations to continue her studies at university, she had gained a well-rounded Christian education and absorbed attitudes of tolerance and devotion to duty that were never to be abandoned during the years ahead.

By now, with the new-found freedom of her senior years, there were boyfriends: 'I was rather fortunate in that I had a lot of charming young friends, some of them who had a rather adolescent interest in you and, of course, one always had somebody who was "The Number One" and you would be waiting for a letter. My boyfriends were mostly from Geelong Grammar and Melbourne Grammar. I'd be invited to their prefects' dances, usually at Nine Darling Street. They were awfully nice boys and we were all good pals. Yes, there were one or two who were quite devoted and we corresponded after I left school. There was an older family friend, Peter Manifold. He took me up flying in his Gypsy Moth and we looped-the-loop. We went to Luna Park too and he took me on the Big Dipper which we both adored. I was a bit intrepid, and Peter was fun, but never a suitor.'

There was another young man who Elisabeth was 'madly in love with' when she was fourteen. He was a family friend from Sydney who was prominent in the wool trade. Sylvia admired him too, but he was happily engaged, had been for years, and only came to see the Greenes because he was lonely in Melbourne. After they were married the couple invited Elisabeth to stay with them in Sydney and he suggested that she have her portrait taken while she still had her two long plaits. As was the custom in those days, the young exchanged photographs and several young men were given the engaging portrait.

'It's one of the nicest photographs ever taken of me. I really didn't have any idea that I was pretty or anything, because my sisters would always put me firmly in my place, but looking back on those photographs I think I was a very nice-looking young girl, with no make-up, nothing. I didn't even use lipstick until I was twenty-eight. It just didn't seem to be necessary. I used powder, of course.

'I was one of the last girls at school to have long hair. I'd had pigtails for all those years, but then the shingle came in and I must have finally persuaded my parents to let me have it done.' Elisabeth was to keep her hair shingled until she was thirty-five. Her husband loved it that way and always admired the shape of the back of Elisabeth's head. But as her schooldays drew to an end there were boyfriends, a few of whom, she says, meant quite a lot to her. 'I had a great passion for one young man in the country. He was a very dashing Scot, an overseer on one of his relations' properties, and he had a motorcycle on which I loved to ride as his pillion passenger. I was still at school and I'm sure that he was a bit of a womaniser and about seven or eight years older than I was, but all that rather attracts you when you are young.

'It was a rather hopeless passion really, but at that age you're very intense. Fortunately, I was deflected from such immature relationships by my sporting interests and other school activities. And then, of course, when I met Keith there was no further interest in former boyfriends.' Yet, years later after this admirer died, his widow sent Elisabeth back the Sydney photograph she had given him in her schooldays.

There were still some 'tortures' for Elisabeth to go through before she finished school and, not for the first time, Rupert Greene was the man responsible for his teenage daughter's distress. Invited to a dance at the Grange Road home of the Brudenell Whites, Elisabeth was told that she must be ready to go home when her father called for her at midnight. But when midnight came, Bairnie had to rouse her husband from a deep sleep and instruct him to collect his teenage daughter.

To make matters worse, Elisabeth recalls, she was chatting to young Geoff de Crespigny, 'a most interesting creature', somewhere in the garden when the impatient Rupert drove up in his office car. 'Oh, the tortures I went through,' says Elisabeth. 'He actually called for me still wearing his pyjamas and I was just so mortified. I don't know if anyone at the party except me realised it because he did have his overcoat on, but I was just so ashamed.

'In those days. of course, you couldn't be brought home by a young man, you had to be called for ... the young really don't understand what one had to do to achieve one's enjoyment and entertainment in those days. Few of the young men had their own cars and Melbourne had not long switched from hansom cabs, or wagonettes, to motor taxis – and you would never expect a young man to hire a taxi.

'Later we took trams and if you missed the tram you had to walk because you'd never dream of letting a young man spend money on you – except, perhaps, for a box of chocolates or a flower. To the young today, taking taxis doesn't seem to mean anything. Yet, I think the use of the taxi and the telephone are to me quite the most outstanding changes in our way of life.

'I still have a funny feeling today about overseas telephone calls, but even people on quite average wages seem to accept such things as part of the cost of living,' says the mother of Rupert Murdoch, the man whose vast News Corporation communications empire was largely built on the results of his constant use of telecommunications. But in the days that Elisabeth was attracting the attention of some eligible young beaux in Melbourne and rural society, local telephone calls were still operator-connected by girls who politely asked 'Number please?' Local calls cost one penny.

The wonderful days at Clyde had to come to an end. Elisabeth played the piano at her final school assembly, and looked out over the rolling plains and distant hills, before Mr South's little service car came to take her and her friends down the mountain to Woodend station for the last time. To this day, Elisabeth regrets that she did not gain her Matriculation Certificate at the end of her happy school days. However, behind her Elisabeth Greene left her name on the school's sporting and honour boards – and, although the tower was strictly off limits when Elisabeth was at school, later visitors have found the name Elisabeth Greene deeply carved into the woodwork near the very top.

It was accepted in those days that the daughters of the well-off and well-connected – and at least Elisabeth Greene was well-connected and had her own bank account, thanks to her doting godfather –

did not need to go out and seek employment after their schooling was complete. Today Elisabeth says: 'It was disgraceful really. I was rising eighteen and there was no question of what I was going to do now for a job. You know, neither I nor my sisters had any job qualifications. There had never been any suggestion that we should be trained to earn our living.

'That was very irresponsible, I know, but that was part of the scene in those days if you came from the kind of home we came from. Our father would have regarded it as a reflection on him if we went out and got a job.' Such attitudes were not confined to the Greene family either. Elisabeth can clearly recall her beloved Granny Forth complaining that the Forth menfolk were unqualified for any occupation – apart from fighting the Empire's wars. 'I certainly had happy times with my friends, playing tennis and dancing and that sort of thing, but I knew something was missing. I used to get on those electric trams that had replaced the cable cars armed with hockey sticks and tennis racquets and set off to old girls' matches at Albert Park or the University of Melbourne ... and, of course, I lived at home – nobody would live anywhere else at that time.'

But Elisabeth already instinctively knew that there was more to life than sport and boyfriends. Within weeks of leaving school, she had volunteered to work one day a week at the Lady Northcote Kindergarten in a very poor part of industrial Melbourne. 'I had no qualifications whatsoever, but you'd just make yourself useful and help those poor, often hungry, children as best you could. It was an eye-opener for a girl just out of school.' In fact, one friend who accompanied Elisabeth on her regular visits to the kindergarten was shocked to find that the poor children, many suffering from impetigo, actually 'smelt'.

But sister Marie sewed for friends in a shop that specialised in babies' clothing. 'My sister sewed beautifully and she did work at that for a while. It was a very exacting employment and very badly paid.' Sylvia, who was now spending most of her time at the beautiful Delatite property of the Ritchies, in the foothills of the Australian Alps near Mansfield, was at this time deeply in love with her future husband, pastoralist Robert Ritchie.

Elisabeth's sporting and kindergarten interests were not generally considered to be pursuits suitable for a young Toorak lady. 'I wasn't really interested in a social life but I came out – or was brought out – as was the ordinary thing for girls in those days and is nothing to be ashamed of now. It was when the Duke and Duchess of York – the late King George VI and his wife, now the Queen Mother – came to Melbourne in 1927 and attended a ball in Stonnington, the old Government House in Toorak. It was a great place to make one's debut and a lot of other girls were there that night. There was Elsa Andrews, who later became Elsa Chirnside, and the darling girl who became Mrs Wally Davenport and a number of my other friends. We were not presented, we just attended the dance and we were squired by glorious young naval officers.' One of the young officers took a passing interest in Elisabeth which, she says, was reciprocated. 'I was won over by his gorgeous naval cloak. I thought he was marvellous. He later became Australian war hero, Vice Admiral Sir John Collins.'

There was another fascinating young man there with the Royal party that night too – John Cochrane who later became a distinguished Admiral in the Royal Navy. Before he left Melbourne he sent Elisabeth a beautifully illustrated copy of A. A. Milne's *Now We are Six*. 'I suspect there was a book in every port,' Elisabeth chuckles.

Elisabeth was looking delightful that night in a flowing taffeta picture frock with a rose pattern and a low neckline. She danced the night away with the gallant young officers and saw the Duchess draw the Duke's attention to her dress as they swept past on the floor. Elisabeth has never forgotten the charm and beauty of the young woman destined to be Queen, on that important night in her life.

Certainly Elisabeth aroused the interest of several very eligible young men at the Stonnington ball that night, but, as she says: 'Then, by a miracle, and it was a miracle for me, I met Keith!'

CHAPTER SEVEN

The Meeting

IT WAS NOW eighteen years since Keith Murdoch had left London and returned to Australia feeling sad and rejected after his first failed tilt at Fleet Street, journalism's 'Street of Broken Dreams'. In those eighteen years the world had been changed forever by the first of its Great Wars and the fortunes of the shy young Australian had changed just as dramatically too. Keith was now the prosperous and influential editor of *The Herald* newspaper with powerful friends in Britain and Australia and – following his controversial disclosure of the folly of Winston Churchill's flawed Gallipoli campaign in 1915 – he had earned a worldwide reputation as a fearless and accurate reporter.

Ruggedly handsome, sophisticated and charming, Keith Murdoch was now forty-two and unmarried – and considered by the society matrons of Melbourne and Sydney to be a most eligible bachelor. The embarrassing stammer was, after expert therapy in Britain and

Australia, now firmly under control and Keith was considered to be interesting and desirable company at dinners and social functions. Australia's awesome operatic diva, Dame Nellie Melba, was just one of many celebrities seeking Keith's company, advice – and influence. Statesmen, artists, politicians and powerful company directors were his friends. And then, looking back, it probably was a miracle, as Elisabeth believes, that led Keith Murdoch to finally meet the vivacious eighteen-year-old debutante. As Elisabeth tells it: 'Keith was being pressed by Mrs Allan Spowers to go to a dinner dance in aid of the Red Cross at the Austin home, Eilyer, in Irving Road, but at the time he was just too busy at *The Herald* and too pressed for time to go out to dinner too often. Really, he was very much in demand as an interesting "odd man" to make up the numbers at dinners but he simply couldn't accept many invitations.' However, although Keith Murdoch's great talents were directed mainly at newspaper production at that time, the company did own magazines, including a *Tatler*-style society-gossip picture magazine called *Table Talk*.

Glancing through the latest issue of *Table Talk* on his desk, Keith stopped at a page featuring a cameo portrait of a pretty, vivacious young debutante – Miss Elisabeth Greene. Keith was enchanted and picked up his phone to re-call the persistent Mrs Spowers. Yes, he could after all manage to come to the charity dance in Toorak that night – but only if she made certain that a Miss Elisabeth Greene was also a guest and he could be introduced to her, he told the amused society matron.

Looking back to one of the most important moments of her life, Elisabeth can remember that she was indeed introduced to Keith Murdoch that night. They did speak briefly, she remembers, but he did not invite her to dance. He seemed too shy, and besides she was there with an escort. 'But I can remember his eyes, big, dark and compelling. They just seemed to follow me around the room for the rest of the evening. Believe me, it was a very significant night,' says Elisabeth.

Elisabeth arrived home at Pemberley that night, her mind in a whirl and still thinking of 'that shy man who realised I was shy too and quite overcome, and was so sweet to me.' Rupert was still awake when his youngest daughter came home and he called to her: 'Well, who did you like better than yourself?' Even the worldly Rupert Greene must have been startled when Elisabeth replied without hesitation: 'Well, Keith Murdoch.'

The next day, Keith phoned to ask Elisabeth to come with him to Sorrento, then a morning's drive from Melbourne on the beautiful Mornington Peninsula. Without hesitation – or permission – Elisabeth said yes, she would love to go. 'He turned up outside Pemberley in his big Itala sports car and immediately there were terrific ructions in the family, but I said I was going and there would be no stopping me,' says Elisabeth, still shaking her head at the memory of the trauma at the time. Back home just a little late, after stopping off briefly at a party at tennis star Norman Brookes' Cliff House at Mt Eliza, and a breezy ride in the big Italian vintage car, Elisabeth was carpeted by her anxious parents and told never to do such a thing again – 'No nice girl ever goes out with an older man like that,' an angry Rupert Greene declared.

'Think of it today. It would be quite ridiculous to get so upset, and Keith was quite oblivious to all the fuss. He moved in a much more sophisticated set who thought nothing of going out for a day's run ... but I suppose it was the difference in our ages that worried my family.' When Keith called the next day to suggest another trip, she had to say: 'I'm afraid my family are rather upset and don't want me to go out with you again.' Undeterred, Keith just said: 'I've asked Mr and Mrs Henry Gullett to come along too. I am looking for a house to rent at Sorrento for the holidays and it would be lovely if you could come too.' Penny Gullett was the daughter of writer Barbara Baynton and Henry Gullett was a distinguished journalist and Federal MP. Elisabeth believes now that the Gulletts' obvious friendship with Keith Murdoch, and their approval of the newspaper editor, helped influence Bairnie and Rupert Greene – and Elisabeth's sisters. Elisabeth, who was to become a lifelong friend of the Gulletts, says: 'I always had the warmest affection and appreciation for them because Penny and Henry were marvellous friends to me. They'd known Keith well and they were very fond of him. I think they really encouraged our romance. They did so long for him to be married and happy.'

Both Sylvia and Marie had met Keith at dinner parties and Marie was able to support Elisabeth as she described Keith as: 'Such a charming, kindly, nice, gentle and interesting man.' Says Elisabeth: 'I think that recommendation from Marie was a notch up in Keith's favour.' Before her meeting with Keith there were quite a number of young men friends. 'Of course, in those days no young couple attached themselves to each other to the exclusion of others. That just wasn't on. I think it's an awful pity when young people just settle on one person without looking at anybody else, because then they never experience any other relationship, and I think that's very foolish.' But there is no doubt that from the first meeting Elisabeth Greene was very attracted to Keith Murdoch. 'How can you explain it, but some people have a sort of certain magnetism and, if you can catch it, how lucky you are. Of course, you could make a great mistake, but I certainly didn't and I still hope and pray that it wasn't a great mistake for him. I don't think it was!'

But, in fact, Elisabeth can now see that early romance was lucky to survive. 'My family could easily have said that you are not allowed to see him any more, because in those days young people more or

The Meeting

less did what their parents said – perhaps it's a pity that now there isn't a little more control. I do think that the present generation mature earlier. At eighteen or nineteen they are very much older than I was. I was very innocent and unsophisticated really – a very well brought up young lady, you see.'

But well brought up as she undoubtedly was, Elisabeth Greene was a very determined young lady too, and, as she says now: 'I owe so much to my mother, father and sisters, because it could have been made an impossible situation and disaster could have overcome me because I might just have dug my toes in and gone off – or perhaps not been allowed to marry ... and look what I would have missed.' As it turned out, Elisabeth was allowed to go on more outings in the Itala as long as she was properly chaperoned by either one of her sisters or responsible friends known to both the Greenes and Keith. A weekend at Sorrento was approved with the Kepple-Palmers – he was an aide-de-camp to the State Governor – in attendance, and Keith and Elisabeth went off alone together for a picnic lunch on the rocky ocean beach near Elephant Rock on the back beach at Sorrento. Keith loved his picnics and proudly produced a wonderful hamper skilfully packed by his manservant. Elisabeth remembers vividly that it was a perfect, warm, midsummer's day, sunny and clear with a flat calm ocean – instead of the usual rolling surf off Bass Strait. Elisabeth had no premonition of danger.

Keith lazed on the beach as Elisabeth, a strong swimmer, walked down the sandy beach to the sea and waded in. After a few powerful overarm strokes, Elisabeth realised that she was in the grip of an undertow, the treacherous current that can drag even the strongest swimmers to their deaths on Australia's beaches. Without panicking, Elisabeth raised an arm and called to Keith for aid. He quickly dived in, swam to her side, and helped her struggle back to the shore. 'Keith and I were quite intrepid in the water in those days. We were both fairly good swimmers, but that experience really did warn us. It was one of those near misses and very alarming. Keith loved the ocean and I did not understand why until we went to Scotland and visited the Murdochs' family property, which marched with the ruins of Slains Castle, built in 1664, on the craggy cliffs of the wild Aberdeenshire coast. The ocean was in his blood. He used to stand on the cliffs and breath in the air with exhilaration.'

Shaken, but relieved, Elisabeth and Keith re-packed the hamper and drove the Itala onto the high cliffs of Cape Schanck, before slowly motoring back to join the Kepple-Palmers. 'He proposed that evening on the verandah of the rented holiday cottage – so that beautiful, but dangerous, day at the beach must have done the trick,' Elisabeth laughs. In fact, Keith suggested that Elisabeth should carefully consider his proposal before giving her answer, but she replied 'Yes,' without hesitation. Keith hadn't even bought an engagement ring for Elisabeth, but the delighted chaperones were told. There was no champagne that night either because Elisabeth feared that her parents might not say yes. 'It was not a foregone conclusion and I know that when I told them, my parents were very anxious, very concerned about what their decision should be. Yes, it was unexpected, and I don't think that I knew what a great conquest I was making. In fact, I was still a bit puzzled why anyone would take a fancy to me after seeing my photograph. It really was most peculiar. I thought I was a gawky looking creature and I had no confidence that I was the least bit attractive. Perhaps I thought of myself as being friendly and enthusiastic and I did seem to make very good friendships – but there were all these raving beauties around, and Keith Murdoch had chosen me.'

At first, Elisabeth was totally overwhelmed by it all. 'It was such a tremendous thing for me, having grown up and just left school and coming out and having a lot of nice friends – it was all suddenly just

The Meeting

swept away to the annoyance of many people. Certainly, I wasn't promised or committed to any young man. I didn't really break any young man's heart, but I did have this little circle that I was very fond of and who wrote to me and that sort of thing, adolescent romances – but not serious or binding ones. Keith was such a kind, considerate man that he knew my problems and he had such a strong sense of duty that he wasn't just going to take off down Toorak Road with me in his great open sports car. He insisted on calling at Pemberley to formally ask my father for my hand.'

Later, Keith told his fiancée of her father's reaction, which clearly had startled the ambitious budding newspaper magnate. Keith had tried to explain his comfortable financial position to Rupert but Elisabeth's father didn't want to hear the finer details. All Rupert said when granting permission for forty-two-year-old Keith to marry his favourite daughter was: 'Well, Murdoch, I suppose you can keep her?' That decided, the couple went to Drummonds in Melbourne to buy a diamond engagement ring. In fact, although Bairnie, Rupert and her sisters were lovingly supportive, many of Elisabeth's closest friends seemed to disapprove and appeared keen on her ending the romance and preventing her marriage to Keith at any price. Her tennis and hockey set were not happy about the match. Neither were old school friends. Teachers from Clyde pleaded with her to reconsider, pointing to her youth and the age of her fiancé.

But the most deeply disturbing opposition came from Elisabeth's benefactor, godfather John Riddoch. His first move as soon as he heard the news was to propose funding an instant overseas trip for Elisabeth to give her time to 'come to her senses'. Then, when that suggestion was flatly rejected by the determined Elisabeth, he angrily castigated the Greenes for allowing such a match. Worse was to come. The lonely old man announced that he was cutting off payments to Elisabeth's bank account and demanded that his wife's jewellery, which he had given to Elisabeth and her sisters, should be returned. Finally, he let it be known that Elisabeth, who was to have been a main beneficiary of his considerable estate, would be cut out of his will unless she ended her engagement to Keith Murdoch immediately.

'I remember that I was stunned and horrified that my godfather could be so horrible about Keith. I suppose it was the age difference that upset him. He didn't even know Keith, but he was so terribly put out. He had this strange proprietary interest in me, because he had been so good to me. I think probably the reaction was understandable, but it was so blind and so foolish of him, because he could have had a great deal of happiness out of my marriage and my children. Later when Helen was born, I said I'd love to push her in the pram to see Mr Riddoch, but Keith told me not to be so stupid. Keith had wanted to go and see him alone, but he was persuaded not to do so in case Mr Riddoch became violent. It was like a Victorian novel, very sad.'

For some time Elisabeth, who had deep affection for her godfather and shared Bairnie and Rupert's gratitude for his contribution to her education, remained distressed and anxious to heal the breach, but John Riddoch would not be consoled. Not then, nor later. Sylvia, Elisabeth's stalwart sister, recalls now the pressures Bairnie had to withstand in the early days of her daughter's engagement. 'That poor mother of ours. She had a lot to put up with over Elisabeth's engagement. You see, some people looked upon it as if she was selling her daughter. Mother really had an awful time.'

Today, Elisabeth can tell Sylvia: 'Well, you were all marvellous to keep these hurtful thoughts from me.' Even now Elisabeth wonders how it all came about. 'I still say that it was extraordinary and

The Meeting

rather terrible to think that, at that stage, I didn't have a little modesty about whether I would be adequate or not. I often look back, but I don't think I was conceited or anything. It just didn't occur to me that I wouldn't be able to manage it. These things don't seem to matter when you're in love!'

CHAPTER EIGHT
The Murdoch Connection

CRUDEN FARM, at Langwarrin, thirty miles from Melbourne, was the name chosen for the ninety-acre farm property Keith Murdoch gave to Elisabeth as her wedding gift. Cruden Investments is the name of the Murdoch family holding company which today controls News Corporation, one of the greatest media empires the world has seen.

Originally, Cruden was the name of a bay thirty miles from Aberdeen among the jagged cliffs of North East Scotland, a safe haven for herring boats sheltering from North Sea gales. The Free Church of Scotland, founded during the 'Disruption' of 1843, gave the name Cruden – from 'Croch Dain', the site of a slaughter of the Danes by the Scots in 1210 – to one of its loyal parishes. Today the name has deep significance for Dame Elisabeth and the entire Murdoch family although, as she reveals now, Cruden Farm, presently enlarged to 135 acres, was often 'in hock' to meet sudden financial demands.

Keith Murdoch's maternal grandfather, George Brown, was minister of the Free Church in Hatton in the Parish of Cruden. A graduate of Aberdeen's ancient university, he was twenty-four when the Disruption split the established Church of Scotland, mainly on the issue that congregations should be free of government interference in appointing their own ministers.

The Reverend Brown ministered to the poor, completed his partly built stone church, constructed a school nearby, and gained the reputation of being an extremely stirring, passionate preacher. During his ministry, he married Mary Smith Shepherd, daughter of James Shepherd, the owner of the large Aldie estate, and a devoted supporter of the established church.

While steadfast in his own stern religious beliefs, the tolerant James Shepherd gave two acres of his land so that his rebel son-in-law could build his new Free Church. During his ministry, the canny Reverend Brown managed to acquire several estates in his parish and, on retirement, he and his wife built a small mansion, 'Longhaven House', which stands to this day.

The man who took over the charge of Cruden Parish in 1878 was the Reverend Patrick Murdoch, himself a son of the manse, whose father James had been a minister of the Free Church in Rosehearty, a windswept fishing village to the north of Cruden. Also a graduate of Aberdeen University, Patrick Murdoch had completed his theological studies at New College, Edinburgh, and then started on what was to be a very distinguished ministry by working for a time in Edinburgh and London.

The daughter of Reverend George and Mary Brown, Annie Brown Shepherd, who to meet the requirements of a family will had taken her mother's maiden name as her surname, met, fell in love with and married her father's young replacement at the Free Church in Hatton. Six years later, shortly after Annie proudly laid the foundation stone of the new church, Patrick Murdoch accepted 'a call' from his elders in 1884 to take up a Presbyterian ministry in Melbourne in far-off Australia – just a little more than one year before his son, Keith Murdoch, was born in the Victorian state capital.

Assured that his new church in West Melbourne would be of solid bluestone with a loyal congregation of respectable, well-to-do middle-class citizens largely of Scots background, Patrick was happy to join other members of his family, including his parents and younger brother Walter on the long trip to Australia.

Walter went to school at Scotch College in Melbourne and soon showed signs of academic brilliance. He went on to the University of Melbourne and graduated with first-class honours in logic and philosophy before becoming a schoolteacher and then a university lecturer and noted author. Always retaining his Scots accent, he began public speaking, writing essays of exceptional depth and beauty, and making his long-term impact on Australian education. Later to be knighted, Sir Walter was to become the Foundation Professor of English at the University of Western Australia.

Sir Walter remained in Western Australia and became a renowned university vice-chancellor. When radio came to Australia, his warm, commonsense weekly broadcasts became favourite Sunday night listening all over the nation. Today, a second university in Perth, the Western Australian capital, has been named 'The Murdoch University' in Sir Walter's honour.

But before that, life was often difficult for Patrick and Annie Murdoch in Melbourne as the boom of the 1880s, which was accelerated by the vigour of Scottish migrant industrialists, turned to depression in the 1890s, and the lights of 'Marvellous Melbourne' were quickly dimmed in inner-city suburbs like West Melbourne.

Faced with a dwindling and increasingly impoverished congregation, Patrick Murdoch was soon assisting another Scottish migrant, his close friend the Reverend James Climie, who had left Aberdeen for Australia two years before the Murdochs. Sadly, Climie's health was declining and Patrick took services for his friend in the church which served the still prosperous Melbourne suburbs of Camberwell and Burwood East. When the Reverend Climie died, at thirty-two, Patrick took over his ministry – a move that was to lead to Patrick Murdoch becoming the much-loved first Moderator-General of the Presbyterian Church in Australia.

But before that elevation to the head of his church, Patrick Murdoch and his wife had to struggle to bring up their six children – five sons, including Keith Murdoch, and a daughter. Patrick's was a large parish, the stipend was modest and then, as now, the clergy were expected to help those less fortunate than themselves.

This was the very devout and loving family into which Keith Murdoch, the eldest of the sons to survive, was born in 1886. When, years later, Keith's son Rupert was called a 'foreigner' and criticised by a British MP for owning so many newspapers in Britain, the *Daily Telegraph* and other publications sprang to his defence.

The *Aberdeen Leopard* magazine, published in the city the Murdoch forebears knew so well, rejected the charge that Rupert was a 'foreigner', traced the solid Scottish heritage of the international newspaper proprietor and his family back to its Buchan roots and commented: 'Heredity is the rock on which everything breaks. Rupert Murdoch has descended from a line of go-ahead, successful people who had courage and strong convictions – a line rooted in the dour, granite-hearted, realistic land of Buchan.'

The case for Rupert's defence would have been even stronger if his mother's Forth connection had also been examined. But despite his heritage, there was nothing granite-hearted in the make-up of Keith Murdoch, a shy engaging lad who, because of that humiliating stammer, was slow to make friends at school. In fact, he had to be taken away from the Camberwell Common School when the endless cruel teasing of his peers often sent him home in tears.

Other schools followed before Keith found peace and sound academic help at Camberwell Grammar School. After two years there he finished his troubled education as dux of the school and immediately made it clear to his anxious father that after much consideration he had decided not to go on to university or enter the Church.

Patrick Murdoch, now an influential figure in the Presbyterian Church in Australia, called on his friend, dour fellow Scot, David Syme, owner of the powerful, but studiously dull, *Age* newspaper, then a publication which migrant readers found as heavy going as the London *Times* of that era to read.

Patrick had told his friend that his son had an 'insatiable appetite' for newspapers, but what impressed the humourless Syme was the fact that Keith Murdoch had actually learned shorthand while still at school – a skill he was to always retain, even when he was more a proprietor than a reporter. But even assisting the son of a friend did not overcome Syme's native caution. His offer to Keith Murdoch was less than the going rate – a penny halfpenny per line for any news items that Murdoch brought in that found their way into *The Age*. Added to that, Syme offered Keith the Malvern area of Melbourne to cover ... an area whose middle-class residents preferred the then more conservative opposition newspaper, *The Argus*.

The fledgling reporter's prospects seemed to be bleak indeed, but faced with such a challenge Keith Murdoch went to work with enthusiasm and vigour, undeterred by the vocal impairment which at times left him speechless in the middle of asking a question. The young man's perseverance won him friends and he soon found useful contacts in the council, police stations, courts and sporting clubs ... added to that he delivered his neatly typed reports directly to the chief sub-editor at *The Age* office every day and soon found that reports from his 'beat' in Malvern were being given prominence in the paper – which in turn resulted in a pleasing increase in *The Age*'s circulation in the area.

Desmond Zwar, in his compelling book *In Search of Keith Murdoch*, recounts how Keith's mother would find him at breakfast in the manse reading *The Age* and carefully marking the paragraphs he had contributed before counting the lines and entering them in a notebook. Before long the reliable young reporter with sound shorthand was being given assignments outside his district to cover. After a few months, he was offered a staff job on the paper. Most young reporters would have gratefully accepted the offer, but Keith was his canny father's son and he soon calculated that he was earning more money working for a penny halfpenny a line than he would on staff wages.

In those days, before immigration laws ended the free exchange of movement between Britain and Australia, it was the dream of every reporter to work on Fleet Street. Keith Murdoch did more than dream. By 1907 he had put away the equivalent of five hundred dollars invested in bonds – sufficient to allow him to pay his fare to London and spend a year there trying to get a break by being given a trial on one of the great London newspapers.

This account of the life of Elisabeth Murdoch began with the sad outcome of Keith Murdoch's first failed assault on international journalism. By 1910, while Elisabeth was being wheeled in her pram by Pemberley nannies, Keith was back in Melbourne as a staff reporter on *The Age* earning four pounds a week.

During his later years, as head of the powerful *Herald* empire, Keith Murdoch constantly urged his young reporters to learn shorthand – a necessity in those days before mini-cassette recorders. For it was his own excellent shorthand that won him swift promotion at *The Age* when he was assigned to reporting the debates in the Australian parliament – then sitting in Melbourne.

Gaining confidence as his reporting skills increased, Keith was soon on friendly terms with men like Labor Prime Minister Andrew Fisher, a Scot with a broad accent which Murdoch, unlike most of his colleagues, had no trouble understanding. Welshman Billy Hughes, soon to succeed Fisher and become Australia's fiery wartime Prime Minister – in which office he won Empire fame as 'The Little Digger' – also became a close friend of the rapidly maturing Murdoch.

Eventually Murdoch was receiving overtures from other newspapers. He switched to the modern and aggressive Sydney *Sun* as their Commonwealth parliamentary correspondent in Melbourne – a post which provided a small office in the old offices of *The Herald*. Keith Murdoch's rise to newspaper fame and fortune was about to begin.

Soon after the war in Europe broke out, Britain invited Australia to send an official correspondent overseas to cover the fighting. The Australian Journalists' Association was asked to choose a man, and an election among the union's members resulted in a *Sydney Morning Herald* editorial writer, Charles Bean, getting the job. Keith Murdoch came second by only a few votes.

Bean went off to the Mediterranean to write part of Australia's history, but Keith Murdoch was not far behind. In fact, in line for swift promotion at the Sydney *Sun*, he was being sent to London to head the group's wartime cable service. He took with him a formal letter from his friend, Prime Minister Andrew Fisher, explaining that

Mr Murdoch would be 'undertaking certain inquiries for the Government of the Commonwealth in the Mediterranean theatre of war'.

Apart from this rather vague *laissez passer*, Keith also had a letter of introduction to General Sir Ian Hamilton, the hard-pressed British General Officer Commanding at Gallipoli, who was also a close personal friend of Winston Churchill, explaining that Murdoch had been asked by the Australian Government to 'make certain inquiries in connection with postal facilities at the base in Egypt . . .'

This Murdoch mission ultimately destroyed Hamilton's career and significantly changed the course of the war as envisaged by Winston Churchill. It began with Keith's arrival at Gallipoli after signing a declaration that he would not dispatch newspaper reports that had not been passed by the censor. The declaration went further. In it he had agreed that he would not attempt to 'correspond by any other route or by any other means than that officially sanctioned'. But an on-the-spot investigation of the campaign which was clearly headed for a costly stalemate, if not the disastrous defeat of the courageous Imperial forces, convinced Murdoch that he had a more important mission than filing dispatches to newspapers.

He left Gallipoli determined to write a report to Prime Minister Fisher in Australia and he also carried a similar scathing report from a fellow British war correspondent, Ellis Ashmead-Bartlett, sealed and addressed to British Prime Minister Asquith. British intelligence officers seized this letter, which had not been sighted by the censors, from Murdoch when his London-bound ship docked at Marseilles.

One of the mildest passages in Keith's 'Gallipoli Letter' to his friend Fisher was: 'I say that the work of the general staff in Gallipoli has been deplorable.' The rest of the savage eight-thousand-word dispatch, long held to be classified information by successive Australian governments, outlined the casualty figures, the hellish conditions the men lived and fought under, and their peerless courage as they tried in vain to push back the firmly entrenched Turks.

Regarding Hamilton, Keith reported: 'For the General Staff, and I fear for Hamilton, officers and men have nothing but contempt... sedition is talked round every tin of bully beef on the peninsula, and it is only loyalty that holds the forces together.'

Always magnanimous, Keith had nothing but praise for the Australian troops. He told his Prime Minister: 'Oh, if you could picture Anzac as I have seen it, you would find that to be an Australian is the greatest privilege the world has to offer.' And of the general he was to surely destroy he had this to say: 'I like General Hamilton and find him exceedingly kindly. As a journalist I admire him, but as a strategist he has completely failed. Undoubtedly, the essential and first step to restore the morale of the shaken forces is to recall him.'

Events now moved quickly. On 25 September 1915, two days after Fisher received the Murdoch dispatch, Murdoch was persuaded by British Cabinet ministers to pass on his vital information to Asquith. He did so reluctantly, stressing that his motive in doing so was 'one of affectionate regard for our soldiers' interests'. Asquith had the Murdoch dispatch circulated as a State paper. At the same time, Ashmead-Bartlett arrived in London after being expelled from Gallipoli, and set about convincing his proprietor, Lord Northcliffe, that the Dardanelles should immediately be evacuated.

In his defence, Hamilton sent off a carefully considered repudiation of Murdoch's charges, the key passage of which read: 'My own feeling certainly is that, in his admiration for the Australian forces, and in his grief at their heavy losses (in both of which feelings I fully share), he has allowed himself to belittle and criticise us all so that their virtues might be thrown into even bolder relief.' But this angry assessment was not accepted. The general and his senior aides were recalled and General Sir Charles Monro was given the command. Somehow lost in the drama that surrounded the secret evacuation is the fact that, after examining the position, Sir Charles telegraphed an assessment to London that was a virtual carbon copy of the Murdoch letter. He recommended that the operation should be abandoned at once and the armies evacuated. Tellingly he added that, with the exception of the men from Australia and New Zealand, the troops were no longer equal to a sustained effort. This signal so shocked Field Marshal Lord Kitchener that he urged an inspection and was authorised by Cabinet to go to the Dardanelles. But when it was revealed that Kitchener had departed on what was termed 'an important mission in the East' the rumour began to spread that he had in fact resigned his office as Minister for War. This was quickly denied, but when a Fleet Street paper repeated the report, it was raided by police, the issue destroyed and warnings were given that a similar offence would lead to the suppression of the paper.

In his fearless style, Kitchener inspected the British camps and went forward to the Anzac positions where he approached to within fifty yards of the Turkish trenches and was rousingly cheered by the Australians and New Zealanders. What he saw convinced him that what Murdoch had said – and Monro confirmed – was correct. Kitchener returned to London and spoke to the Imperial Cabinet which authorised Monro's plan to begin the evacuation.

Plans already drawn up were set in motion and the secret and highly risky evacuation of Imperial troops from that terrible battlefield began. At the Royal Commission later set up to examine what had gone so tragically wrong in the Dardanelles, Keith Murdoch was aggressively cross-examined on the question of censorship . . . rather than the accuracy of his assessment. Why had he carried the letter from Ashmead-Bartlett to the British Prime Minister – a letter that had not passed the censor?

Murdoch's reply was that his acceptance of a sealed letter marked 'personal' to Asquith was absolutely justified and had been done in a completely open way. Murdoch told the Royal Commission that he knew he had been risking his whole career by writing his report, but he insisted that correspondents – and indeed troops – had the unquestioned right to correspond with ministers of the Crown without censorship.

'I am always prepared to offer everything I have for Australia,' he added. Keith Murdoch's understanding of the censorship rules were upheld by the Commissioners, and have been confirmed many times since by the action of outspoken correspondents in the Second World War – and with even more dramatic results when US correspondents breached censorship to highlight the failure of the military leadership in the Vietnam War. The Commission recognised General Hamilton's undoubted personal gallantry, his 'sanguine disposition' and his determination to win at all costs, but he was recalled and Gallipoli was successfully evacuated.

Later Ashmead-Bartlett wrote a book in which he revealed that Murdoch and he had believed that the evasion of censorship was essential if the Imperial troops were to be saved from the horrors of a futile winter campaign. Yet to this day there are journalists who criticise Keith Murdoch's action and champion the cause of their trade union's enshrined code of 'ethics' without ever having to face a situation – as Keith Murdoch did – where their journalistic silence could cost the needless loss of thousands of lives.

Years later, in his notable history of the first thirty years of the Commonwealth of Australia, A. N. Smith was to write: 'There was much bungling by every country that took part in the war. It is, perhaps, inseparable from war. But it is doubtful whether the mismanagement at the Dardanelles was equalled elsewhere.'

On one of the Sundays Keith spent at the front in Gallipoli, his father was back in Melbourne preaching: 'We must love men as men, pitying them if they have fallen wounded by the wayside, condemning their sins, fighting against them if they be our enemies, but still loving them, however wicked and in spite of their hostility, for they are men and God loves them, and Christ died for them.' It is doubtful if such lofty Christian ideals would have been shared at Anzac Cove that Sunday.

But soon, his major contribution to the war effort discharged, Keith took up his London post as editor and manager of the United Cable Service, jointly controlled by Australia's newspaper groups. His friendship with Fisher, Hughes and senior British Cabinet ministers who admired his courageous Gallipoli intervention, resulted in the young journalist becoming an unofficial Australian ambassador in the heart of the Empire. When Billy Hughes became Prime Minister, Murdoch's activities on both the political and military fronts took on an even more official complexion. He arranged London dinners for Hughes which were attended by ministers and press barons like the brilliant but erratic Lord Northcliffe. Everyone was impressed by the hard-working, influential Australian journalist with access to the offices of the highest in the land.

Keith Murdoch had actually attended a conference during his first unhappy visit to London at which Lord Northcliffe spoke. Then he had not been able to meet the great Anglo-Irish publisher because he did not have a frock coat which would have allowed him to attend an official reception. Now Keith was able to meet and address the powerful owner of both *The Times* and the *Daily Mail*, as 'Chief'. Letters exchanged between the two men show a degree of respect and affection which confirm reports at the time that Northcliffe and Murdoch were almost like 'father and son'.

Alfred Harmsworth and his brother Harold were in many ways the fathers of modern journalism. Alfred, later to become Viscount Northcliffe, and Harold, who became Viscount Rothermere, founded the *Daily Mail* in London in 1896 and then the outrageous *Daily*

Mirror in 1903. Together they opened several other papers and – just as Rupert Murdoch was later to achieve – saved *The Times* from closure.

Lord Northcliffe was not without his flaws. He had delusions of grandeur, worshipped Napoleon, and even chose the Northcliffe title so that he could sign his correspondence with the Napoleonic '*N*'. Visiting Fontainebleau and being handed Napoleon's hat to try on, he was delighted to discover that it was too small to fit him. Doubtless Keith was aware of some of the chief's famous foibles but he told friends that the otherwise astute Northcliffe had offered him senior posts in his vast newspaper empire. However, in mature letters home to Melbourne he maintained: 'I do not want to alter my present relationship with Northcliffe. I value him as a friend, but would certainly quarrel with him as an employer. He cannot resist making his employees feel that they are the puppets of his will ... he would not permit development as I wish to develop.'

Unaware of Keith Murdoch's reservations, Northcliffe was now telling his friends that Murdoch had the makings of newspaper greatness. Mirroring the devastating tactics of Beaverbrook and other great press barons, Northcliffe showered praise on the Australian, gave him invaluable advice and insisted that he join him for a holiday at his villa on the Riviera. Flattered and grateful, Keith nevertheless kept his head and was unwavering in his determination to return to Australia and take up a senior editorial position on *The Herald*, Melbourne. In fact, he returned to his homeland in fine style aboard HMS *Renown*, the pride of the Royal Navy, bringing the Prince of Wales, later the ill-starred Duke of Windsor, to Australia for a Royal Visit – a visit which Keith was covering for *The Times* and a group of Australian papers. These were heady days for Keith Murdoch and he lost no opportunity to take advantage of his growing stature in journalism.

The Murdoch Connection

In Melbourne, he met Theodore Fink, the chairman of the Herald and Weekly Times, who offered him £2000 a year to edit *The Herald*, a tired old broadsheet which he was quickly to transform into one of the finest evening newspapers in the world. From the start in his new job, Keith made a point of getting to know his staff, remembering their names and even the names of their wives and children. In the days before his marriage to Elisabeth, *The Herald* was his whole life, and his staff repaid his interest and enthusiasm with undying devotion.

In the twenties, the Herald and Weekly Times went from strength to strength and Keith Murdoch went with it, even hosting a visit to Melbourne by his old 'Chief' who told a gathering of prosperous Melburnians: 'The only way to make money in newspapers is to back the man, and this young Murdoch is the man to back.'

While Elisabeth was still climbing her beloved trees at Pemberley, then going off to school, Keith was leading the life of a dynamic and prosperous executive, attending conferences, building circulation and making hurried trips overseas. He was well paid and soon learnt to make wise personal investments. He liked to dress and live well, although usually in rented, serviced apartments close to his office. His friends outside the office were usually rich and famous or politically powerful, although he was never happier than when chatting to his reporters or printers.

For a while, he lived at Cliveden, an old Melbourne mansion once owned by the Clarke family and then converted into large apartments on the site of the present Hilton Hotel. But the need to be able to entertain visiting business and political leaders persuaded him to move into a charming and spacious house in Walsh Street, South Yarra. Keith took over the house on a walk-in walk-out basis from Mrs Fred Fairbairn, an ardent collector of antique furniture and ceramics, so he inherited some fine pieces which gave impetus to his own collecting instincts. He had only to add a butler to lay out his clothes and staff to keep the house and prepare the meals for his dinner guests.

At this time, Keith had been paying court to Peggy Mills, the daughter of a wealthy Riverina Merino stud family. When Peggy became ill and bedridden with a serious and perplexing spinal complaint, Keith stood by her, and they became engaged. But with her eventual recovery, the couple sensibly agreed that they were incompatible and the engagement was broken off. The matchmaking society matrons now saw the charming Keith Murdoch as a confirmed bachelor wedded to his demanding profession.

But then, in 1927, he thumbed through that fateful copy of *Table Talk* magazine on his desk and saw that photograph of the enchanting Miss Elisabeth Greene. Looking back now, Elisabeth says: 'I think I was very lucky that I came along when I did. You have to face facts. Keith was probably very vulnerable at the time. I wouldn't like to think that I was on the re-bound – but that's what a lot of people did say. I did realise that Keith wanted to get married. I knew when he was courting me that he didn't want a long engagement, because I think he felt he was getting older.'

CHAPTER NINE

'I'd rather have twenty years with Keith...'

IN THE YEARS between the wars, Melbourne remained a conservative bastion of traditional British values, especially at the upper-limits of the economic scale. 'Big business' and 'society' maintained Victorian standards now rapidly vanishing even 'at home' in London or Edinburgh, and certainly the engagement of Keith Murdoch and Elisabeth Greene was the talk of the town in Melbourne in 1928 as Australia unknowingly waited, poised on the brink of the Great Depression.

'She's just a babe in arms,' one Toorak matron complained bitterly on hearing the news that the charming Keith Murdoch was about to be removed from the bachelor circuit. 'Yes, but she's a babe with arms,' replied the perceptive Mrs Ruth Whiting, a brilliant and attractive friend of Keith's and sister of Mrs Allan Spowers, part owner of *The Argus*, who had already recognised exceptional strength, intelligence and devotion in the character of the young woman Keith Murdoch had chosen.

Rupert Greene had to run the gauntlet of elderly members of the Melbourne Club who, amazingly, were critical of his daughter's engagement to an older man. Dorothea Tucker, Elisabeth's former headmistress, was particularly upset when she heard of Miss Greene's engagement to forty-two-year-old Keith Murdoch. She told her: 'You know, I know someone who sadly married a man twenty years older than herself and after twenty years she was a widow.' It was then that Elisabeth halted all attempts by friends or relatives to change her mind. Suddenly a schoolgirl no more, Elisabeth stood up and looked directly at Miss Tucker as she said: 'I'd rather have twenty years with Keith than forty years with any other man.'

The passing of all those years since Keith Murdoch's death has done nothing to change Elisabeth's mind on that score. But before their June wedding in 1928 the critics had begun to change their tune as the protective Keith introduced his fiancée to his rich and famous friends and business colleagues.

Snubs from some of Keith's close admirers, including Dame Nellie Melba, then in her domineering sixties, just passed over the head of the happy Elisabeth. 'Dame Nellie always made a great fuss of Keith and, after we were engaged, she invited us up to Coombe Cottage for lunch. Unfortunately I wasn't well that day and Dame Nellie was very bossy and I resented the rather proprietorial attitude she took to Keith, but her daugher-in-law, Evie Armstrong, was sweet and took me to rest after lunch and told me not to worry about "Madre's" bullying.

'Even after we were engaged, Dame Nellie was making use of Keith and wanting to stay at Walsh Street – she'd done that before and everything had to be laid on for Dame Nellie. I don't know why it was, but Keith had a party for her after one of her farewell concerts and she behaved rather badly. When she was older she wasn't very loveable and it was hard for me at the age of nineteen to hold my own with her ... But I wasn't going to be downed by her. I knew that I had to hold my ground, as it were, but I did resent her a bit because I think she made use of Keith.'

But the behaviour of Elisabeth's godfather, Mr Riddoch, became more of a worry. He had cut himself off from all contact with the Greene family as Elisabeth quickly fitted into the exciting, sophisticated adult world of her husband-to-be. Bairnie was troubled by the now open rift between the former close family friend and her youngest daughter. It was only during a 1991 discussion with her sister Sylvia, that Elisabeth learned the full facts of the sad episode.

At the time, only recently married to Robert Ritchie of Delatite, Sylvia had received a bitter letter from Mr Riddoch demanding that she return the jewellery he had given her and her sisters. 'I thought that would be a dreadful thing to do, but Mother wrote to me telling me I must do it, so I decided to go to Melbourne and see Mr Riddoch,' Sylvia said. 'So I did go to see him and he was quite peculiar. He went down on his knees and prayed that this dreadful thing – Elisabeth's marriage to Keith – should be averted ... most extraordinary!

'Then he went to his library and got a dictionary and said to me: "Do you known what a philanderer is?" and I replied: "Yes I think it's 'a male flirt'," although that was the last thing in the world you would have said Keith was – the very, very last thing. But then I was completely made mincemeat of, and realising that he was almost deranged, I went home, packed up my jewels and sent them back.'

But worse was to follow. Marie, who had lost the diamond brooch given to her by Mr Riddoch, received a solicitor's letter saying that if the brooch 'said to be lost', was not returned its value would be . . .

'Poor father, who was always very hard up – usually through his own fault – had to cough up the money,' Sylvia told Elisabeth.

Elisabeth: 'I never knew that. They kept it from me, which was ridiculous.'

Sylvia: 'Well, we didn't want Keith to know because we realised that he would feel he had to replace all those things. Mr Riddoch was very difficult. I think he really felt that if Elisabeth was going to marry someone twenty-two years older than herself, why couldn't she have married someone forty years older, as he was?'

Elisabeth: 'Oh Sylvia, I don't think so at all.'

The Riddoch drama now apparently controlled, Elisabeth continued to enjoy her short engagement. She was soon introduced to Keith's parents and was delighted at the warmth and friendship of the Scottish couple, who were in turn overjoyed that their son had, at last, made such a happy match.

There was a cloud or two on the horizon however. Sylvia's wedding at St John's, Toorak, the year before had strained Rupert's always limited financial reserves, and Elisabeth knew that he would find it difficult to cope with a full-blown society wedding with expensive reception to follow, so favoured by the wealthy Toorak set at the time. Apart from that Elisabeth says: 'I did feel a little shy about marrying someone so much older than myself. I was conscious of that. I didn't want to make it a big splash – that was not my line. Although my parents wanted me to have a generous wedding, I begged that we should just have a small one . . . and, although Keith was very good about it, it was a foolish decision of mine.

'With just the absolutely essential people the guest list was one hundred, and of course we should have invited two or three times that number, because a number of people were hurt that they were not invited. It was hard for Keith with his many friends and business associates, but I was very young, very ignorant really, and I insisted on a small wedding.'

Elisabeth's wedding gown did not quite meet with her approval either but it did fit in with the 'something old ... something borrowed' tradition. 'I thought that it had an ugly uneven line in the front, but then it was, as usual, a hand-me-down from Sylvia,' she laughs. Certainly few photographs of the wedding seem to have been retained in the family collection. But Elisabeth remembers the beautiful choral service at Scots Church lovingly performed by Keith's father, the Rev. Patrick Murdoch, who by now, Elisabeth says, 'I simply doted on.' In the congregation the unmistakable voice of Dame Nellie Melba could be distinctly heard as the guests sang the old familiar hymns. There is one photograph of Elisabeth looking beautiful in her wedding gown and carrying a bouquet of what appear to be lily of the valley sprays.

Although 1920s society weddings were frequently front page news with big pictures and stories by social writers, the Murdoch wedding on a rainy Wednesday, 6 June 1928, and the reception that followed at Pemberley, with champagne and sandwiches for afternoon tea, seemed to attract very little newspaper or magazine attention. But it was a happy day for Elisabeth and Keith with their parents and closest relatives and friends around them as they cut a splendid wedding cake.

Elisabeth had her sister Marie as bridesmaid for, as she says: 'I could have had a dozen lovely bridesmaids, but I didn't think it was suitable. There had been so much controversy over my engagement to Keith that I just wanted to keep it quiet and simple.' Obviously Keith respected Elisabeth's desires, but after the wedding was over, he did say: 'You know dear, it was rather difficult. I think we offended a lot of people.'

Eventually, Elisabeth was driven up Toorak Road past the familiar houses and shops to begin her new life. The wedding car was Keith's new Sunbeam with a *Herald* driver at the wheel and the destination was their honeymoon cottage at Cruden Farm, where more gifts from the groom to the bride were waiting.

In those days the house was really a single-storey weatherboard farm cottage with roses growing over the surrounding verandah and noisy possums in the roof. Keith had sent his cook, manservant and maid ahead to prepare for their arrival and they were waiting at the front door when the newlywed Mr and Mrs Keith Murdoch were driven up the long bumpy track from the road. The manservant, 'a little raw, low Scot named Alec', was, according to Elisabeth, 'Impossible!' and had to be dismissed after the first two days.

It was a happy but short stay for Keith soon found he had urgent newspaper business in Brisbane that required his presence there. Would Elisabeth object to continuing the honeymoon 'Up north'? From the day she had met Keith, Elisabeth always fitted in with his business plans, so she immediately agreed. On this occasion, however, Keith's usually immaculate planning went astray. Calling at Thomas Cook's, Keith obtained a glossy brochure giving details of a wonderful new holiday resort with a golf course, polo ground and swimming pools at Maroochydore, on the coast north of the Queensland capital.

The happy couple set off by train to Sydney and moved into the grand Hotel Australia where Elisabeth soon met some of Keith's friends. 'I was rather shy and I remember walking into the dining room for the first time followed by George Lambert, the famous Australian artist. He slapped me on the back and said "Stand up, girl, stand up and I'll paint you" – obviously I was not holding myself very well, but it was so humiliating and I was always very allergic to George Lambert after that.

'He was very colourful and he'd done quite a lot of work for Keith – including a portrait he drew which I think I'll burn one day. He was such an arrogant man and he made use of Keith by living in his flat at Cliveden for a long time. He did do a beautiful drawing of Ruth Whiting, which I gave to her family after Keith died. George Lambert did paint a wonderful portrait of Keith's mother which won the Archibald Prize. But he never did paint a portrait of me,' says Elisabeth with a rare glint of uncharitable mischief in her eyes.

The drive up the coast to Maroochydore was pleasant, but the 'luxury resort' was a shock. 'We checked in but it was too awful! You can have no idea what it was like. It really was still a drawing on the architect's plan when we arrived and we had to stay in this corrugated iron and timber hut on stilts. There was no indoor sanitation and there was always this smell of phenyl – awful, awful! We quickly moved on to Brisbane.'

In the Queensland capital, it quickly became clear that Keith's urgent business trip was connected with an offer for an interest in the *Courier Mail*. Keith told Elisabeth that John Wren, a millionaire Melbourne businessman and Roman Catholic philanthropist with a poverty-stricken Collingwood upbringing, was involved with him in the business bid. Elisabeth was alarmed. With her father's background in horseracing, she had heard rumours about the alleged gangland connections of Wren and his illegal off-course bookmaking operations.

'I had never met him. But I'd had the impression that he was a rather sinister man. But Keith, who was always wonderfully frank with me for all those years that we were together, assured me that whatever the negotiations were they would in no way embarrass him,' Elisabeth says.

Indeed, in future, dedicated enemies of the 'Murdoch Press' did try and embarrass Keith and his family with unsupported innuendo about the Wren–Murdoch connection. In fact, it was conducted on the most proper business basis at all times.

Looking back now Elisabeth believes that the wonderfully frank discussions Keith had with her about business matters on their honeymoon continued because he really didn't ever confide in anyone else. 'You know, I learnt from very early on that off-the-record was something that was absolutely sacrosanct and, as a result, I think I was awfully dull with my friends because so much of my life was off-the-record and I never could tell them anything very interesting.

'At the same time I was very lucky to know so much about what was going on. I was so interested, and, occasionally, I was anxious – just as I have been anxious when certain things have been happening with our son Rupert.

'Keith was very communicative and this made me awfully lazy about reading newspapers. Even today I have to bully myself to try and read our papers every day,' says Dame Elisabeth, who is still kept fully briefed on significant moves in the family's vast international News Corporation activities.

But Elisabeth's life as a newlywed in fashionable South Yarra was not overwhelmed with matters of big business in 1928. She had a large house in Walsh Street to run, with well-trained staff accustomed to carrying out their duties without direction, but Elisabeth was determined to take charge and, although she could always call on Bairnie for advice in an emergency, she had inherited her mother's cookbook from Pemberley – the one with the chapter on how to train a 'green maid'.

'I'd rather have twenty years with Keith ...'

However, the cookbook did not tell her how to correctly seat four married couples around a dining table and, at her first formal dinner party as Mrs Keith Murdoch, the nineteen-year-old was in a quandary and some wives did end up sitting next to their own husbands. 'Keith liked everything to be perfect, but he was so patient,' Elisabeth recalls.

At an early afternoon tea party for Keith's friends at Cruden Farm, Elisabeth now admits she was making a rather 'slap-dash job' of tea pouring. 'Keith loved his tea, and he loved everything to be just so and I wasn't handling it in a very adept or civilised manner. Penny Gullett noticed Keith's discomfort and said to him: "Cheer up Keith. It's no good. She hasn't come to grips with the tea ceremony yet."'

However, things settled down remarkably quickly with Elisabeth soon able to run the staff, and the entire household, in the smooth style to which her perfectionist husband had by now grown accustomed. Keith was happier than he had ever been in his life. At work his colleagues remarked that he looked years younger. His workload increased, but he now rushed home in the Sunbeam and made certain that he was able to collect Elisabeth early on Friday evenings for the drive to Cruden Farm, where already they were planning alterations to the cottage and a garden of which they could be proud.

Keith Murdoch liked beautiful possessions, fine works of art, handmade leather shoes, and the best of clothing for formal and informal occasions. Although he was not mechanically minded or particularly keen on driving, he liked big luxurious motor cars and he mistakenly believed his young wife was keen on them too.

But Elisabeth was anything but impressed when he arrived home and asked her to step out the gate. For parked outside in Walsh Street was a gleaming second-hand Rolls Royce, the first Keith had ever owned. 'Too ostentatious!' said Elisabeth firmly, even rejecting

Keith's invitation to 'go for a spin' in his new acquisition ... which was soon taken back to the dealers.

By then Elisabeth was expecting their first baby and, although she has always accepted the importance of genes in the wider scheme of things, she dislikes the modern concept of all-powerful family dynasties, and bristles if she is referred to as a 'matriarch'. Yet in 1929 a new branch appeared on what was already a remarkable family tree.

CHAPTER TEN

New Horizons

On their return to Melbourne, Mr and Mrs Keith Murdoch soon established a comfortable position in the city's society, with Elisabeth taking firm control of the Walsh Street household and learning to be at ease with the political leaders, businessmen, artists and interesting international visitors Keith regularly invited home.

Before long the delighted newspaper executive saw that he had married a young woman with the natural talent to be a charming hostess, and the staff, who had at first openly shown their resentment of the Master's young bride, were soon fitting into the happy and efficient routine Elisabeth had borrowed from Bairnie. Her dismissal of Alec, the raw Scottish manservant in the first week of her honeymoon and the disciplining of a lax housemaid soon ensured that, entirely supported by Keith, she was now the mistress of the house.

Then, to everyone's delight, Elisabeth found she was pregnant.

But, despite her youth and robust health it was not an easy pregnancy. Elisabeth often suffered from nausea and sometimes had great difficulty sitting through long formal dinner parties, and waiting for the women to finally withdraw and leave the men to their cigars and conversation. 'It was difficult for me, and Keith, but we had to keep going and I was under a fair amount of strain, but I was still beautifully cared for and loved, and happy,' says Elisabeth.

There are happy photographs of the Murdochs' first Christmas together at Cruden Farm. Henry and Penny Gullett were there. Artist Will Dyson was another guest and so was Jimmy Bancks, the creator of one of Australia's greatest comic strips, *Ginger Meggs*. 'In those days so much more fuss was made about pregnancy, so it was a quiet, but very happy Christmas,' says Elisabeth.

The New Year was made even happier by the news that Keith was to be elevated to the post of Managing Director of the growing Herald and Weekly Times. Helen Murdoch finally arrived on 9 April 1929, and Keith was as proud and happy as Rupert Greene had been when Elisabeth was born twenty years earlier. There is no doubt that Keith doted on his daughter, and naturally Elisabeth adored her first born too.

Today, in many subtle ways, Helen seems to have inherited more of the characteristics of her father than either her sisters, Anne or Janet. But sixty years later Elisabeth still regrets the decision Keith persuaded her to take just four months after Helen was born. To stay in touch with new newspaper techniques and technology, Keith had to travel to the US and Europe, and Elisabeth, he insisted, was to accompany him.

Today, the Murdoch children accept that their mother, while devoted to their upbringing, naturally regarded the interests and well-being of Keith as high priority requirements. Certainly at the time Elisabeth was emotionally torn, but in the end she relented and accepted that baby Helen would be perfectly safe in the care of a trusted and highly skilled English nanny, Sarah Russell, inherited from Ruth Whiting, as she accompanied Keith on the first of the overseas working trips she was to take with him.

'I had to go. It was one of those things that today would probably have been frowned upon, but I knew I was leaving Helen in the hands of this superb nanny who was to stay with us almost forever and who was really the most wonderful surrogate mother,' says Elisabeth today.

So Keith and Elisabeth set sail for the US leaving behind plans for a few alterations to the Cruden Farm cottage. Artist Daryl Lindsay, husband of Clyde old girl Joan, who was now a near neighbour of the Murdochs at Langwarrin, offered to oversee the project and M. H. 'Jac' Baillieu produced architect and friend, Harold Desbrowe Annear, who, although well regarded, was anxiously seeking new assignments.

Elisabeth was certainly keen to have the possums removed from the roof because they were marking the ceilings, but she was enchanted by the verandahs all around the small cottage with their honeysuckle and creeping roses and wanted few major changes. 'Now we had Helen and we were hoping to have a large family and really that was the only reason we wanted to make the Cruden Farm cottage a little larger,' says Elisabeth, who still laughs as she thinks back to the last time she was to see her little farm cottage before they left for America.

In those days of slow travel the Murdochs sailed across the Pacific with Keith taking the opportunity to visit newspaper contacts in Hawaii and Los Angeles. They drove around the homes of Hollywood stars and they met Scripps-Howard newspaper chief, the charming Roy Howard. Then they set off by train for Chicago where they were guests of the McCormack-Blairs, a prominent US family with banking and business interests.

At every stop Elisabeth anxiously looked for letters from Nanny, exciting, almost daily, letters that detailed the day-to-day progress and activities of baby Helen and were full of understanding for the concerns of the absent mother. 'I missed my daughter so. I think, probably, biologically, as well as in so many other ways. It was such a wrench and the separation made me feel a bit numb – so much so that it probably took away from my wholehearted fascination with the trip,' she says with a sigh.

In Chicago, Keith and his young wife were overwhelmed by American hospitality, as Keith called on his many newspaper contacts and Elisabeth was enthralled by the articulate and well-informed American wives. 'I was stunned. I was very much out of my depth at my first introduction to American business society, but although the women did rather take the stage when it came to conversation, I liked and admired them,' says Elisabeth.

From Chicago Keith took Elisabeth to the Grand Canyon then Salt Lake City and Detroit, always calling on newspaper proprietors and paying special attention to new production techniques and, in particular, inquiring about the suitability of the new Goss presses. 'He always worked so very, very hard,' Elisabeth says.

After three weeks of travel, the Murdochs spent three weeks in New York. The days of prohibition were still in force and it was on the eve of the Wall Street collapse ushering in the Great Depression. Taken to a nightclub Elisabeth was so excited that she took off her precious engagement ring and left it in a washroom, where it vanished. However, when Keith reported the loss to the maitre d'hotel the ring was quickly returned. 'In those days of prohibition, nightclubs couldn't afford to have the police called in,' Elisabeth chuckles.

Then came the Atlantic crossing, a memorable voyage on the

Berengaria. Keith took a separate day cabin for his books and typewriter and was hard at work as soon as the ship sailed. But it was not all work and the couple joined in the usual shipboard activities and Keith discovered that there was an illustrious fellow passenger aboard – Winston Churchill, the man Keith's Gallipoli letters had almost destroyed. No record remains of the first shipboard meeting between Churchill and the Australian journalist who had effectively ended Winston's sadly flawed design for shortening the war by using the Dardanelles as a springboard for an allied advance on the Black Sea.

Elisabeth, on first meeting, was unimpressed by the great British statesman who would sit up all night playing cards and drinking champagne. 'I was very young and intolerant and asked Keith how anybody so great could possibly sit up all night drinking and gambling. I can still remember him replying: "Look my dear, I have lived a long time and met many great men, and I would say so often in my experience, the greater the man, the greater the failings."'

Winston, then enduring his long spell in the political wilderness, was returning to Britain after a successful tour of lecturing and writing in the US. He had witnessed at first hand the stock exchange crash and had written for the *Daily Mail,* London: 'Under my window a gentleman cast himself down fifteen storeys and was dashed to pieces.'

Although Keith did not join Winston's nightly gambling forays, every morning on that Atlantic crossing the two men would meet in the shipboard Turkish baths to relax in the steam. At the traditional ship's benefit concert on the last night of the voyage, Elisabeth's view of Winston Churchill was to be changed. In good humour, Winston performed, telling witty anecdotes about his recent meetings with Charlie Chaplin and other personalities in the US before making a wonderful, spellbinding speech. 'He was a great man and

Keith was so right to correct me,' Elisabeth recalls. 'It was a lesson to me, something I've always remembered that you mustn't be judgmental of people who are very much larger and better than yourself, you mustn't pick on small things that put you off people. That is very foolish. Keith taught me to be very much more tolerant,' says Dame Elisabeth.

The arrival in London on the boat train amazed Elisabeth for they were met and ushered to a London cab. 'I thought someone was playing a joke on us. I had never seen a London cab before,' Elisabeth says. At the time, Granny Forth was in London for an eye operation and there was a joyous reunion, after which Elizabeth and Keith went to stay for a few days with Ruby and Clive Baillieu at Parkwood where Elisabeth succumbed to her first severe attack of English hayfever. But the happy memories predominate and Elisabeth still recalls the kindness of Lady Dawson of Penn, the delightful wife of the King's physician, and mother of Ursula Bowater, then living with her husband in Australia. Lady Dawson took Elisabeth around London and introduced her to her friends and all the right shops.

When he was not working, Keith delighted in showing Elisabeth the London he knew so well, visiting galleries, theatres and shops. They enjoyed Sir Max Beerbohm's witty and touching play, *The Happy Hypocrite*, together, and Keith introduced Elisabeth to the friends and contacts he had previously made in the opera, music and arts world. Elisabeth was enchanted by the beautiful musicals of Ivor Novello then playing in the West End.

Elisabeth's aunt, Ethel, Mrs Claude Macdonald – her father's eldest sister – was very modish and determined that her young niece should follow her advice about clothes. They visited Victor Steibel to have two beautiful evening gowns made, but Aunt Ethel was determined that Elisabeth was to have 'the best fur coat in London', despite the cold winds of the Great Depression now reaching Britain, and Keith was happy to agree.

So, to Elisabeth's amazement, five superb fur coats were delivered to her hotel room on approval and she was told by a delighted Keith to make her choice. Aunt Ethel urged her to take a mink. But to Elisabeth, still with that Rolls Royce in mind, that was just 'too ostentatious'. 'There was an astrakhan coat – beautiful, beautiful and, I felt, much more suitable for one as young as myself. But Keith and Aunt Ethel insisted on the mink. I forget how much it cost, but in those grim days it was a frightful amount of money, and I hardly ever wore it. Only two women I knew then wore mink in Melbourne and they were both much older than I was. I was never very happy wearing my fur coat and I had it gradually cut down and finally I gave the remaining cape, when it was about forty-five years old, to an elderly relative in the country. So it did its stuff.

'Of course, it was kind and generous of Keith, but I do feel he was rather managed by my aunt,' says Elisabeth, who was made to feel less spoilt by the fact that Keith took the opportunity while in London to have suits tailored in Savile Row, and had some beautiful handmade shoes fitted. 'Keith loved his London suits and shoes,' says Elisabeth, who to this day has kept some of her husband's fine shoes and leather cases neatly stored at Cruden Farm.

'Another thing, of course, was that Keith was determined that I should have some beautiful riding clothes made in London – and what a fuss it was. The Savile Row habit was a lovely charcoal grey, almost black, and then the boots were made at Maxwells round in Dover Street and I had to have jodphurs made and take them to Maxwells to make certain the boots fitted over them. I wore that wonderful riding outfit for quite a few years but, alas, finally grew out of it.'

And Paris was the next stop as Keith showed Elisabeth the world.

Living in Paris at the time was the ageing Dame Nellie Melba. Keith and Elisabeth called on her and she said she'd like to go out to dinner. Keith booked a table at the Cafe de Paris. Dame Nellie didn't care for the famous restaurant so Keith quickly found a table at a fashionable restaurant run by a group claiming to be White Russians.

But now Elisabeth was to see the towering artistic temperament of the Australian Diva in full cry. She didn't like the White Russians or their restaurant and told them so before sweeping out followed by a humiliated Elisabeth as Keith went in search of yet another restaurant. 'I was so ashamed that anyone could behave like that, but then again I was so young and intolerant. She was ill and she wasn't herself – but I didn't ever see the attractive side of Melba that others saw when she was younger, and that's a shame. My experience of Dame Nellie Melba could have been a rich experience if I'd known her earlier or when I'd been older. But I was too young. Probably the fault was mine.'

Elisabeth loved London and Paris, but couldn't wait to board the Orient liner headed back to Australia – and Helen. There was the excitement of a trip to the pyramids in Cairo before the passage through the Suez Canal, then the heat of the Red Sea, before the run down to Colombo and at last, Fremantle. 'I will always remember sailing into Fremantle in a beautiful sunrise and being greeted by this wonderful smell of Eucalyptus – the distinctive Australian smell.'

Elisabeth's lifelong awareness of the cost of telephone calls was on this special occasion forgotten as she picked up the phone in Fremantle and called home to Walsh Street, South Yarra, to be told by Nanny that Helen was a healthy, happy baby, waiting for her mother. The trip back to Melbourne seemed to Elisabeth to take a lifetime and then, when they did finally arrive, the happy Murdochs were in for the shock of their lives.

CHAPTER ELEVEN

A Most Eventful Year

ELISABETH WAS overjoyed to be reunited with her baby daughter, now eight months old, who had flourished under the expert care of Nanny Sarah Russell. But with the effects of the Depression already being felt in Melbourne, Keith had to go into immediate action to head off any possible crisis in his growing newspaper and broadcasting empire.

On their first weekend at home, they decided to drive down to Cruden Farm with Nanny and Helen to see how far the refurbishing of Elisabeth's romantic little honeymoon cottage had advanced while they were overseas. They arrived to find work still very much in progress but already the Cruden Farm cottage had been outwardly transformed into a stately two-storey Kentucky-style southern mansion with tall columns where once the side verandah had been. The small cottage garden was still more or less intact.

The house looked grand from most angles, but Elisabeth and

Keith were furious. 'How dare you! What do you mean by this, Annear? It doesn't in any way resemble the plans you were commissioned to carry out,' said Keith in some anger. But the elderly architect was unrepentant: 'Oh, you can't complain. You gave me a picture of a house like this ten years ago and said: "That's a lovely facade. You should put it on one of your houses one day," so I thought I would give you a surprise old fellow,' Desbrowe-Annear said mildly.

A shocked Elisabeth believed that their friend Daryl Lindsay had conspired with Annear, with what he considered to be their best interests at heart, to transform the farm cottage into a scaled-down 'Tara' from *Gone With the Wind*. Elisabeth and her family have long since grown to love the house, which remains tastefully comfortable, relaxed and functional, rather than luxurious, behind those grand columns. And Elisabeth, to whom Cruden Farm remains the precious family seat full of happy memories and dreams that came true, says: 'We were lucky that old Annear did what he did, because without him we would never have had such a distinguished house. But, of course, it cost so much, much more money than we could possibly afford at the time. And when we first saw it, the house wasn't nearly as nice as it is now.'

While Keith and Elisabeth were overseas, the electricians had been allowed the free run of the project and there were triple sets of power points and eight or ten light fittings in every room – and the painters and other craftsmen were still at work, much to the dismay of Keith and Elisabeth. Added to that, there had been problems with the builder and delays during the Murdochs' absence. When they got home, work resumed – slowly.

'We came down another day for a picnic with Helen and Nanny and they were still working on the house and Keith said: "I can't stand this any more." Then he went to the builder and said "Out by the end of the week! I don't care what's not finished. Out!" So there are still a few little unfinished touches even today, woodwork, a touch of paint. They were just little things, but it was all we could do because we saw our money melting away and it meant a lot to us in those days,' says Elisabeth, who still points to an unpainted corner of the house which she has always kept in that condition: 'as an example of Keith taking a strong hand'.

Keith was also being forced to take a strong hand at the Herald and Weekly Times as the grip of the Depression tightened. Already the Scullin Labor Government in Canberra had called for cuts in public service pay. There was even a call for cuts in the pay of ministers and members, but this was defeated in the House by a vote of 49 to 20. A plea to the Bank of England to nominate experts to advise the Commonwealth Government on its financial woes resulted in Sir Otto Niemeyer being sent out with Professors Gregory and Kershaw. Soon after their arrival they dined with Keith and Elisabeth at Walsh Street. They talked long into the night with Keith impressed by the British team's depth of financial knowledge.

Sir Otto was adamant that the only way out for Australia was for the Commonwealth and State Governments to balance their budgets – no matter what the sacrifice. Then, and at later meetings, Keith took their sound advice to heart. Almost immediately he negotiated a thirteen per cent pay cut for all his employees, while he and his fellow executives and directors took a similar cut, and a reduction in their annual bonuses. The belt-tightening even extended to the Murdoch servants with the maids, the butler and Nanny having the situation explained to them and all agreeing to take a percentage wage cut.

Rivals were soon calling Keith 'Lord Southcliffe' as, despite the economic climate, the Murdoch empire expanded to other states and his newspapers took on the sparkling, professional look of the

Northcliffe publications he so rightly admired. But to the journalists who worked for him, he was 'KM', the most respected of Australian newspaper proprietors. 'KM's young men' were proud to work for him and they knew that a Murdoch cadetship would almost certainly open doors for the more adventurous when their turn came to try and break into Fleet Street – often with their fare to London paid for by the Herald and Weekly Times.

But, despite his business acumen and in-depth knowledge of newspaper production, Keith seldom seemed relaxed behind the wheel of his car. Noticing that 'Keith did not concentrate on his driving', Elisabeth quickly learnt to drive Keith's big British Sunbeam with its VIC 12 number plates. 'I got my licence in Frankston simply by driving the car round the block and back to the police station,' she laughs.

Soon, whenever *The Herald* driver was not available, Elisabeth was taking the wheel as a skilled and confident driver allowing Keith to concentrate on more important issues. Since then, many cars driven by Elisabeth have carried the transferred VIC 12 plates. It was the registered number of Keith's grey chauffeur-driven Daimler just before he died and it was thoughtfully passed on to Elisabeth when the family connection with *The Herald* was temporarily severed in the fifties. These days such early, low-number registration plates are avidly collected by car enthusiasts. VIC 12 could be expected to raise thousands of dollars at auction, but when young car buffs flag her down, as they often do, and ask Elisabeth if the plates, now on her Peugeot, are for sale she replies: 'Young man, I was courted in a car with these number plates and I'm going to my funeral with the same number.' But if people make remarks about her valuable number plates, Elisabeth is quick to say that she's been driving with them for more than sixty years. 'I wouldn't want people to actually think I'd paid some outrageous price for them,' she says.

A Most Eventful Year

Eventually work reached completion on the Cruden Farm residence – although Elisabeth says 'those possums were still in the roof' – and their weekend escape to the farm became a delight for the Murdochs, with Nanny and Helen joining them for the picnics on which Keith loved to take his family ... out across the green paddocks and along the narrow bush tracks into the thickets of ti-tree that grew so prolifically in the sandy soil of the Mornington Peninsula.

After a busy week in the city, arranging Keith's frequent lunches and dinners at Walsh Street, Elisabeth was always delighted to relax at Cruden Farm at the weekends where she occasionally had Keith to herself away from the constant and growing demands of his newspapers, magazines and radio stations. Helen was thriving and delighted at the attention she got from her father and from her grandfather, Rupert Greene.

With the new house at the farm finally free of builders, some additions were made to Walsh Street. A new nursery was added and the kitchen modernised. Elisabeth had some of the more ostentatious curtains and furniture coverings inherited by Keith removed. But, as busy as she always was, Elisabeth never forgot others less fortunate than herself. She maintained her interest in the Free Kindergarten, always conscious of the sharp contrast in the upbringing of herself and her own Helen, and the struggle of those Port Melbourne waifs. Even more remote from Elisabeth's experience was cruelty to children but in 1933 she allowed herself to be persuaded to join the committee of the Royal Society for Prevention of Cruelty to Children – the first of many such committees she would serve on in the future.

Several years later the president of the Free Kindergarten movement, Mrs Harry Creswick, asked Elisabeth if she would consider succeeding her as president. The busy young mother was honoured but had to decline, for by that time her growing involvement with the Children's Hospital, her husband's interests and their own children would have made it impossible. 'I felt that my work at the hospital was very much my duty. I think that people who want to help must realise that they have an absolute commitment and it is dishonourable not to turn up unless you are ill or bereaved,' she says, reflecting the philosophy that has been the guiding light of both herself and her family. But before her future great work with the Children's Hospital began, Elisabeth started planning what became one of her other great missions in life – to create one of the finest gardens in Australia and encourage others to follow her lead.

At this time, Elisabeth had no real desire to move from Walsh Street, although she knew it would be a little crowded after the new baby she was expecting arrived. But Keith knew that the Depression had forced property values down and calculated that now would be the time to buy. On 11 March 1931 a son was born to the overjoyed Murdochs and proud Rupert Greene was able to tell his friends at the Melbourne Club that, by his daughter's choice, the boy was to be named Rupert after him. However, Keith moved swiftly and personally registered the boy's name as Keith Rupert Murdoch. In fact, he was to always be called Rupert in the family – a solution that pleased everyone.

By now Keith had become an avid collector of fine glass and porcelain, and Elisabeth was glad to join her husband in his new out-of-office enthusiasm. He gained the expertise, which he shared with his wife, but Elisabeth's natural eye for quality was a great asset as the collection grew. With, for the times, a remarkably liberal view on art, Keith had chosen to sponsor an exhibition made up of works by Matisse, Modigliani and other modern artists then held in private Australian collections. It was his first major venture as a patron of the arts and Elisabeth had been delighted, just as she was when, in 1933, Keith was appointed a member of the joint board of trustees of the Public Library, Museum and National Gallery of Victoria.

Now, as Elisabeth and Nanny coped with the two young children in the Walsh Street house, Keith heard of a grand residence that could soon be coming on the market. He told Elisabeth that Heathfield, the old Baillieu mansion in Kooyong Road, Toorak, a brisk uphill walk from Pemberley, would soon be up for sale. Elisabeth knew it was one of the largest houses in Melbourne – and it was set on five acres of carefully tended land. Apart from that, Keith knew and loved the house, because he was very fond of the Baillieu family – particularly Claire, one of the Baillieu daughters. 'I think that at one time W. L. Baillieu may have considered that Keith would make a very nice son-in-law,' says Elisabeth. 'However, I was very worried about Heathfield. For one thing, I didn't think we could afford it and I knew that instead of four servants we would need at least eight to run it.

'It was a colossal step to take and I knew that it was no good moving to a new house unless we could run it properly. I remember saying to Keith, "Now look, darling, if you really want it I'll run it, provided we can afford to do it properly. I couldn't face it if we were going to be understaffed and it smelt of stale cabbage and dust like some old houses I have visited." So we bought it, but I never had any grand ideas about refurnishing and renovating and spending a fortune – one just went on gradually replacing things in those days, unlike today. No wonder some people get into trouble,' says Elisabeth, who to this day, can point to curtains from Heathfield still hanging in the sunny rooms of Cruden Farm.

'It was a large house though. You entered through this small ante-hall and then there was this vast entrance hall and several other large rooms, including a huge drawing room and a library where we used to spend all our evenings when we were alone,' Elisabeth recalls. 'I had my own beautiful little sitting room which opened out onto a raised bluestone terrace. In the next room was the children's school room and nearby a huge nursery.

'At the bottom of the staircase was the beautiful formal dining room and upstairs there were many bedrooms and bathrooms. Of course, there were all the staffrooms, storerooms, larders and office. It was a very large house on the grand old scale. There was a big billiards room – but we immediately turned it into the nursery. It was a wonderful house for children.

'In the evenings we had a fire in the library and the children always came down to be with us before they went to bed. I usually used my little sitting room during the day to take afternoon tea and sew. I know it sounds luxurious, but really it wasn't and I do remember when Helen married and Mrs Handbury, her mother-in-law, was amazed that Helen made her own bed. I think people expected that they had servants to pick everything up for them, but I never allowed anyone to pick up anything for them – although in those days, I'm afraid a lot of children were brought up in that style. My children were always brought up to do chores and to consider the people who did things for them. It might be a smug thing to say, but I think it paid off because they are all pretty considerate.'

One key factor that eased the move from Walsh Street to the vast reaches of Kooyong Road with two babies who were still very much in arms, was the presence of Sarah Russell, who was known to the family and friends as 'Nanny Murdoch'. 'She was a wonderful woman, because contrary to the image of the English nanny, she was very unpossessive. Her sense of values was so right, but when I first met her I was perhaps a bit resentful that this older woman was perhaps going to manage an area in which I should have charge.

'But I soon realised that we fully understood each other and that I should be very grateful that she had come to us. She was so loyal and devoted to us all, and she adored Keith and he adored her. It's

20 Keith Murdoch in the 1930s

21 Keith and Elisabeth at a wedding in the 1930s follow her parents 'at a respectful distance'

22 Keith's parents, the Rev. and Mrs Patrick Murdoch

23 Keith - war correspondent, Gallipoli

24 War correspondent Keith Murdoch, with map, with other Australian journalists in the forward area near La Maicourt between Flamicourt and Perrone, France, 4 September, 1918

25 Elisabeth's wedding day with sister, Marie, as bridesmaid

26 Cruden Farm cottage before the architect's renovations in 1929

27 Cruden Farm 'cottage' after the architect's renovations

28 Elisabeth holding Anne, with Rupert, 4, and Helen, 6, at Heathfield

29 Rupert and Helen at Cruden Farm in the mid-1930s

30 In the garden at Cruden Farm in 1932: (standing from left) Aunt May Forth, Bairnie Greene, Rupert Greene, Rev. Patrick Murdoch, (seated from left) Aunt Helen Murdoch, Rupert Murdoch, Keith and Elisabeth Murdoch, Helen Murdoch, Mrs Patrick Murdoch and Anne de Lancey Forth

31 Elisabeth ready for a ride at Cruden Farm in the mid-1930s

32 Keith and Elisabeth on their tour of inspection of Tasmanian forests in 1935

33 Keith and Rupert Murdoch in the mid-1930s

34 Elisabeth with Helen and Rupert at Pompeii in 1936

35 All day picnic in the early 1930s at Pt Leo. Elisabeth, centre, with Rupert and Helen, and, at left, Kimpo and Aunt May Forth, and Joan Lindsay, in big hat, at right

36 Elisabeth, holding Anne, with Keith, Rupert and Helen in the mid-1930s

37 Lady Gullett and Rupert in the mid-1930s

38 Rupert - Wantabadgery holiday in the 1940s

asking a lot for both parents to have this terrific rapport with a nanny, because so often there is jealousy and conflict of opinion over discipline, but we soon understood that we would never do anything but support each other whether we agreed or disagreed. In all matters affecting the children we were absolutely in unison,' says Elisabeth. 'We were also fortunate to have two wonderful English maids who, with Nanny, were the core of the large staff.'

The move into the big house over, Elisabeth was able to step out into her other domain – the five acres of garden on the top of what was then the Toorak Hill. There, she soon met Kline – a well-trained old-school gardener resplendent in leather apron, inherited from the Baillieus along with old Bob Simmons, who remained on as a gardener and 'useful'. Bob's main duty under the Baillieus was to milk the family cow – a practice abandoned, along with the cow, just before the Murdochs moved in. 'It was marvellous what those two men did in the garden. It's hard to imagine that it could be done today, but they were dedicated to their job. We had beautiful flower gardens and a big vegetable garden, and a grass tennis court, which old Kline felt was a bit of a bind to keep up.'

Already tactful beyond her years, Elisabeth heaped praise on her gardeners as she began to make suggestions about what needed to be changed in her garden. 'That was rather one's job in life to manage one's own menage and you only got the best out of people when you really took a lot of interest in their own welfare as well as what you wanted. I simply loved the garden and got enormous pleasure out of it. In spite of my childhood at Pemberley, I really didn't think of myself as being any sort of gardener – and I'm still not,' says the woman who created a garden now listed among the most notable gardens in the world.

Despite his love for Elisabeth and desire to please her in every way, Keith had taken an earlier step at Cruden Farm that clearly still rankles with Elisabeth to this day – because he was such a perfectionist, he persuaded her that they should call in Edna Walling to design the new garden. The no-nonsense Miss Walling was a cult figure in thirties garden design in Australia. She was at the height of her power and writing for Keith's influential *Home Beautiful* magazine at the time. Keith clearly thought she was the ideal woman to design the perfect garden for Elisabeth – but from the moment they were first introduced Edna Walling almost ignored the young Mrs Murdoch and set about designing an Edna Walling garden with brick paths, flowerbeds and tree plantings.

The ebullient Mr Desbrowe Annear had included a very formal Italian garden in his grandiose plans for Elisabeth's original cottage. 'Too elaborate!' Elisabeth had proclaimed with her unerring instinct of what was right for an Australian country garden. But, as Elisabeth says: 'Edna came and planned the garden without any regard for my wishes, and I was not experienced enough to know then that it was really not a good siting of those gardens and, anyway, they were too small.' Nevertheless she appreciates the beauty and design of Cruden Farm's stone walls and admires much of Edna Walling's work. In the years ahead, there were problems with the humidity and the heat of the Australian sun, and gradually Elisabeth moved the rose garden to a better site, made more natural beds without the Walling brick pathways and planted major trees in her own chosen positions. Later her re-designing was to be assisted by bushfires and gales, but today the garden of Cruden Farm is unmistakably an Elisabeth Murdoch garden, admired by all who see it.

After her brief association with the autocratic Edna Walling, Elisabeth was able to rely on the devotion of Duell, the skilled Cruden Farm gardener who, assisted by some local lads, set out to plant and nurture the plants preferred by Elisabeth at the time. Two of the many outstanding features of the Cruden Farm garden are its stately elm trees and the beautiful avenue of Australian lemon-scented gum trees winding up to the house from the front gate. Although she planted the trees with Keith, she cannot remember who chose the lemon-scented gums that look so spectacular today, but thinks it could have been their friend Sir Russell Grimwade.

Now with two gardens to run, Elisabeth was often up at dawn or watering through the night in summer because of the poor water pressure on top of the Toorak Hill – a problem that was to repeat itself as the Cruden Farm garden grew. Later, Cruden Farm was to supply all the vegetables needed at Heathfield. A hamper would be sent up by train every week from Frankston to Armadale station where it was picked up. In the hamper would be cream, butter and eggs and eventually there would be several dressed chickens and a tender lamb and, always, flowers.

During the worst days of the Depression, Keith had been approached by a number of local unemployed family men, including stonemasons who had built the walls, looking for work. Keith decided to give them what they regarded as a decent living wage to make the beautiful stone stables, dairy and garage block to the design of leading Australian architect, Percy Meldrum. They are now a much admired feature of the farm complex.

Two gardens, two children and a husband reaching dizzy heights in the publishing world would have been enough to occupy the average twenty-four-year-old but that wasn't all fate had in store for Elisabeth Murdoch in the eventful year of 1933. First there was the knighthood bestowed on Keith in that year. He became a Knight Bachelor – the most ancient of the British Imperial Honours – for services to journalism. In fact, with his natural Presbyterian caution he had felt it prudent to reject the offer of such an honour from both Prime Ministers Lloyd George and Hughes in 1919, because he knew what controversy it would generate after his Gallipoli intervention.

Besides, when younger, Keith had little time for such trappings of the old Empire – a view his son, Rupert, shared years later when, as a major Fleet Street media 'Baron' based in London, he too was to reject suggestions of even more exalted Imperial honours. Elisabeth Murdoch was proud of her husband's title and happily became Lady Murdoch – although to her close friends she was Lady Liz, and to her loyal staff, M'lady.

The year 1933 also marked the beginning of Elisabeth's first great involvement in Australian public life. 'The President of the Children's Hospital, Lady Latham, came to see me and put the hard word on me to join the Management Committee. In fact, it didn't require a very hard word because I thought it was something I really should do. I was only twenty-four years old and I already had two very healthy children and I was extremely fortunately placed. I had wonderful help for them and, of course, being invited to join the Children's Hospital in those days was, I knew, a tremendous honour – at least if I hadn't known that, Lady Latham would have very quickly told me. I think she sincerely believed that a young mother with the ability to give time had almost an obligation to help in some way or another and she was a very formidable person – and I'm not saying that unkindly. I had a tremendous respect for her. I admired her enormously and I think I was just mature enough to realise that there was another reason that Lady Latham invited me ... and that was because I think she was very aware of Keith, who she and her husband, Sir John (then Deputy Prime Minister in the Lyons Government and later to be Chief Justice of the High Court of Australia) knew. I didn't even then kid myself that it was just that I was perhaps being chosen because of what I could contribute,' says Elisabeth.

'Lady Latham thought that Keith would not only be sympathetic, but, perhaps, would be indulgent with his use of *The Herald* and

The Sun . . . so, although I didn't ever feel uncomfortable or embarrassed, I am quite sure that was the overriding reason she invited me to join her. And that didn't worry me at all. I was honoured to be asked and I knew that I would try and, of course, very quickly I became tremendously interested. I must say that Lady Latham was very good to me and I was very careful not to be in any way presumptuous or precocious, or to be impertinent enough to question or argue. However she always sought your view and allowed you to express it. I met marvellous people over my years at the hospital.'

But, as Elisabeth settled into her new home and supervised the upbringing of Helen and Rupert, while being a loving and supportive wife to the busy Keith, there came a near disaster. An energetic tennis match in 1933 with Neville Fraser threatened in an instant to jeopardise the whole future of the Murdoch family.

Una and Neville Fraser, whose son Malcolm would one day be Prime Minister of Australia, had come from their Riverina property to see the running of the 1933 Melbourne Cup . . . to be started, as usual, by Rupert Greene. At the time, Sir Keith's responsibilities at *The Herald* were enormous. He was now at the head of Australia's first national media chain with publications and radio stations in every state. He was preparing for a difficult annual general meeting of the Herald and Weekly Times and was planning an overseas trip with Elisabeth. He was also suffering from the pain of a badly infected tooth. Since childhood, when he had first begun to try and cope with his distressing stammer, Keith had clearly been prone to nervous tension. There are suggestions too that he had contracted rheumatic fever as a child, and Elisabeth was now aware that her husband was a workaholic who simply refused to take proper holidays or relax for longer than the few hours it took to have a family picnic at Cruden Farm.

Keith was always on the go, always planning for his growing family's future. Despite his strong, robust appearance his health and hectic lifestyle had been causing his doctors concern. He had been told to slow down, and ignored the advice. On this warm spring day on the grass court at Heathfield he played a strenuous game of singles with Neville Fraser. It was a game which, in typical Murdoch fashion, Keith was determined to win but, at the end of a furious rally, Keith appeared to falter and was persuaded to sit down. Later a doctor was called and initially diagnosed a heart attack.

Treatment and further urgent tests were quickly arranged but, in those days of less precise diagnostic equipment, it was eventually decided that Keith had 'strained his heart'. Complete rest was ordered and a trip Keith had been planning to Peking, with Elisabeth, in search of more precious glass and porcelain, was cancelled. He was told he must stay away from his office for one entire year.

Sixty years later, Elisabeth believes that the medical advice Keith received then was 'unsound'. Although, with his father's faith, Keith had no fear of death in itself, he was alarmed that a heart attack could end his career before he had carried out his great plans for the future security of Elisabeth and their children. 'I think the doctors made him too anxious about his health – over anxious,' says Elisabeth. 'That's where today's doctors and psychologists are so important. They ease the anxiety.'

Keith did not ever really slow down, but for the rest of his life he worried about the consequences of his workload as doctors continued to warn him to guard against 'straining his heart'. Today, proper medication and medical advice would probably have removed the need for such anxiety, but following his first collapse on the tennis court, Keith had regular episodes of 'heart trouble'. During times of high stress, and when his brother Frank passed away suddenly that same year, Keith would experience fibrillation, or irregular rhythm of the heart.

Always a loyal and emotional man when it came to human relations, Keith would 'suffer agony', according to Elisabeth, if he had to dismiss anybody, knowing that he would have to hurt them and the families they had to support. The aftermath of such a confrontation in the office would even on occasions lead to Keith taking to his bed for a day until his heart beat returned to normal. Yet, despite his understandable anxiety about his health, Keith seldom spared himself. His unfailing safety valve was Elisabeth, their children and the close, loving family lifestyle they were creating at Cruden Farm.

CHAPTER TWELVE

Weathering the Storm

DESPITE THE DOCTORS' stern warnings, Keith kept a close watch on *The Herald* and his other business interests, although he no longer attended board meetings and was forbidden, by Elisabeth and his doctors, to go near his office. Although she says now 'it was a very unhappy time', Elisabeth decided that the best possible thing she could do for her husband was to try and carry on their lives at a normal pace, while watching for any telltale signs of stress or strain.

The cancellation of the Peking visit, although regretted, allowed her to devote more time to the Children's Hospital as Keith tried to relax while fuming at his enforced absence from the helm of *The Herald*. Tennis was out, but games with Helen and Rupert, now four and three, as well as swimming and picnics, remained on the relaxing weekly agenda at Cruden Farm. But whether in Toorak or Langwarrin, Keith always had a radio at hand – usually tuned to

3DB, *The Herald*'s trendsetting radio station. 'I never could understand this,' says Elisabeth, 'but Keith liked the wireless on while he was working. He always loved to have his music in the background. Really I could never concentrate if I had it there. But I love the radio on at night when I can listen in bed. Keith used to listen to 3DB because he always made it his business to know what was going on in the world.'

The Murdochs' 1933 Christmas at Cruden Farm was certainly more subdued than those first happy occasions, but Elisabeth was determined that her husband should quickly return to living a normal life as soon as his heart problems showed clear signs of improvement. But, early in 1934, there were secret moves at *The Herald* which would really put Keith's stamina and resolve to the test.

Throughout his recuperation, Keith had kept in almost daily contact with friends and associates within the widespread Herald and Weekly Times empire. They came to Cruden Farm where they sat with him under the trees already growing in Elisabeth's garden and he soon heard that there was a growing plot, hatched by a group led by Theodore Fink, the wealthy and powerful original chairman of directors, to force Keith's retirement or have him stripped of his executive powers. The plan was to replace Keith with Fink's young son, Thorold. Elisabeth says that at the time 'horrible' rumours were spread about Keith's health. 'They were very harmful and, of course, they were designed to be,' she says.

Indeed, when he was able to return to work, Keith found there was a new board member, George Caro, on whose vote the Finks were relying to remove the Murdoch influence. As it turned out, when the vote came in the boardroom, Caro sided with Keith. Now the way was open for Sir Keith Murdoch's *Herald* to become the finest evening newspaper in the English-speaking world with memorable editors, a fine Australian reporting staff and distinguished correspondents in the world capitals. At the same time, Keith's breezy tabloid morning *Sun News Pictorial* was setting the pace in Australia – just as Rupert Murdoch's *Sun* would do in the UK nearly forty years later.

Looking back now, Elisabeth says: 'They were easier days, more pleasant really, for the next few years. There was no TV, of course, but we did have a gramophone with a pile of old records... a lot of them Melba's arias – and Keith's wireless sets. Keith was not really very well educated musically. He didn't know a lot about it. He had seen opera and he loved that, but then Keith had an extraordinary ear and eye for quality. He could discern what was a good performance although intellectually he couldn't tell you very much about it, but he had this discernment and he was very quick to hear things that weren't good,' says Elisabeth, a longstanding benefactor of the opera in Australia.

'At school I had longed to learn music and I was supposed to be quite good at it. I continued my music lessons after I left school and had a very good music teacher, Miss Annie Cocks, whom I went to privately. I remember she wanted her pupils to have accompanying lessons and there was a very well-known violinist named Eduard Lambert who was commissioned to come and have some sessions with us, just before I became engaged to Keith.

'I've never forgotten the shame of it!' says Elisabeth now. 'I had to accompany him in a Beethoven violin sonata and, of course, I was stiff with fear and I got off on the wrong foot and couldn't get back on to it so, at the age of eighteen, I fled from the room in tears. I was so mortified and so ashamed. I don't think I have ever quite got over that,' says Elisabeth. 'Poor Miss Cocks must have been ashamed too. The other students did well but it was just terrible, terrible!

I continued my lessons and, of course, Keith got me my beautiful piano for a wedding present. It was just after the war when you still couldn't get German pianos and so it was a Broadwood, a famous English piano, which is still in my drawing room today. I continued with my lessons for quite a while then I had the children and I gave it up altogether for many years.'

Much of the fine antique English furniture at Cruden Farm today was bought by the Murdochs after their return from their trip to the USA and Europe in 1929 but it was not until their next overseas journey, in 1936, that the couple had 'a big spend-up'. Elisabeth explains: 'I think Keith always wanted very much not to live up to his income – a very Scottish thing. When we first married he was very careful, although always very generous to me, but his objective was to save at least one quarter of his income. But our big spend-up in 1936 was to our absolute limit. Keith had worked frightfully hard after recovering from his heart attack and always he set himself to save part of his income to give himself equity to proceed further. That's how he got on so well. We bought all the lovely oak, the tables, the dresser and the Windsor chairs, in London – at Woolseys, Buckingham Gate. At that time we bought the wonderful ship prints that are now in the dining room. They were very expensive, very high quality. So we really did have a lovely buy and I think Keith felt rather anxious. However, we soon did get on an even keel again.'

But before that memorable London trip with his family, Keith was able to devote time to a major project he had often discussed with Elisabeth: the setting up of an Australian newsprint industry to cushion his newspaper interests from any world shortages – and the coming world conflict he was already predicting. Keith saw the thickly timbered island state of Tasmania, with its rainforests and bountiful supply of hydro-electricity, as the ideal venue for his first pulp mill and soon he had mounted an expedition to personally check on the reserves of fast-growing mountain ash in the island's northern forests.

To Keith it was a great adventure, for Elisabeth more of a trial as, clad in her Savile Row riding gear, she set out on horseback with Keith and a support staff to set up camps along the steep bush tracks into the vast timber lands her husband was interested in. There was a long way to go before the coarse, yellow newsprint made from the eucalypt pulp was to be refined into the acceptable paper that undoubtedly enabled Australian newspapers to continue publication during the war. For Elisabeth the long, gruelling Tasmanian ride was very different to her teenage rides on the Melbourne 'tan' or the relaxing gallops around Cruden Farm. But, as always, she was delighted to be at Keith's side when he was enthusiastically involved in one of his great projects.

Meanwhile there was the Children's Hospital. Today Elisabeth says: 'It was almost a full-time voluntary job and I'm afraid I used it largely as an alibi – which, I suppose, sounds a funny thing to say, but it made very good sense to me. You simply can't join too many committees and do justice to all of them and I already had my hands full looking after Keith and the children, so I thought if I went boots and all into the hospital it would be the best thing I could do at that stage of my life.'

Carefully feeling her way on the Children's Hospital management committee under the watchful eye of Lady Latham, Elisabeth soon made important friends. 'I was absolutely devoted to Mrs Higgins, widow of Mr Justice Higgins. She was a tremendous influence, a remarkable person, as was Mrs Fogarty. Although I respected and admired Lady Latham enormously, I think as human beings I really had tremendous affection for both Mrs Higgins and Mrs Fogarty. Whereas, perhaps, I wouldn't have asked for Lady Latham's advice when I wanted information in-depth I always felt that I could turn to Mrs Fogarty and Mrs Higgins who were very wise women without, perhaps, the enormous intellectual strength of Lady Latham. It was a wonderful education for me as a young woman,' says Elisabeth.

Commenting on today's moves away from voluntary hospital and other charitable committees and auxiliaries, Elisabeth says: 'I think it is sad really because, although there have been changes in direction – very important changes – I still believe that it is the human touch which is so frightfully important.'

Today, more than sixty years later, with their son Rupert now in control of Keith's old newspapers, and many more of his own, Elisabeth continues on the same theme: 'It's what I've heard happened at *The Herald* too. It's not just the hospital, it's everywhere. *The Herald* went through a period – before the Murdoch return – where nobody from upstairs or downstairs ever saw a soul. And when my daughter Janet went there as Chairman it was partly because Rupert wanted her to represent the family and put a bit of Keith's humanity back into the place. That's what she did too. She went through the whole place. I don't think there was an area she didn't visit in an unobtrusive way, and she found people there who hadn't seen anybody from "upstairs" for years. She's marvellous, and when people retire, Janet always knows and she has them up for a cup of tea and a yarn about the old days.

'Now we are in a period right through our society where we're losing that kind of thing. I do think that the great joy for me in my time at the hospital was this close contact with everyone, from cleaners to surgeons to management. That's just a personal thing though, some people don't need that. I think we did have it in those days. It was valued. I think people were probably a bit simpler then. I think the successful institutions must rely very much on the relationships of the people within them, and that has to come from the top. It's the same with our schools. Leadership has to come from the top. There are loads of good people underneath, but if the example isn't right at the top, you're in trouble,' insists Elisabeth.

In the early thirties, Elisabeth was at the threshold of her lifetime of public service but today, looking back to the traumas and joys of the thirties, she says: 'Being part of the hospital for so long and meeting the children and their families has been very enriching. I suppose it's a part of my great feeling for my family too. Of course, the most satisfying thing I ever did was to marry my husband because from that came so much. I never would have been involved in the Children's Hospital if I weren't Keith's wife, I know I wouldn't.

'What I mean is I used to knit singlets for the Children's Hospital at school and as a child I was taken with the idea of poor suffering children, but as for ever dreaming I would be in any way involved ... that was a different matter altogether. Then, of course, I never would have been involved in the arts either if it weren't for Keith.

'You know, I've had at least two lives. I mean I had a fascinating life with Keith and the children and that was a wonderful, full, rich period. And then, of course, I got very responsibly involved in the Children's Hospital. And when I gave that up, along comes the National Gallery of Victoria. That really opened up a lot of things too, and, of course, the gallery down here (the acclaimed McClelland Regional Gallery) is absolutely charming. The whole place is beautiful and it's got some very notable sculptures around the park.'

CHAPTER THIRTEEN

The Travelling Murdochs

ALWAYS AN ENTHUSIAST, Keith Murdoch, with his young wife, pursued his new interests with zest, reading and learning about horses and riding, cattle breeding, fly fishing, and collecting silver, glass and ceramics. In many of these pursuits he was assisted by the Murdochs' close friends and neighbours, the Lindsays, Daryl and Joan, who lived a brisk canter away from Cruden Farm at delightful Mulberry Hill. 'Keith was always inquisitive,' says Elisabeth, 'and a lot of what he learnt rubbed off on me without me having to do the hard work. It was wonderful to be at Keith's side when he was pursuing knowledge about the arts and so many other interesting things.'

Back at *The Herald* with his health and confidence returning, Keith was soon in an unassailable position at the helm of the growing Australian media empire; so much so that by mid-1935 he was able to tell Elisabeth that he was planning a lengthy family trip to Europe. Now Rupert and Helen were able to explain to Kline, the gardener, why Elisabeth had stopped climbing on her stepladder to pick the lush sweetpea blooms in the Heathfield gardens. 'We'll tell you a secret,' Rupert told the amused old gardener. 'Mummy is getting a baby for us, but you must promise not to tell Dad.'

On 20 September 1935, Elisabeth's baby was delivered a month early at Epworth Hospital and, following a long family tradition, christened Anne. Planning for the overseas trip continued but this time it was understood that the whole family – including Anne – would be going along. There would be no repeat of the 1929 trip when Elisabeth was parted from baby Helen for several months. Before the trip began, the Murdochs consulted Keith's heart specialist who told Elisabeth that he could really find no evidence of anything particularly serious in the condition of Keith's heart and urged that this information should be used to boost her husband's eroded morale – a suggestion which Elisabeth acted on with enthusiasm. 'It was wonderful. Keith was reassured and from that time on he was very much more confident and able to handle any situation,' Elisabeth says.

At Heathfield with the new baby, Elisabeth had the loyal support of six maids living upstairs and a valet living downstairs along with a butler and his wife. There was also a full-time laundress living in. 'It's fantastic thinking of it today. Looking back, it was a very feudal system, but we were a very happy household and I made sure that nobody was overworked and, unlike other big households in Melbourne at that time, we gave all the staff three weeks' annual leave. It was quite a business organising it all really. You had to be a juggler when you were entertaining, as we were, with past, present and future prime ministers, businessmen, musicians and artists visiting us for dinners or musical evenings.'

Early in 1936, the Murdochs boarded the *Otranto* bound for Europe. There were Helen, seven, Rupert, five, and baby Anne, four months, along with Nanny and Edith, a house sewing maid. Edith went along to look after packing the clothes and as a back-up to Nanny taking care of excited Helen and Rupert and caring for baby Anne. Also on that voyage were Bob Menzies and his wife, Pattie. Today these two notable Australian Dames are still friends. As usual, on the traditional Australia/UK route, the ship stopped for a day at Naples and Keith took Elisabeth and the family to inspect the ruins of Pompeii. It was a winter's day and Elisabeth still treasures the photograph of herself wrapped in her mink coat nursing baby Anne among the ancient statues and columns.

The family voyage ended at Gibraltar where Keith and Elisabeth went ashore leaving Nanny and Edith to take the children on to London. Elisabeth says now: 'I suppose it was a terrible thing to do. We were out of touch with the children for such a long time but you see we trusted Nanny completely and knew that she would be taking them on to her home in Leicestershire to await our arrival. But, unfortunately, the three children contracted gastroenteritis and poor Nanny was left to nurse them the rest of the way to England. Nanny was very English and to her horror when she finally got to her sister's farm that she had talked about so much she discovered there was no water laid on in the house – everything was in the yard – and she had these three children with gastroenteritis having the most awful time while we were gallivanting around Spain.'

Passing through the border at Algeciras, Keith and Elisabeth drove into Spain then just on the brink of its civil war. They drove to Granada where they visited the Alhambra Alcazar and delighted in the gypsy dancing in the famous caves before driving on to Valencia and then Madrid. In the uneasy Spanish capital they were met by the *Times* correspondent who over ten days took them to the Prado, home of one of the world's finest art collections, and to other fascinating places off the regular tourist tracks. The Murdochs crossed into France just days before the Spanish Civil War broke out, leaving behind a fearful, deeply divided country.

The Murdochs then drove through France to Paris where Keith insisted that Elisabeth should buy three beautiful gowns at a well-known fashion house. 'He was awfully keen that I should have some really beautiful clothes. He also wanted to add to my pearl necklace which he had given me when Helen was born – and I didn't want to because I knew we couldn't really afford it and I thought it was foolish. However, we went to Cartiers and a very persuasive gentleman insisted on putting three beautiful pearls in the centre.

'At the time I was determined we were not going to have them. It was just too much money and we had other things to do. But Cartiers said: "Just take them to London before you decide." You see, they thought that once wearing them I would never part with them. But the minute we got to London, I insisted on them being taken back. I don't think they ever forgave me. I never had much more to do with them after that,' says Elisabeth.

In London, the Murdochs moved into a rented flat in Queen Anne's Mansions and were soon reunited with Nanny and the delighted children. While Rupert and Helen were given riding lessons in Hyde Park – with young Rupert objecting to the 'proper' clothes and the formality of British riding – Nanny proudly took Anne for long walks through the park in a new gleaming English pram with all the fittings, which Nanny would stay up until midnight polishing. 'Nanny wasn't a snob, but she liked the best. Elitism is a terrible thing, but the pram marked excellence and she wanted top of the line,' says Elisabeth.

Helen and Rupert, still two 'dinkum Aussies', were sent off to Holland Park School for a term. Keith was soon resuming his contacts and introducing Elisabeth to the powerful British newspaper barons and politicians he had met in London after the First World

War. 'It was a sad time in England because Edward was in trouble over his liaison with Mrs Simpson and there was all this speculation going on about their illicit romance. It was awful. Everywhere we went this was the main talking point, although I noticed that the women we met were also incessantly complaining about the lack of kitchen maids.

'I was rather shocked by this. I didn't think that it was really polite conversation to talk about that sort of thing. I mean, one got on with those things and coped with them but you didn't talk about them,' says Elisabeth now. 'I remember after we returned to Australia and told my darling little Granny Forth about the topics of conversation she was quite shocked. She said, "Oh, dear, I don't think you could have been mixing with very nice people." She was very Empire-minded in a nice sensible way and generations of being British and loyal to the Crown was a great thing in our family.'

Just before Elisabeth had set sail with her family, Nanny Russell had said to her: 'M'lady, I beg of you, will you and Sir Keith find a good governess for the children because I haven't had the education. I am a children's nanny. I think that Helen and Rupert are now needing somebody with more education.'

Says Elisabeth: 'It was such an unusual thing for this very devoted Nanny to talk like that. In my experience, I thought it was extraordinary. But although I hated the thought of it, I knew she was right and, in London, we set about looking for a governess. I got in touch with a well-known agent. She advertised for us and she got ninety-three answers.'

As Elisabeth went through the names of the applicants seeking a job as a governess in far off Australia, Keith decided he should take a look at Hitler's 1936 Olympic Games. Before leaving, Keith insisted that Elisabeth should take her sister, Marie Greene, for a ten-day holiday in Paris while he went on to Berlin. 'Marie and I had a wonderful ten days in the French capital where we were escorted to museums, nightclubs and restaurants by one of Keith's young journalistic friends, Ted de Pury. It was splendid. I was able to give my dear sister a splendid holiday, which was necessary at that time, and it wasn't long after our trip that she decided to get married – to John Durnford, later to be a distinguished Royal Navy Vice-Admiral.'

Keith, meanwhile, had been shocked at what he saw in Nazi Germany and wrote scathing articles for his newspapers warning of new threats of war in Europe. 'He was very critical indeed, although at the time some people in Australia saw this as war-mongering. Keith didn't actually meet Hitler but he left Germany well aware of the man's evil spell and feeling very alarmed indeed. He had a great feeling of foreboding that there would be another war.'

By the time the Murdochs returned to their flat in London, three governesses had been shortlisted for them by the agency. 'One of them, Miss Joan Kimpton, came to see me at Queen Anne's Mansions. I had come back from Paris with a beautiful tartan cotton blouse which she saw hanging with the washing while she waited for me. I was a bit late and poor Miss Kimpton looked at this blouse for a while and thought, "Oh, dear, some large and intimidating Scottish woman will be arriving to interview me."

'When she saw me, I suppose it put her mind at rest and seeing that she was a very shy and charming woman, I told her: "We'll do everything to make you happy and find you friends and hope you'll be one of the family but, in fact, you'll be living a great deal in the schoolroom with Nanny and the children."

'Miss Kimpton drew herself up to her six feet and said: "I would prefer that." So she was my girl and she turned out to be the most wonderful person in the family for many years. I was about twenty-seven then and she was one year older and she had had a pretty sad and difficult life and her expectations were nice and admirable. She knew what her job would offer. That was the great thing – people should know and accept what conditions are and go out and make the best of them and be happy. Miss Kimpton was rather stern, because I think she was anxious to keep her authority in the kindest possible way.

'The one thing I didn't say to her then was that she had to get on with our wonderful Nanny. But, of course, she did. They got on very well together indeed and respected each other even if they didn't always agree. I told them both: "My husband and I don't always agree with our edicts about the children but we stand up to them together in face of all opposition because you have to have a united front. You will always have us to support you as long as you always support us in matters of discipline."

'From then on, we had a wonderful family life. The only time I had to chastise Rupert with a slipper was when he was rude to Nanny, although he might have been a bit older then, still finding his feet. You see, children are so defiant and blatantly disobedient if they are never checked. We never had any trouble with our children. We really didn't. They understood when we said things we meant it, and we always tried to say things that were fair, proper and suitable. But if we did say something they resented, they would never give us cheek. That was the way you brought up children then and I think young people today are having the most hideous time because they are confused. With teenagers, of course, it's different, but it shouldn't be so difficult with the very young,' says Elisabeth.

Then it was time for the Murdochs with 'Kimpo' – as she became known until her death in 1993 – now part of the family, to return to Australia where Keith would immediately begin to tell all those who would listen about his forebodings of war.

CHAPTER FOURTEEN

At the 'Country Seat'

BACK IN AUSTRALIA with Kimpo soon conducting classes for Helen and Rupert in the Heathfield schoolroom, Elisabeth resumed her active role on the Children's Hospital committee and other voluntary interests, while tuning the household staff to fit in with Keith's increasingly demanding social and business life. Today, although she admits that the lifestyle at Highfield and Cruden Farm appeared to be lavish for the times, Elisabeth says she was unaware of the financial details of her husband's obviously improving fortunes, and indicates that prying into such details would have been 'vulgar' – a view certainly held by Bairnie throughout her long life.

Yet, she says: 'At the time I wasn't conscious that ours was a very grand establishment but perhaps other people did think that. Today, if you saw someone living like that you'd say "How extraordinary," but isn't it funny how you're not always aware of how your lifestyle looks from the outside? Sometimes you go into a house and it looks rich and you know it's all really just there for looking at – and that's to be avoided if at all possible.'

In the days at Heathfield, Keith had no expense account for home entertaining, nor was such entertainment tax deductible, but Elisabeth recalls the fine detail of her dinner parties. 'Our table could seat twenty-four. That was the limit and it was a bit crushed with that number of guests. I had a lovely Wedgwood dinner service – twenty-four of everything in gold on plain white and I can tell you I still have twenty-two settings today, nearly sixty years later. That says a lot. My staff were so careful. I've only had one chip in one plate in all these years. I'm a very fast worker and if anyone breaks something it's me.

'In those days we didn't have huge marquees and caterers because we had a wonderful household and it was really quite nice to have a dinner party knowing that the butter, cream, chickens and flowers all came from Cruden Farm. Everything came by train from Frankston to Armadale station in big wicker baskets which were collected by the chauffeur in Keith's great big blunderbuss of a Cadillac.

'Keith loved his treasures and was very lucky to acquire beautiful things like pictures, silver and glass. But, you know, beautiful things don't have to be ostentatious. Fortunately, Keith and I had very good rapport, similar tastes. I quickly absorbed his appreciation and feeling for things. My mother had good taste but never the means to do anything significant about it. Looking back at Pemberley it was always very charming with good Edwardian taste but even though the pictures on the walls may not have been of much value, they were good. Sadly, there was nothing inherited from the de Lancey Forths. Granny once told me there were some beautiful Raeburn pictures in the family but they disappeared. I think they were spenders. They lived their lives and somehow their possessions got shed on the way.'

Clearly, although Sir Keith was now Australia's leading newspaper proprietor, he did not share the lifestyle of a Hearst, Beaverbrook or Rothermere with villas in France, steam yachts and great country estates. Yet Keith, always the astute businessman, was an early entrant into Australian broadcasting with interests in more than eleven radio stations nationwide. He also made several profitable property deals and, setting an example which his son, Rupert, was to later follow, he was adept at buying up unprofitable newspaper properties – including his majority holding in Queensland Newspapers – and skilfully building them up into profitable quality publications.

As Elisabeth clearly recalls, there was at times pressure from banks. Cruden Farm, her wedding present, was often 'in hock'. At *The Herald*, Keith used his office boardroom to entertain politicians like Prime Ministers Joe Lyons and Robert Menzies, as well as senior businessmen and visiting media executives. Elisabeth seldom attended these functions although she would often visit *The Herald* and be introduced to senior staff members as well as young cadet reporters by her proud husband. In those days before industrial confrontation and aggressive trade unionism, Keith and Elisabeth would know the names of almost every employee at the Herald and Weekly Times from the editorial floor to the print room. Occasionally, when Keith was heavily engaged, Elisabeth would arrive at the office to find that the chief of staff or senior reporter had been delegated by Keith to 'take Elisabeth to tea'.

Although Saturdays were usually strictly family days at Cruden Farm, Sundays often saw important house guests taken for picnics or formal lunches around the English oak table. Former Prime Minister Lord Bruce, and his wife, who were also near neighbours, were frequent guests as were the Lindsays. 'We were very friendly with the Bruces in a superficial way but I never felt we got very close to either of them because they were so particularly close to each other. It was almost a closed book.

'Then, of course, the Gulletts, Joe's parents, were always very close friends of ours. I owe a great deal to Lady Gullett. She was a loving friend and encourager when we first met. She knew how much Keith wanted to be married and have a family life and I loved her dearly. She was a very amusing woman who could be absolutely devastatingly funny. I can remember one occasion when Henry was just rising in politics and it was rather important that he should be giving this party on a public holiday and I was taking all the flowers. The car was absolutely stacked up with flowers and I was driving up Point Nepean Road through Chelsea when I saw there was a car following me. Of course, the more it followed, the faster I went, and I thought it must be a friend from Portsea. But, of course, it was the police and that was the only time I have ever been in serious trouble with the police.

'I think I was perhaps going about sixty miles per hour but it was an outrageous speed in those days and, oh, I was terribly upset. The police took my name down and when I arrived at the Gulletts I burst into tears, and Henry said: "The brutes! I will go and see them about it." That was a disgraceful thing. I should never have let him go but I have always been absolutely craven about getting into trouble. I'm stupid like that. And he went to the police and, of course, it was the worst thing he could do and I was fined ten pounds! Dear Henry was such a loving friend but I should never have been going so fast.'

At this time, Keith's long association with Australia's wartime Prime Minister Billy Hughes was still continuing but Elisabeth says 'the little Digger' was very much a 'fair-weather friend'. 'Keith did feel that Hughes, who had a chequered career in Australian politics, had rather let him down after making great use of Keith's important contacts in London after the war, and there had been a coolness for years. He stayed at Cruden Farm one night and was very amusing but I couldn't bear to see people like him ingratiating themselves and trying to use Keith. We went to see the Hughes at Lindfield once because Keith was very forgiving, although he felt Hughes had let him down after Gallipoli, and when we got to the front door after these years of coolness, dear old Mary Hughes met us and we were amazed to see on the hall table a picture of Keith. It's a long time ago but I always remember it.

'Keith was never completely close to Labor politicians but because he was a very broad person I was never quite sure about his political persuasion. Although at first he was clearly a small 'l' liberal, he did become more conservative. I think if Keith felt someone was doing something that perhaps he didn't think was very good for Australia he could be quite intolerant. Certainly, he was intolerant of Scullin and I don't think he was very appreciative of Labor Prime Ministers Chifley or Curtin.'

But while Keith was kept busy insisting on excellence of reporting and objectivity in his newspapers, Elisabeth was now overseeing the upkeep of two great gardens and often moving hoses from sunset to dawn to cope with low summer water pressure in Toorak or Langwarrin. 'I had been very busy having babies for ten years, but I knew now the National Gallery really called for some sort of effort from me. Keith, now the Chairman of Trustees, was very keen that I should help to get a Gallery Society going. I was already doing the flower arrangements in the old gallery for receptions. The flowers came from the Heathfield garden in those days.'

In 1904, Alfred Felton left Victoria a great £383,163 legacy and directed that half the income be used to buy works of art – a bequest which helped Victoria accumulate one of the world's notable art collections.

'We had quite a few gatherings at Heathfield on behalf of the gallery trustees and the Felton Bequest. I remember one awful occasion, I blush when I think of it now, but it wasn't that Keith wasn't awfully generous. He didn't quite understand, nor did I. We had a musical evening with Spivakovsky, the great violinist, and his quartet. I don't know how Keith knew them but they were asked and they were delighted to come. And when they played, I can see them now, our guests weren't really interested in this lovely music. It really wasn't a big party, but I thought it was lovely chamber music and when Keith said goodbye to them he asked them what their fee was and they said "nothing, nothing," and he said "you must, you must," and so he gave them one hundred pounds.

'But apparently you either give them nothing or you give them rather more. I know Keith said to me, "They don't seem terribly pleased." It was pure innocence, the sort of mistake anyone could make but he really should have found out from a professional body. There was no way he could have known but he was very uncomfortable about it.

'On another occasion we had a group of singers from the university, and a famous harpsichordist, over for the evening. Heathfield was absolutely packed and my little sitting room opened up into the big drawing room and into the hall. I remember sitting at the back next to a man while this woman was playing away. I didn't like it and I said to the man sitting next to me: "Awful, isn't it. Not my favourite instrument, do you like it?" And he replied: "I have to, she's my wife,"' Elisabeth laughs.

'However, most of our parties were with our friends many of whom had something to do with the office.' Indeed Keith and Elisabeth delighted in asking young staff members and new executives home for formal dinners. Few could be anything but overcome by the servants, Elisabeth's table settings and Keith's conducted tours of his antique glass and china collection. Elisabeth still chuckles as she recalls Keith, in a bid to put one young wife at ease, asking 'Do you like old things?' The nervous reply which Elisabeth says nearly caused her to splutter in her soup, was: 'Oh yes, Sir Keith, I'm very fond of you.'

Keith was now captivated with Wantabadgery, the large grazing property he had purchased in 1938 in New South Wales, with rolling, rocky hills and river flats spread along the meandering Murrumbidgee River between Wagga Wagga and Gundagai – although he rarely found time to visit there. 'Keith loved Wantabadgery, which had been owned by the Macdonalds (close kinsmen of Elisabeth's). It already had splendid cattle, and his great challenge was to improve the stud. Altogether it was quite a testing time. Keith was terribly interested, but it was a very large property and, of course, we soon had all the trauma of the challenge of a soldier land settlement scheme with the government compulsorily taking half the land, with Keith retaining about 6000 acres.

'There were a lot of negotiations over that. There was a great conflict of opinion about what would be viable. We had an enchanting little modern house built by Ian Macdonald right up on the hillside away from the original homestead which was the scene of an historic siege with the notorious bushranger, "Captain Moonlight". When you got there you thought you could stay there forever. That was where I nursed Anne after her serious illness and that's where we had a number of our school holidays. We all rode and had lovely picnics on the Murrumbidgee.'

But it was also a very sad time. Elisabeth's cousin, Hamish Macdonald, had been posted as missing in action during the Fall of Singapore. He was never found. He had married Nancy Syme, who was living with her young children in Wantabadgery West and the Murdochs and the Macdonalds saw a lot of each other with Nancy steadfastly refusing to give up hope for her missing husband.

'My uncle, Claude McDonald, who was very frail, came out and Nancy looked after him marvellously for two or three years,' recalls Elisabeth. 'Keith came when he could but I was always disappointed because he would come up for ten days and by the third day something would come up in Sydney or Adelaide which needed his presence. The family was always disappointed that we didn't have more of him. The children hardly ever brought chums home from school but perhaps that was because I felt that, as they were away from home so much, we'd like to have them on their own when they did come home. Keith couldn't bear for them to go away. On the whole, we look back on those days as being very precious because they were such family times.'

Clearly Keith loved the experience of being a 'Collins Street Farmer' – the slightly derogative Australian term for city businessmen with rural interests – and soon he had juggled his finances sufficiently to allow him to look out for other grazing properties within range of Canberra, and he next purchased Bredbo in the Australian Alps near Cooma, more than one hundred miles from the Australian Parliament House. Elisabeth remembers that another property inspected by Keith was overrun with rabbits and subject to flooding. Keith described it as 'a most attractive place'. But despite Keith's expanding interests, Cruden Farm was still the refuge that the Murdochs loved most.

In her book, *Time Without Clocks*, Lady Lindsay wrote this evocative contemporary account of the Murdochs of Cruden Farm:

'Although the Murdochs lived most of the year at Heathfield – a splendid boom-time mansion in Toorak, where they did their formal entertaining – it was at Cruden Farm that the whole family had their fullest flowering. At the farm we watched the children growing up,

Helen and Rupert learning to fish and ride and swim, Anne and Janet getting through chickenpox and measles.

'Sometimes, we joined them at a gymkhana or a picnic at Point Leo, then a wild, almost deserted beach; when Keith, lying full length on the yellow sand, tipped his hat over his eyes, forgot *The Herald* office and for those few glorious sun-drenched hours, became the family man.

'If only he had lived in the 18th century – a period in which he would have been very much at home – what a splendid subject he would have made for a conversation piece by Joseph Highmore: *The Murdoch Family at their Country Seat*, with Keith in a Georgian armchair dandling the latest infant on an elegant silken knee.

'The Murdochs out riding on Sunday mornings made an unforgettable spectacle – a sort of medieval cavalcade of children, servants, outriders, horses and dogs – along the rough tree-lined roads of Baxter and Langwarrin.

'At the head of the gay motley procession rides Keith, mounted on a massive charger, an upright rather heavily built figure immaculate in English tweed and riding boots; proud and happy, as well he might be, in the company of his lively affectionate brood, enjoying the sights and scents of the bush tracks, the anticipation of an excellent midday dinner with claret and roast beef at Cruden Farm. Beside him rides Elisabeth, slim and fearless, sometimes on a half-wild racehorse liable at any moment to bolt the last few miles to the home stables.

'Friends and children rode animals of varying quality according to their skill and experience – shaggy ponies begged or borrowed for extra children, stock horses spelling from a drought-stricken station, a quiet hack or two reserved for timid house guests.

'Sometimes Daryl would join the procession at our crossroads, perhaps on Pompey or Mickey the flighty Arab brought up on the treeless northern plains, who would dance halfway across the sunflecked track at the mere shadow of a leaf.

'Amongst the riders could occasionally be seen poor Basil Burdett (later *The Herald* art critic), who hating and fearing all horses, jogged his unhappy way on a solid little old pony, with his long legs almost touching the ground, and once (in a macintosh cape and black beret) looking remarkably like the Friar from Chaucer's *Canterbury Tales*.

'And lastly, alert and loving in the rear, Kimpo the adored English governess, on horseback with the younger children or driving the pony cart, with little tow-headed Rupert bouncing up and down on Joy Boy the miniature Shetland, a present from Godfather Daryl, attached by a leading rope to the tail board.

'Keith will not ride our quiet country lanes again but the pattern continues, with other happy children and other Joy Boys, equally cunning, belaboured and beloved ...'

Elisabeth too has affectionate memories of both Daryl and Joan Lindsay, although, she says pointedly, she never met Daryl's younger brother, Norman Lindsay, the wildly brilliant author and painter of voluptuous nudes who was perhaps the best known of that richly talented family. 'I suppose I never met Norman because in those days Daryl didn't speak to him and there was very strong feeling against him amongst conventional people ... today, when you think what we all accept and look at ... but they were different times. It is funny to look back now and see how one's attitude has changed and been conditioned,' Elisabeth muses.

CHAPTER FIFTEEN

The War Years

THE FRIENDSHIP BETWEEN the Murdochs and the Lindsays, with Keith seeking Daryl's advice and encouragement as his interest in collecting works of art grew, was warm and close. 'I was very fond of Joan. She was an unusual person, not easy to know and somewhat unpredictable at times because she had very definite ideas about people. As they grew older, Joan became more eccentric and Daryl became very deaf and very irascible,' Elisabeth recalls.

On occasions, another of the famous Lindsay brothers, Lionel, was a guest at Cruden Farm. Elisabeth still remembers the 'agony' when, at half past ten, the fish course still hadn't been completed because Lionel, although a great and fascinating conversationalist, could be very argumentative. 'I can just see him now with the fish poised between his mouth and plate and never getting to the mouth. And all the while, our wonderful loyal staff were waiting with the second course spoiling.'

The War Years

By now, Keith's forebodings about the Second World War were being widely acknowledged but at Cruden Farm life went on smoothly. The Murdoch children all agree that while Keith was the indulgent father, Elisabeth was the disciplinarian in the family – an assessment she accepts today. 'All through our family life, Keith was older and naturally more inclined to spoil them so I think I had to balance that a bit by sometimes being a bit stricter and a bit repressive of Keith's more extravagant indulgences.

'I think the children knew that. It's not easy but I suppose one parent always has to show a little more restraint. Sometimes, Keith did feel a bit anxious about discipline for the children. And, although she wouldn't like to know this, he did feel at one stage that Kimpo was being rather too strict. In the early days, it was very touch and go as to whether our planned regime would be carried out because of his anxiety that perhaps the discipline in the schoolroom was a little too severe. But Kimpo and I soldiered on and I think Keith gradually began to appreciate it,' says Elisabeth, whose most severe sanction was usually confined to periods of standing the children in a corner.

'Rupert was born nearly two years after Helen and they became tremendous mates. They were close and Rupert has always maintained his tremendous respect for Helen – in fact, that is a wonderful thing about the family, we all respect each other and it was the two older children who set the pattern in a way.

'In the late thirties, we seemed to be incessantly on the road moving between Melbourne and the farm and that was quite a job. Although I had lots of help, there always had to be two cars. There were the children and Nanny and myself and sometimes three of the staff would come too. Keith always had a *Herald* driver to call on to drive one car and I'd drive the other. It was always quite an undertaking at the end of a busy week to organise the trip down to Cruden

Farm and Keith often wanted to ride and have various visitors at weekends.

'Although I had all those people to help, I had to mastermind it all and keep everything running happily. Of course, Keith had been a bachelor a long time and had been spoilt by the people looking after him. He was very, very busy and there was never any certainty about the time for meals, so thankfully I had a staff who were devoted to him. I'd go through agonies thinking we were keeping them up too late but they never seemed to mind. Our houses really did run on oiled wheels but I don't think Keith had a clue as to how those wheels went around,' she says.

The Murdochs became members of the Davey's Bay Yacht Club, at Mt Eliza, a small friendly bayside sailing club with family swimming contests and barbecue lunches. Keith bought a little sailing dinghy and delighted in taking the children out into the clear waters around the clubhouse jetty.

On 1 January 1939, Janet Murdoch was born and the family was complete. But just one month later, there was a scare that was to deeply affect the family. Anne suddenly became seriously ill with a high fever and doctors who were called in diagnosed osteomyelitis, a serious complaint that, in those days, could result in loss of life or limb. Fortunately, Elisabeth was quickly told of an orthopaedic surgeon, Mr David Officer Brown, who had just returned from the United States with a new technique for dealing with the disease.

Critically ill, Anne was rushed to Melbourne and immediately operated on. A second operation was needed and for a while the little girl's life was in the balance. 'I was in this awful position of being told that for the next ten days it would be touch and go whether she would recover. We had this splendid trained nurse who said to me: "Lady Murdoch, it is going to be tough but if I am to pull this child through, you must leave her to me," so the agony

The War Years

began for me, but I simply had to leave her to this devoted nurse who put in a tremendous effort.

'For a long time in Anne's subconscious mind remained the belief that I had not been at her bedside when she was so ill. She felt terribly deprived that I hadn't spent all my time with her. Yet others thought I was too wrapped up in Anne, that I allowed her to become too important in relation to the others. I don't think I did, but I must agree I was very close to Anne. You have to be when a child has been stricken like that. That was the way they did things in those days. It wouldn't happen now but I know Anne was wondering why I wasn't at her side and it certainly caused me great distress,' Elisabeth says now.

Years later as Dame Elisabeth Murdoch, President of the Royal Children's Hospital, Elisabeth told a televised 'Meet the Press' programme that parents should be allowed to visit their children in hospital at any time they were able, and at the Children's Hospital that was certainly the enlightened policy.

Anne's recovery was slow and painful but eventually she was allowed to return home where Keith's sister, Helen, a skilled physiotherapist, aided the recovery of her little niece. Meanwhile, Rupert had been enrolled in his first school, Adwalton, a private preparatory school in Malvern intended for boys destined to enter Geelong Grammar School.

Helen had followed her mother's course and was enrolled as a day girl at St Catherine's in Toorak before going off to board at Clyde, at Woodend. At home, Kimpo was on hand to supervise homework and provide extra tuition and Elisabeth was determined that all her children would matriculate, but Rupert was rebellious about what he regarded as a daily double dose of schooling.

Soon, just as Keith had been predicting, the world was at war again as, on 1 September 1939, Hitler's forces invaded Poland. Keith was now immediately working around the clock organising war correspondents and coverage for his newspapers and rallying support for Australia's war effort. At this time, he made several trips to Britain and the US and saw wartime leaders, including President Roosevelt. In Australia, he was among the first to warn of the threat posed by the Japanese militarists. At home, Elisabeth continued to nurse her sick daughter, care for her new baby, and look after the family properties, now including Wantabadgery.

In May, 1940, Prime Minister Menzies told the Australian War Cabinet: 'The morale of the people is going to undergo a terrific strain and, regardless of everything else, we should get the best publicists and journalists in Australia to ensure that the press and the people are caught up into the national effort.' With Cabinet approval, Keith was appointed Australian Director General of Information on 8 June 1940.

It was an honorary appointment and Keith immediately severed all active connection with his newspapers. But, as Desmond Zwar recorded in his book, *In Search of Keith Murdoch*, Keith's acceptance of the post was a 'gaffe' – 'the greatest in Keith Murdoch's professional life; it was a thunderbolt that made him a failure as Director General of Information; it was a negation of all the things on which he had built his life as a newspaper man.' Powerful newspaper groups outside the old Murdoch empire objected strongly to the stern censorship regulations Keith introduced. They referred to his government department as a 'dictatorship'.

Not surprisingly, by November Keith announced that he felt he could make a more effective contribution in the strengthening of public opinion and the winning of the war by resuming active association with his newspaper interests. His departure from the department came just before the Japanese attack on Pearl Harbour, on 7 December 1941, plunged the United States into the war.

The War Years

Pearl Harbour also changed the settled lifestyle of the Murdoch family for ever. Senior US officers setting up a base for General MacArthur in Melbourne were soon seeking suitable accommodation. When Keith was approached he immediately offered Heathfield to the US rent free. Within hours, Elisabeth and the staff were evacuating their home, leaving it fully fitted out for the arrival of Lieutenant General George H. Brett, a US Air Force officer then in command of all American troops in Australia.

In research for their book, *Disaster in the Pacific*, Peggy and Denis Warner uncovered clear evidence of General MacArthur's well-documented paranoia at its worst. From the moment of Brett's arrival, the Warners discovered, MacArthur slighted the Air Force general and cabled the War Department in Washington that it was 'most essential as a fundamental and primary step' that Brett should be relieved. It took MacArthur two months to get rid of Brett and his lieutenants and, meanwhile, MacArthur had astonished Australian officials by referring to Brett and his men as 'Murdoch's spies'. Then, the Warners' research in Washington shows, MacArthur branded Keith as 'an Australian quisling'.

MacArthur also claimed that Keith Murdoch had made overtures to H. R. Knickerbocker, war correspondent for Marshall Field's *Chicago Sun*, to act as a United States agent by publicising a critical attitude in regard to MacArthur's conduct of operations. He had positive information, MacArthur claimed in dispatches, that Murdoch had issued instructions for his military achievements to be 'written down'. Senior US General Henry H. Arnold, who had seen MacArthur at this time, noted in a signal to Washington that MacArthur's hands twitched and trembled. He bluntly diagnosed 'shell shock'. Murdoch executives, John Williams and Theodore Bray, who also saw MacArthur at the same time, reported that even this diagnosis did not adequately describe MacArthur's troubled mental state.

Recalls Elisabeth: 'It was a time for me fraught with anxiety and tension because as well as the war there was my preoccupation with a very young baby and soon after that Anne got her osteomyelitis and it was more or less two years before she was properly mobile. After her second operation, we went to Wantabadgery for Anne to recuperate in the sunshine and have lots of open air treatment.

'The sun was considered very important in those days, but I was left looking after her without professional help because the marvellous sister who had come with us was called up, and Anne's surgeon and the other sister were both sent off on active service overseas, so it was a difficult time for us. It was a very anxious time for the Children's Hospital too because a number of the young doctors joined up and staffing was quite a problem. Lady Latham was a masterful president who had a grasp of all our problems.

'After we evacuated Heathfield and moved down to Cruden Farm, we took a tiny flat in Wallace Avenue, Toorak, and Keith used to go up on Mondays and stay there through the week. He had a marvellous Swedish woman in *The Herald* office at that stage and she used to cook the luncheons at *The Herald* and she would sometimes go out on a Monday and cook Keith's dinner. On Tuesdays, I would drive up to town and look after him on Tuesday and Wednesday nights. I'd never had much experience of cooking, I'm ashamed to say, but dear Keith always said he had the best meals ever on those nights. In a way, it was a rather lovely intimate time together. The children weren't there and I was thrilled to be able to look after Keith and try and ease his burdens. Then on Thursdays, I'd come home to look after the children and make sure everything was running properly at Cruden Farm,' says Elisabeth.

'Anne and Janet were growing up at Cruden Farm and we still had Miss Kimpton who was determined also to meet her commitments to the two or three children who had been sharing lessons with our children in Melbourne and she went up and looked after them at Rosemary Manifold's home in Domain Road, South Yarra. She'd divide her time between there and Cruden Farm which meant of course that Nanny, the ongoing wonderful person, was here, sitting on the nest and I also had to be here a good deal. You just had to manage in those days and everybody was looked after happily and well.

'By this time, Keith was going overseas regularly. He had some quite testing times, going to see bombed cities and writing and speaking about what he saw. I think he was miserable at times but he was always driven by his sense of duty. I remember on one occasion in London he took our RAAF Battle of Britain boys out and gave them a wonderful dinner. They were so thrilled that he was really telling Australia about how well they were doing. They were very appreciative of Keith and his championing of their cause and they gave him the most beautiful silver model of a Spitfire.'

The Children's Hospital was also taking up some of Elisabeth's time. She was on the board of management and had to go up to meetings at least once a week. Normally it was the board of management or the board of management house committee. At that stage, she was junior vice-president and had quite a bit to do although without having sole responsibility for the running of the hospital. 'It was work which I was proud to do and very happy to be doing,' Elisabeth says.

But the war was still on and food, clothing and petrol were strictly rationed. The Murdochs soon had a cumbersome charcoal-fired gas producer on the back of their car which became the bane of Elisabeth's life. 'Then there was food rationing, although compared with Britain I often felt we really didn't know what it was in Australia. We had meat rationing which was not in any way really difficult because we still had quite a houseful and we'd put all the tickets together which went to buy one huge bit of beef for Sundays.

'We had roast on the bone and that was a problem. Keith never realised that it had to last right through the week and he was always so generous he'd be saying "Come on you must have some more" and my heart would go to my boots. It was amazing what a big piece of beef you could buy with nine ration tickets, but by Monday the remains had usually been made into mince.

'We made our own butter. We had our own milk, our own hens, and the occasional lamb. We were very fortunate and I used to sometimes feel a little ashamed at our good fortune. Of course, tea was rationed. I always remember our dear English maids pouring the cold tea off and then heating it up for themselves. The only thing one could do was send as many food parcels as we could to Britain.

'We had given up Heathfield because we felt it was one contribution we could make ... of course, there was no question of asking the Americans for rent or anything. Our old butler was kept on there but I think he was quite overwhelmed by the Filipino servants the US officers brought in. The gardening staff remained there too. The house was full and the Americans entertained madly.'

The memories of Heathfield remain but Elisabeth says: 'After the war when the Americans left Heathfield, we never went back to live there. We never had a hope. It was a house that needed about nine servants. I was very spoilt because I was allowed to keep a cook and a nanny and two maids at Cruden Farm because they were considered too old to go anywhere else.

'Keith and I did go back once to have a look at Heathfield. The butler was still there. The schoolroom had been turned into a billiards room where they had obviously had a great time. Upstairs, in our bedroom, the ceiling had stamps stuck all over it, but that was nothing. On the whole, the Americans had behaved very well and we had no complaints but there was no hope of us going back. We simply couldn't have afforded it,' Elisabeth insists. 'Then, when that was over, we loaned it to the Salvation Army for their servicewomen, and later, the Children's Hospital for their night nurses' house.' Eventually, in 1947, Heathfield was sold to the Colonial Mutual Life Insurance Society which resold to the Children's Hospital for £30,000.

'Then we bought 39 Albany Road, Toorak, designed by Geoffrey Somers. It had a beautiful exterior and inside it was a very charming house, a delightful house, built in 1939 by S. O. Woods. It had been the home of the British High Commissioner, Sir Ronald Cross, and his wife, who had rented it for two years and adored it. There was quite a nice garden at the side and another sunken garden on land that had originally been a part of Heathfield. It backed on to the Ramsays' tennis court and I think that in the end we bought the tennis court from them. I built up a very nice perennial border at the back.

'At that stage, I would have loved Keith to live down at Cruden Farm and he would have liked it too. But we knew it was impossible now that Helen was going to university, so in order to give her the background we thought she ought to have, we decided we would have Albany Road as a base and support. Of course, in a way it was ironic because when she did go to university, in our rather old-fashioned way, we wouldn't give her a car and it took her almost an hour to get to university by tram.

'She's got a good brain, Helen, and was doing Arts. I think at one time she would have liked to be a teacher. And, of course, when she got home she was too tired to come to any of our interesting dinner parties and Keith was very disappointed. He doted on her and he wanted her to take part in our lives and benefit from all the interesting people who came to our table. But she became quite "anti" because she was so tired and she'd set her eyes on Geoffrey Handbury and really didn't want to have anything divert her. So

Albany Road was, in a way, disappointing. But we got over that and after a year Helen gave up university. She said it was useless and she wanted to get married.'

At this time, at Bairnie's urging, Helen was sent off on an overseas trip. Keith and Elisabeth were to have taken her but that plan was cancelled when Keith was sent to hospital for a serious operation. So Helen made the voyage with Mrs Osborn-Fairbairn, a family friend who offered to take the eldest Murdoch child under her wing. It was a trip any Australian girl would have dreamt of, for as fellow passengers she had the Australian cricket team, including the young and handsome Keith Miller – later hailed by Fleet Street as 'Killer Diller Miller' – one of the greatest of cricket's all-rounders.

'Of course, she took a great fancy to them, and Keith Miller became a great friend, but she wasn't really too interested in anyone because she had left her Geoffrey behind,' Helen's understanding mother says today. 'To my dear sister Marie's concern, when she got to England Helen didn't want to do anything she had organised for her. All she wanted to do was be with the cricketers. It was all very trying until the Test matches got under way and Helen was able to see more of Britain.' At the time, Helen wrote a letter to her mother telling of *The Herald* London Bureau's reaction to a forthcoming visit from Sir Keith: 'It's terrible, Mum, all the office is taking vitamin pills against Dad's arrival,' she reported. But an English summer failed to divert Helen and she returned home to be with her Geoffrey. The couple were soon engaged and, after a wedding at Toorak Presbyterian Church, on 10 May 1949, began a happy and successful marriage.

But before the wedding, Elisabeth still recalls Keith's concern as he lay awake saying 'It's after midnight. Where are they?' to which Elisabeth could only reply: 'Don't forget, darling, that I was only nineteen when you used to keep me out later than that!' Elisabeth smiles as she says: 'Well, she had her reception at Albany Road and it all worked out very well although by that time Keith's mother and father were not alive to see it.'

By now, Rupert had been sent rather reluctantly to Geelong Grammar School and his mother says that the man who has today built a vast international media empire was 'always struggling at school. He was right down the bottom of the class usually. And I can still hear him saying defiantly: "I was twenty-first out of twenty-four, Mum, I might have been twenty-fourth." He was trying hard but it was a difficult time at Geelong Grammar at that stage for children who were not academically brilliant. But we always thought he should try and do better. I remember at Wantabadgery during the holidays trying to help him a bit with Latin verbs because we felt he needed coaching and I was not capable. But he was always good at things he was really interested in.'

Looking back to those days, Elisabeth reveals a long-held concern that her devotion to Keith may have at times left her children feeling deprived. 'I often feel I was so tremendously involved with Keith, and though we were very devoted and I hope good parents, I think that I myself sometimes did put Keith before the children. It worries me but I don't think they suffered. I think Keith needed my full attention and because of the difference in our ages I gave it to him. I hope the children didn't feel any deprivation. I was talking to Helen the other day and she was saying "But Mum, you and Dad were so marvellous. You were so different from other parents."

'I'm glad to think that perhaps the children do seem to have that opinion. They seem to think that we were very unselfish. We endeavoured to give them a good example without worrying about any sacrifice to ourselves. Rupert has always been very open in all that he's done and been working for. I think he still likes to keep me informed and feel that I am approving but he is not dominated by that. Rupert was always very independent. He has always had to do things and go forward in various ways that were quite challenging for me to accept. I've been lucky enough to have a lovely relationship with Rupert in that he would always tell me things, even if I didn't agree with him or he didn't agree with me. That has never altered our close affection. In many ways we're perhaps a strength to each other. He has always had, I hope, a great respect for me. He wished that whatever he was doing I would see and understand.'

At the time there were some concerns about Kimpo's obsessions over Rupert's interests. 'Many times when Rupert was growing up, and especially at Christmas, Kimpo would infer that the girls always had much more than Rupert. Late on Christmas Eve we used to assemble all the presents around my bedroom and there were piles for Helen, Rupert, Anne and Janet. Of course, boys' presents were knives and smaller things like that and Kimpo would say, "Oh, Lady Murdoch, Rupert's pile of presents is very small." She just adored Rupert and she did think that when it came to material things he came off worse than the girls. It's funny, isn't it?' Elisabeth laughs.

CHAPTER SIXTEEN

The Great Fire

By 1944, the Allied drive to push the Japanese out of the Pacific had begun. With Keith either overseas or rallying his media empire behind the war effort, Elisabeth was very much in control on the homefront, driving endlessly between Langwarrin and Melbourne and often on the day-long trip between Melbourne and Wantabadgery.

With petrol strictly rationed, her car was fitted with a dirty and unwieldy gas producer which needed constant stoking with coke carried in heavy bags. 'To keep the thing going was pretty difficult but it meant we got to Wantabadgery on very little fuel. But I'll never forget the one glorious occasion on the way there when, just outside Wagga, the most wonderful thing happened – the gas producer unit just fell off,' says Elisabeth, with a chuckle.

It was also difficult for Elisabeth to keep Cruden Farm running. 'By this time we had only one old Irishman who was marvellous with the horses. We also had some sheep and cows. I think he milked the cows and I don't think that he had any help at all. The garden was smaller during the war but I really worked very hard in it.

'One summertime the two children, Anne and Janet, were here, and they had measles. Helen and Rupert were away at school. Nanny came to me and said: "M'lady, I really want another baby." And then she suggested that she leave us and go and look after John and Elisabeth Baillieu's baby. That was her great gift, looking after babies,' says Elisabeth. So for a time, 'Nanny Murdoch', as she was known, left Cruden Farm and became 'Nanny Baillieu'. But she returned to Cruden Farm in her old age living in a cottage Elisabeth and Keith had built for her near the main house.

Although Geelong Grammar took a leaf out of the English public school system and subjected its pupils to cold showers or early morning swims, Keith and Elisabeth were concerned about Rupert growing up in a 'house full of women'. In an operation commented on in the numerous biographies written about Rupert, a wooden hut was built not far from the colonial entrance of the Cruden Farm homestead. Instead of glass windows, unnecessary in the Australian heat, flyscreens were fitted and 'Rupert's hut' with no electricity or running water became his spartan summer sleeping quarters. Rupert's sisters remember he also had his own comfortable room inside the house for cold winter's nights when he was home from school and Rupert remembers this 'toughening up process' as a pleasant part of the adventure of growing up. 'Perhaps that hut is why Rupert is so adaptable,' Elisabeth says proudly. 'He can make himself comfortable and be at home anywhere.' However, he could be a mischievous boy and his sisters recall dead snakes being slipped into beds and other pranks that were invariably traced back to Rupert. Rupert's sisters still recall the happy times when they willingly collected manure and trapped and skinned rabbits as part of Rupert's early

The Great Fire

business enterprises. 'The girls did the work while Rupert collected the money,' says Elisabeth with glee.

Elisabeth says she never had to spank her children and that anyway Keith did not approve of physical chastisement. 'I think I took a slipper to Rupert once or twice. He still teases me by opening a conversation with "when my mother beat me",' she laughs.

There were few workers at Cruden Farm during the war years. Fire breaks had not been cut for some time and Elisabeth had to manage the water supply which came in by gravitation across from a nearby hill into a tank. 'All the water we had for the house and the garden was what could be pumped up and I had to do the pumping every morning,' says Elisabeth. 'I had to struggle very hard to let the air blocks out of the pipes but even when the children were sick upstairs I somehow managed to keep the lawns at Cruden Farm green.'

Today, Elisabeth sees Cruden Farm as the 'continuing factor in our lives – the anchor of our family'. But on 14 February 1944, a hot summer's day with a blistering north wind, Cruden Farm was nearly destroyed. Elisabeth was up in town for the day having lunch at the Alexandra Club when she got a call from Keith to say he was sending an office car – a little English Morris as it turned out – and driver to pick her up to go down to the farm.

Although Keith had a broken ankle and was on crutches after a horseriding accident, this was the day he was leading a delegation of trustees to the Victorian State Government in a bid to secure the old Wirth's Circus site on St Kilda Road as the location for a grand new National Gallery of Victoria.

The farm was threatened, as a bushfire near Frankston was sweeping towards it, Keith told Elisabeth. 'I was to get down at once. But by the time we got there over an hour later, the paddocks were already ablaze and the fire was swirling towards the house. So we went in the back way to the house with the fire right on our heels,' Elisabeth says. At the house she discovered Nanny, the maids Edith and Alice, and the widowed Mrs Duell, but Kimpo had already driven the children off to safety in Cranbourne in the utility. 'At the time my greatest concern was to get in the house and get the books and cashbox of the Clyde Old Girls' Association. I was then the secretary and treasurer and I had to get those books out.'

Nanny and the maids had already gathered up the silver and any other precious things they could carry and put them in the centre of the tennis court. 'It seems that before I got there, Alice had been washing up after lunch and she said to Nanny: "Nurse, I think it's time we packed the silver." So, she packed the silver and two or three rugs Keith loved, but Mrs Duell wouldn't leave her cottage nearby, despite everyone's urging. When I got there, Mrs Duell was struggling with Nanny who was putting the hose down her neck, and Mrs Duell was saying "I know you never liked me, Nurse, I know you never liked me" – in the middle of all this!'

Elisabeth brought garden hoses and played low pressure jets of water on the weatherboard walls of the homestead as the fire drew closer. But as flames exploded in the tall eucalypts, Elisabeth and the household ran to the centre of the tennis court and watched as surrounding trees burst into balls of flame. 'We had pushed the little *Herald* car under the trees. The fire took all the trees around the tennis court and jumped the drive and went right through the front paddock.'

By now volunteer firefighters and naval ratings from the Flinders Naval Depot had arrived to fight the blaze which had already destroyed fourteen houses near Cruden Farm. 'They had the good sense to open all the gates so the stock could look after themselves and the cows were in the dam. One of our own cottages was burnt but the fire flared over the walled garden and up against the stone stables. The tree there was flaming up to the top but it was amazing the house didn't go. The fire literally went round the tennis court. The big bank at the bottom stopped it and it went right across the paddocks and killed a lot of sheep. It was a horrible experience.

'Poor old Kimpo had gone off with Anne and Janet. She wasn't very experienced at driving and on the way to Cranbourne she met a lot of children coming along the road because the school master had just told them to get home as best they could. So she picked up too many and the car broke down but she somehow got them all safely to the police station in Cranbourne. Soon as the smoke drifted away we had I don't know how many people sheltering in the house and on the tennis court. Many had lost their homes and everything in the fire and we had to set to and find them food and somewhere to sleep.

'The next morning the Governor's wife, Lady Dugan, came round with the Red Cross. Ours was not a good district because many families had never recovered from the Depression and their housing wasn't good. But in the end they all got good compensation and better homes than they had before which was wonderful after that terrible trauma. Of course, there was not much manpower, and no firebreaks had been cut around the district.'

But there was one amusing moment on the night of the great fire. Recalls Elisabeth: 'At about half past eight I had just settled myself exhausted on the flat roof with a mattress and was keeping a watch in case the fires flared up again, when up the blackened driveway came our car carrying a triumphant Keith, Russell Grimwade and Daryl Lindsay. They believed they had secured the site in St Kilda Road for the gallery Keith was dreaming of.

'I was a bit tensed up sitting up there on the roof and feeling I was responsible for the whole district when I ran down and met them. Obviously, they had had a very good dinner at the Melbourne

Club and they were celebrating. I remember Keith saying "Oh darling, how are you, what can we do for you?" And I just said: "Go home at once!" They couldn't do anything so they all went back to Melbourne feeling rather ashamed of themselves I think. But before we got any sleep that night, there was the aftermath of looking after the firefighters who had done a great job but were now looking for a good time. We coped with that too.

'But the next morning the sight was really terrible. There were dead sheep in the paddocks, our beautiful lemon-scented gum trees in the driveway were blackened and all the fences were gone. We had to quickly replace those, and at the end of the war wire was very hard to get. The fire was quite an event in the family's life.

'The trees in the driveway took a long time to recover. I was desperate about what to do but I thought Russell Grimwade would be the one to ask because he had written a book on eucalypts and was quite an authority. I said: "Russell, what are we to do? Do we cut them back or start again?" They were fifteen years old and beautiful. He said: "I don't know, Elisabeth. I think we leave them and pray."

'Most of them recovered, although perhaps five or six didn't. I think possibly the fire is why they are as beautiful as they are because they lost a lot of their low growth. They're unusually effective. People adore that drive. The orchard had gone, as had the fifteen-year-old tulip tree which was just about to burst into flower – and they take fifteen years to flower. We lost apples, pears, everything.' Also lost in the blaze was a copse of about twenty birch trees which Elisabeth describes as 'Edna Walling's theme tune'.

Out of the devastation of that black day Elisabeth would create one of the Australia's finest gardens.

CHAPTER SEVENTEEN

'I think he's got it.'

IN THE LAST years of the war, Keith maintained a tremendous workload. On one trip in 1944 he covered 28,000 miles, mostly in the slow propeller-driven service aircraft then available. Because he still had the international contacts that few other journalists or proprietors could match, Keith was able to have private meetings with Churchill and Roosevelt and interview Generals Eisenhower and Alexander, Lord Louis Mountbatten, and Admirals Nimitz and Halsey – who, with 'Bomber' Harris, Chief of Britain's RAF Bomber Command, Keith described as the 'most ruthless minded men I have ever met'.

On this journey around the world's battle fronts, he visited the front line in Italy, saw the launch of the D-Day invasion of Europe and then flew to India as the guest of the Viceroy, Lord Wavell, before flying on to the Pacific war zone interviewing Allied commanders and reporting as he went for his own Australian newspapers as well as the Fleet Street dailies.

Few US or UK war correspondents or commentators were allowed such access to the top, but in the Second World War there was no suggestion that Keith ever breached censorship, although he certainly again made his views known to the political leaders in the UK and Australia. In Australia, his fellow proprietors were agreed that Keith's pre-war initiative in setting up the Australian newsprint industry had allowed the Australian press to continue publishing throughout the long war.

As the war ended, there had been new concerns for Keith's health and, after the Japanese surrender, it was decided that a prostate operation was necessary. A straightforward procedure with today's medical technology, in the 1940s the operation on the enlarged prostate gland was major surgery, and it was some weeks before he could leave hospital. Worried about a growing bank overdraft, and aware that his plans for a secure future for Elisabeth and the children were far from realised, Keith called his legal and financial advisors to his bedside and re-drafted his will. But the surgery was at least partially successful and Elisabeth was able to nurse her husband back to health at Cruden Farm and later, briefly, Wantabadgery.

Elisabeth recalls that in the late forties Keith was spending more and more time with his son. They were becoming close companions, although Elisabeth remembers saying to him: 'Oh Keith, Rupert is only sixteen, far too young for that,' when she came upon them in deep discussion on matters of newspaper finance. 'I think every father of an only son sees his son as a successor. Keith always hoped for that, but he was very anxious Rupert should be worthy of it – and very anxious that there should be no nepotism. Being older, it was very difficult for Keith,' Elisabeth says now. 'I thought it was

'I think he's got it.'

wrong for Keith to talk about business to Rupert that early, but he was right. I remember him saying. "I don't know how long I've got to go." He really did talk to Rupert a lot after he was sixteen and now I think it was a very good thing that he did.' As he became increasingly close to Rupert, Keith confided some of his concerns to Elisabeth.

At Geelong Grammar, the young Murdoch had earned the nickname 'Red Rupert' after invariably taking the side of the left in school debates and in articles for the school magazine and newspaper. Elisabeth still believes it was her son expressing his independence from his father's conservative publishing empire. But after the war there were left-wing influences at work at the school in the shape of teachers like Manning Clark, later a noted historian whose monumental history of Australia many feel was flawed by unacademic left-wing political bias, and charming left-wing academic, Stephen Murray-Smith, neither of whom had much time for the 'Murdoch Press'. In fact, despite the persistent folklore, Rupert never met Manning Clark at school, although he knew and liked Stephen Murray-Smith.

Keith was also concerned that his son and heir's love and admiration for his grandfather, 'Pop' Greene, could result in Rupert becoming far too interested in horseracing and gambling in general, and there is no doubt that while at school Rupert was using the proceeds from rabbit catching and manure collecting to bet on horses. Unknown to his parents, Rupert kept a motorcycle or more accurately a 'put-put' – a cycle with a small motor driving onto the back tyre – hidden at a shop near the school and sometimes used it to ride to the races.

By 1947, with the circulations of Keith's newspapers reaching record levels, the Murdochs received another shock medical report on Keith's health. 'Keith was told that he had cancer of the bowel –

an advanced growth that had to be operated on immediately,' says Elisabeth. In those days the prognosis was bad, almost beyond hope. Elisabeth was warned that Keith might not even survive the operation and, if he did, a colostomy was the likely outcome. For ten days after the operation Keith's life was in the balance and Rupert, determined to be at his father's side, hitched a ride from his school at Corio to St Ives Hospital forty miles away in Melbourne — in a passing hearse.

At it turned out, brilliant surgery removed all the cancerous tissue and the need for the colostomy, and Keith was soon conducting family and *Herald* business from his hospital bed. During the six weeks he remained in St Ives he dictated a penetrating assessment of his personal business affairs and the action that should be taken after his death to ensure his family's welfare. The five-page memorandum FOR MY EXECUTORS begins: 'My estate will be worth some hundreds of thousands of pounds, apart from settlements made on my wife and the three elder children, all of which are substantial.'

Showing an extraordinary grasp of finance, share prices and percentages, Keith also gave a run down of his properties with fine detail of stock numbers and an assessment of the strengths and weaknesses of his staff. Deeply concerned about the death duties at the time, Keith wrote: 'It would, I fear, be quite necessary, to get probate duty, to have a substantial sale of furniture, glass and silver and pictures — in this I am sure my wife would co-operate.' This, and the many codicils he was later to add to his will, became a blueprint for the family's future and a clear indication that he wanted Rupert to follow him into a career in journalism.

Throughout the war, Elisabeth had dedicated much of her time to work at the Children's Hospital — a hospital suffering from shortages of key medical and nursing staff as well as equipment and supplies. Conditions did not improve rapidly after the war either but

'I think he's got it.'

at least there was hope on the horizon as plans for a grand new hospital were taken out of mothballs and behind-the-scenes discussions on the way ahead were held.

Then in 1948, an arrival from England gave the hospital staff the renewed initiative and drive it badly needed. Lucy Sechiari was the newcomer's name. She was the Children's Hospital's new matron and Elisabeth soon grew to greatly admire her. 'She was a "blind date" in a way, but she came highly recommended from London and she was so different from anything we had ever seen in the nursing world before. She was tall, blonde and elegant and had quite a different outlook on the place of nursing in society.

'She gave the nursing world quite a shock, but she was greatly appreciated and I think she did a lot to bring a better understanding of the nurses' standing and role in society. She rather enjoyed meeting people and inviting them to her flat – always after hours, of course – and she really won a very respected place in the Australian nursing world.

'The young nurses were devoted to her and when she married Anton de Neeve they became very much a part of fundraising drives and the team supporting the new hospital. She was a pioneer in the nursing world, with a better understanding and respect for nursing, although she was quite a controversial character. She was an interesting, strong, colourful personality. I was always very interested in the nursing and very close to the nurses.'

* * *

In 1949, Rupert Greene became ill while visiting his friends, Wallace and Ann Meares, in Forbes, New South Wales, and was rushed to hospital. Rupert took his grandmother to Forbes to be at her husband's side, but to the family's sorrow, the irrepressible 'Pop' died at seventy-six.

Supported by Rupert, the grieving Bairnie had Pop Greene brought back to Melbourne. The funeral of the man who started more than 6000 horse races and every Melbourne Cup between 1914 and 1944, left from Pemberley but Elisabeth can remember few of the events of that sad day. 'It is as though I block out deep grief,' says Elisabeth of her much-loved father's funeral.

Keith regained his health after his operation, and Elisabeth insisted on a relaxing holiday on Queensland's sunny Gold Coast, but by Christmas, 1949, he had decided to retire as managing director of the Herald and Weekly Times while retaining the position of hands-on chairman. Then, with Rupert very much in mind, he began consolidating his own small group of newspapers and magazines, in Melbourne, Brisbane and Adelaide.

Jack Kennedy, the original secretary of the Murdoch's family company, Cruden Investments, and a director of the company until 1993, remembers £50,000 being drawn in cash from Keith's account and taken to the office of Harry Giddy at the National Bank. Then, as the family sat around Giddy's desk, Keith handed gifts of £10,000 to Helen and Anne, while the same amount was set aside for Rupert, then at Oxford. Janet, who had been too young to receive the settlement previously given to the older children, was handed £20,000. Keith then told the family to hand back the cash to Jack Kennedy for the allotment of shares in Cruden Investments. This simple handout involved all of the family in the media company that would one day dwarf that of the Beaverbrooks and Northcliffes and even eclipse the ostentatious empire of William Randolph Hearst.

Now for Keith, spared responsibility for some of the day-to-day operations of his newspapers, there were short trips overseas with visits to the US, where he saw President Truman and senior US officials on the eve of war in Korea. In London, all doors remained open to the Australian newspaper executive and on one visit there he

'I think he's got it.'

made a move which was received with mixed feelings by Elisabeth. He engaged Pentecost, a British army veteran who had been recommended to him as a fine chauffeur. 'Pentecost was very proper, and very decent – and very grand – and had actually been chauffeur to the Governor-General of Canada and the British Ambassador in Paris,' Elisabeth recalls. 'He had been blown up in Italy as a sergeant during the war and I think that had affected him.

'He was horrified at what I did domestically and I remember one occasion when I was, perhaps not scrubbing, but down on my knees washing our bathroom floor, and I sensed someone standing behind me and heard a "Hmm, hmm," and the jangle of keys. He said: "Shall I put the Daimler or the Rover out, My Lady?" and seeing his expression, I got up and said: "You'll have to get used to this, Pentecost." He just stood there and said: "I wouldn't allow my wife to do that, My Lady," and I said "Well, that's very bad luck for you",' laughs Elisabeth.

The staff, Elisabeth says, were 'very irked by his grandeur', and Keith was aggravated by Pentecost's repeated failure to get through traffic jams in his grey Daimler when he was running late. When he took on Pentecost in London, Keith had planned to use him to drive from the city to Cruden Farm where he could stay the night and make the return trip in the morning. However, that plan was thwarted by Mrs Pentecost. On their arrival from the UK, Keith had bought the couple a little house in Malvern, but the nervous wife refused to be left alone at night so Pentecost's usefulness was somewhat limited. Still, Pentecost always dressed the part in chauffeur's uniform complete with peaked cap and driving gauntlets.

By 1950, plans were in train for another overseas trip by Keith and Elisabeth. This time, installing Rupert at Oxford after he left Geelong Grammar would be a part of Keith and Elisabeth's mission, although a stopover in Rome for an audience with Pope Pius XII followed by a visit to Canada before returning to the UK, were also included on the itinerary.

With time to fill in, Rupert was shown the ropes at *The Herald*, assigned to police rounds in the tiny press room at Melbourne's Russell Street police headquarters where he fitted in well with the tough crime writers and their band of keen cadet reporters. In April, the Murdochs flew to Europe with Elisabeth now in charge of packing the luggage for her husband and son. The days of the travelling household of maids and nannies were over, as were the slow trips in ocean liners and trains.

In Rome, they were met by *The Herald*'s London correspondent, the man who would be Rupert's first editor, Rohan Rivett, a former prisoner of the Japanese in Singapore who Keith had asked to drive down to Rome with his wife, Nan. In a letter to Rivett asking him to make the trip and then drive the family back to the United Kingdom across Europe, Keith had said that he had 'toyed' with the idea of hiring a Rolls Royce and driver for the journey. No doubt recalling Elisabeth's cry of 'ostentatious!' when he brought his first Rolls Royce home to Walsh Street soon after their marriage, Keith had thought better of the idea. He also warned Rivett that they did not want to stop over at 'expensive hotels'.

But this was a sad time for Elisabeth, who knew that her much loved grandmother, Anne de Lancey Forth, 'The Little Trojan', now in her nineties, was dying and would not survive until Elisabeth could return to Australia.

So that he could make a late start from his office, Keith sent Rupert and the luggage off ahead to the airport with Pentecost for an early check in, while Elisabeth made a more leisurely drive from Albany Road. 'Keith and Rupert had all their lumber packed and I had a very modest suitcase and, just as I was about to leave home, there was a frantic call from Keith asking me to rush to the airport

'I think he's got it.'

because they were eighty pounds overweight,' Elisabeth says. 'I can see it now, unpacking their luggage at the airport and trying to leave behind the typewriters and books that were causing the trouble. Of course, I had to leave half my own things behind, to make room in my bags for all the things they insisted they needed, so I was furious,' Elisabeth now recalls with a chuckle.

'When we got to Rome, there was the great sadness of receiving a cable saying that my wonderful grandmother had died.'

Keith had booked his family in at a modest Rome hotel and Elisabeth had just finished unpacking when officials from the Australian Mission, who had first promoted the idea of Keith and Elisabeth having an audience with the Pope, arrived to instruct them to move. They couldn't possibly stay there. It wasn't at all the sort of hotel suitable for their station in life, the Murdochs were told. Elisabeth repacked yet again and they moved into Rome's grand Excelsior Hotel as the men from the Mission arranged a suitable sightseeing itinerary for them.

'We spent far too long breaking our necks looking up at the ceiling of the Sistine Chapel and running around galleries for two days. Then the day we were to dine with the British Ambassador – which I was looking forward to with true British reverence – Keith had another heart attack. Not a stroke or anything, but one of his distressing fibrillations, so he had to rest for two days to be ready to meet the Pope,' says Elisabeth.

On the day of the private audience, Elisabeth borrowed a black mantilla from the wife of the Australian representative and the trio set out in a hire car for the Vatican. 'Of course, Rupert thought it was all a lot of hooey, but he came along for our audience and on the way our car broke down. It was terrible, a most stressful experience thinking we were going to be late and running along past the Swiss Guards to make it in time,' says Elisabeth.

'As it was, it was all quite impressive, although I cannot recall what the Pope said to me. I was quite overwhelmed. He spoke about Australia to Keith and as we left, Rupert said he was unimpressed, particularly with the little silver medals the Pope gave him. I do remember I had to curtsey, bend the knee,' Elisabeth says.

The audience over, they returned to London and then on to Canada where Keith had to attend meetings of the Empire Press Union, at which he was leader of the Australian delegation. 'Rupert absolutely scorned dancing lessons while he was at school, but one night in Canada when we were very tired he came to me and said "Mum, you must give me some dancing lessons," so I did. We loved that trip. People were so kind to us. It was really a dazzling and happy time.

'But then we went back to London and took poor Rupert to Birmingham, where he was to get some more newspaper experience before going to Oxford. It all seemed pretty grim. He was thrown into the deep end there, although he stayed in a comfortable old boarding house and went off to work at *The Birmingham Post*.'

In London, Keith and Elisabeth were invited to dine with Lord Beaverbrook, the crusty Canadian-born proprietor of the mass-circulation London *Daily Express*. Elisabeth recalls the night with horror. 'We arrived at eight o'clock because Keith was determined not to be late – and, of course, you never arrive that early in London. Lord Rothermere, proprietor of the rival *Daily Mail*, and Lady Rothermere arrived an hour late and I was shocked, because they offered no apology. I was wearing this beautiful white pleated chiffon dress. It was really simple but very pretty and Beaverbrook was shaking one of his cocktails which he shook all over me. Young Sir Max Aitken, who I remember liking very much, was marvellous. He rushed out for a cloth and water and cleaned me up.

'After dinner we sat around and Brendon Bracken, proprietor of

'I think he's got it.'

the *Financial Times* and close friend of "The Beaver", sat on the floor and was really very mischievous. I had been told that Lady Rothermere was having an affair with Ian Fleming, the James Bond spy author – who she later married – and, of course, I was very unsophisticated and shocked at that sort of thing. I couldn't imagine how people carried on their lives, having these things on the side,' says Elisabeth. 'It was quite an interesting evening, but I was shocked to the core that people behaved as they did.'

After his parents flew home, Rupert spent three months in Birmingham and then took up residence at Worcester College, Oxford, in October, 1950. Soon he joined the Oxford Labour Club and made it clear that his sympathies remained with the left of politics. More conservative students criticised his advocacy of socialism while occupying the De Quincey Room, one of the biggest in the college.

Later Rupert was to work for a time at Beaverbrook's *Daily Express* – then considered by journalists to be the world's most exciting and innovative newspaper. As a young down-table sub-editor, Rupert is still remembered by old hands as a wizard at tipping horserace winners around the world and checking the results as they came in on the newspaper's international sporting cable services.

With Rupert away, Keith continued to make plans for his family's future. There were reports after his death that Keith had planned to sever his links with *The Herald* and move in with the London Daily Mirror group which had taken over *The Argus* and turned it into a breezy morning tabloid rivalling *The Sun*.

Keith did move some of his senior editorial men over to his small magazine company, Southdown Press, then the publishers of *New Idea*, now one of the world's top-selling women's magazines. But Elisabeth casts doubts on the widely accepted version of Keith's plans at the time. 'I think Keith played with these ideas. He often did make calculations like that, but I don't think he would have ever left *The Herald*.

'Keith and I were very close. He always talked to me a lot – not every detail – but I knew enough to know how his mind was running and I would have been very surprised if Keith had decided to get out of *The Herald*. I have no doubt Keith did play with the idea and even looked closely at it – after all that's what Rupert does all the time. I think Keith saw Southdown as a very good asset – which it was, and still is. He always told me that *New Idea* was such a good family publication, but it made me laugh that we later owned *Truth*, which was far from being a family publication,' says Elisabeth, who years later encouraged her son to dispose of *Truth* with its page three girls and massage parlour advertisements.

There were tense days for Keith towards the end. His health was questionable and a follow-up operation for his prostate trouble, although a normal medical procedure, was causing concern. In the mid 1940s, Keith had decided that the *Canberra Times*, run on a shoestring by Arthur Shakespeare, would be a valuable property to buy. With this in mind Keith kept looking around for property close to Canberra suitable as an operational base for entertaining politicians and other important contacts. He was shown Booroomba, a lush station property of 13,000 acres in the beautiful and rugged Tidbinbilla Ranges overlooking the Australian capital. He paid £64,000 for it and it was soon heavily mortgaged. Keith told executors that it was 'very worth holding on to' and that private valuations far exceeded the price he had paid for it. Sadly, visits by Keith and his family to Booroomba were to be rare.

'He loved the idea of breeding stock, running cattle and, as he did with all his interests, he got literature and read up all the information and decided that Belted Galloways would be ideal for

'I think he's got it.'

that wild country,' Elisabeth remembers. 'There was nothing enormously grand. It was just a nice station property and we furnished the main room of the house and put in Tasmanian wood panelling and I chose the material for the curtains. We sent up some beautiful furniture and pictures and Keith was looking forward to fishing in the mountain streams and lakes. Keith had several lovely little holidays there with Rupert but I only had one and I found it very frustrating and tedious trying to cast a fly and getting caught up in the trees behind. In winter it was so bleak, and, of course, we had beautiful Wantabadgery.'

Finding time for holidays in Keith's busy schedule was always difficult. Elisabeth still remembers such a rare break after one of Keith's early stays in hospital when there had been a holiday for the couple in a small boat off Queensland's Great Barrier Reef. 'We moored off deserted Dunk Island for about a week and slept under the stars and picked paw-paws off the trees. It was a joyous time for us both – and Rupert repeated our holiday voyage a few years ago on a much grander scale,' says Elisabeth.

But, although Elisabeth always had hopes, this time there could be no repeat of that memorable respite. In St Ives for what was to be his final operation, Keith left more instructions for his executors including this rather frustrated entry: 'It may be that Rupert's strong political views will make his career in our newspapers impossible; it could be arranged that he should have Booroomba instead, probably mortgaged!' he wrote from his hospital bed on 29 April 1952 – just five months before his death.

He also urged his executors to examine the possibility of some recognition by *The Herald* of Elisabeth's tireless contribution to his own years of service. 'I think she should get a pension,' he wrote – a suggestion that *The Herald* board was not to take up.

A letter from Rupert, now twenty-one, and sharing a small flat in Oxford with his friend, John Piper, concerned Keith. Rupert suggested that on his return to Australia it would be better for the family if he had a small flat of his own in Melbourne. 'Keith just didn't want it to be like that. He hadn't been brought up that way – look at him. His family thought it very peculiar when he came home from London at the age of thirty and wanted to have a house of his own,' says Elisabeth.

But then, during his vacation, Rupert attended the Labour Party Conference at Blackpool and wrote an objective and penetrating account of what he had seen and heard for his father, who on reading it looked up joyfully at Elisabeth and said: 'I think the boy's got it!' In a touching and loving letter to 'My beautiful and good Anne,' written to his daughter at Clyde, just hours before his death, Keith proudly mentions that letter: 'We have had a splendid letter from Rupert and he is forgiven some of his misdemeanours...' Keith wrote.

Sadly, Rupert's letter is no longer in the Murdoch family archives, but Elisabeth fills in the gaps: 'Reading that letter Keith finally believed that our son was going to have not only a good mind, but also a very good attitude,' she says. 'Rupert's letter arrived just two days before Keith died and I was so glad because there had been a three-week gap in his letters which had caused Keith some anxiety. That it arrived when it did was wonderful and I will always hang on to the comfort it gave me at the time, knowing that Keith was not at all anxious about Rupert when he died.'

Even today Elisabeth recalls the fortuitous timing of Rupert's last letter to his father and still trusts her intuition when it comes to making contact with friends and relatives when they are in her thoughts. 'I have always found that if you have a feeling – call it a premonition, if you like – that you must see someone or write to them, or give them a ring, there is nearly always a good reason for it. It is always the sin of omission that catches up with you,'

'I think he's got it.'

says Elisabeth, who always seems to have had an unerring instinct in such matters.

Keith had seemed to make a wonderful recovery from his last operation and had received an excellent medical report, but Elisabeth knew that he was still under a heavy strain. At *The Herald*, Elisabeth says, there was now 'an atmosphere of suspicion and intrigue'.

In fact, Elisabeth now recognises, 'I think he was under much more tension than anyone realised, which was unfair. You see, he was sixty-seven and I suppose that it was natural for him to say that he wanted to do much less. In fact, in those last few hours he lived, he was feeling very happy about Rupert and spoke enthusiastically about the trip to London for the forthcoming Coronation that we were all going to make.'

It was a balmy early spring evening on Saturday, 4 October 1952, as Elisabeth and Keith walked together around the Cruden Farm garden after driving down from the city for the weekend together. After the fire that had swept away so much of Edna Walling's concept, the garden was now very much Elisabeth's creation, with the gum trees in the driveway recovering magnificently from the damage caused by the flames.

Keith spoke of his plans for complete retirement to Cruden Farm. 'I promise that next year we'll live here, we really will,' he told Elisabeth. By this time Helen was married and Keith said: 'We'll build a little pavilion out here in the garden for my library and, of course, we'll have the house heated. We can't live here without the house being heated.' Forty years later the house at Cruden Farm is still unheated, although on chilly winter days when guests arrive, Elisabeth constantly stokes open fires and a slow combustion stove with logs cut on the farm. Keith told Elisabeth, then concerned about their £40,000 bank overdraft, 'Financially I think I can see my way.'

'He had borrowed money – today it would be peanuts but in those days you didn't have overdrafts in banks without worrying a little. But that night Keith was saying that we could now be free of financial worry and the overdraft would be reduced.' Elisabeth recalls. They talked about the trip to the Coronation in London early the following year and Elisabeth says: 'Looking back, it was so marvellous that Keith was so happy. Really we couldn't have had a more contented evening, and then we went off to bed early.'

As was his habit, Keith undid the leather strap and placed his wrist watch on the bedside table, before lying back on the pillows. Then with a slight tremor that shook his body, Sir Keith Murdoch lay back and died, peacefully, without pain, or any alarming forewarning. Looking back now, Elisabeth says: 'It was so wonderfully easy for Keith – but so very difficult for all of us.'

Sir Keith Murdoch was sixty-seven when he died. Elisabeth was forty-three and about to begin her 'second life'. The 'few short years' Elisabeth had been prepared to have with the man she adored had, in fact, become twenty-four happy and eventful years and now she was left with a farm, challenging debts, and the wisdom and fierce determination that were to inspire her son and daughters to reach such extraordinary heights.

CHAPTER EIGHTEEN

A New Life Begins

ALTHOUGH AT LEAST forewarned by the episodes of serious illness her husband had faced and conquered over the years, Elisabeth was devastated by Keith's sudden death, but well aware of the awesome responsibility that now faced her. Her first thoughts were for the children, and Miss Kimpton was quickly dispatched to Clyde to break the news to Anne and Janet and bring them home in the car with Pentecost.

Helen was soon at her mother's side, but Rupert had to be told, and a cable was sent to his friend and principal tutor at Oxford, the brilliant academic, Asa Briggs, who woke Rupert early on that Sunday morning at his student digs, at Headington outside the university city, to tell him of his father's death half a world away.

Rupert had last seen his father the previous summer when Sir Keith joined him on a crowded car trip through Italy, Austria,

Yugoslavia and Greece. It had been a happy and memorable adventure and, with no presentiment that this was to be their final meeting, Keith and Rupert parted in Athens. Now, Rupert was flying back to Australia alone and still unaware that he would arrive too late for his father's funeral.

Always conscious of Keith's circle of powerful and influential friends around the world, his widow was still staggered by the tributes that flowed in from prime ministers, statesmen, press barons and proprietors in the UK and America. Few, if any other Australians, have earned the outpouring of grief, affection and respect accorded to Sir Keith Murdoch on his death.

In London, the great Fleet Street dailies ran long obituaries, reinforced by personal tributes from their proprietors. The perceptive Lord Beaverbrook said of Keith: 'His counsels in war and his wise advice on all public affairs served the British race in triumph and disaster over forty years. His death at the apex of his fame is a sad blow to the Empire.'

In an editorial headed 'Man of Empire', obviously inspired by Beaverbrook himself, the *Daily Express*, then the world's top-selling English language daily, said: 'A great newspaperman is dead. Sir Keith Murdoch saw history made and reported it. He had a hand too in its making. In the First World War he sped from Gallipoli to London to bring home the truth.'

The Australian Prime Minister, Mr Robert Menzies, said of Sir Keith: 'For all the spread of his interests, every one of which was his by his own efforts, he was regarded as a model and human employer. As a nation, Sir Keith Murdoch left us in his debt.'

Irving Benson, a charismatic Wesley Church preacher and broadcaster, said of his friend: 'Sir Keith Murdoch was a very great man when judged by any standard, and he was a prince of journalists.'

Arthur Sulzberger, the *New York Times* chief, wrote: 'No community can afford to lose men of Sir Keith Murdoch's stature.' Powerful Canadian Press magnate, Gillis Purcell, described Keith as one of the world's best informed newspapermen and added: 'The same dynamic force that won him fame as a reporter and editor, set him out as an international leader in the development of journalism and the defence of its principles.'

The US Ambassador in Australia, Mr Pete Jarman, saw Sir Keith's passing as 'a tragic loss to his friends, to Australia and the world'. He added: 'He was a great Australian and a great citizen of the world. It can ill afford his loss.' Future Prime Minister Harold Holt, whose own life was to end mysteriously in the wild Australian surf fifteen years later, paid this tribute: 'Sir Keith Murdoch was one of the big Australians of his generation ... he brought to his work the devotion of the patriot and the broad vision of statesmanship.'

Sir Christopher Chancellor, chief of Britain's Reuters News-agency, saw Sir Keith as 'one of the great journalists of our generation,' while Reuter's editor, Walton Cole, said: 'I never knew anyone who tried so hard to give young journalists a break.' In Washington, Assistant Secretary of State J.D. Hickson said: 'In my years of acquaintance with Sir Keith Murdoch, I knew him as an outstanding man who would have been an outstanding figure in any country of the world. Australia, and the whole free world, has suffered a grievous loss.' *The Times* gave Keith Murdoch its highest accolade when it described him as 'the Northcliffe of Australia'.

In a moving tribute, *The Herald* carried an editorial headlined: 'We Lose a Leader', and said: 'Today, the people who work in this company may be forgiven if they take space to say that they feel in the death of Sir Keith a loss greater and more personal than could be felt in any other place outside his family.'

In front page reports in his own and other Australian newspapers which appeared on the Monday after his death, headlines proclaimed him as 'Keith Murdoch – a great Australian' and 'Tireless Man of Vision'.

At her Albany Road home, Elisabeth was visited by executives of the Herald and Weekly Times seeking her views on the funeral arrangements. Elisabeth was, as always, in control of her emotions but had as a vital consideration the need for Rupert to be given time to get home from Britain for his father's funeral. But *The Herald* hierarchy had other ideas. 'They wanted Keith to be given something like a grand State funeral, not at all what I would have wanted,' says Elisabeth. In those days it was not the accepted thing in Australia to delay funerals, and it was decided that the service would have to be held at the Toorak Presbyterian Church on Tuesday 7 October. In that pre-jumbo jet era, there was absolutely no way that Rupert could get back to Melbourne in time.

Federal and State politicians, diplomats, archbishops and media executives rubbed shoulders with Keith's own reporters, copyboys, printers and industry union officials, in the crowd that overflowed the church. Hundreds of wreaths with messages from all over the world were placed outside the church as Elisabeth arrived with her daughters, to join Keith's brothers, Alan and Ivon Murdoch, and his sister, Helen, for the service. In his panegyric, the Rev. A. C. Watson told the mourners: 'The faith in which he was nurtured provided Keith Murdoch with that quality so difficult to define, yet so clearly recognisable – his democratic spirit. He gave men respect for what they were and what they did, and in return they gave him their respect.' It was an astute summing up of Keith's character, and one with which most of that congregation would agree.

The cortege that followed Keith to Melbourne's Springvale Crematorium stretched for more than two miles, but the Murdochs did not join the sad procession. In the 1950s, Melbourne women did not follow their loved ones to Springvale and it was a crowded men-only gathering at the crematorium chapel as Mr Watson said a final prayer and announced that a memorial service would soon be held for Keith at London's St Dunstan's in the West to be attended by high commissioners, ambassadors, and Commonwealth leaders.

Meanwhile, Elisabeth and her daughters were at home sharing their grief after standing at the windows of the house to watch the long cortege pass slowly by the front drive. 'Thinking back, it was awful of me, but I simply couldn't invite anyone back to the house after the funeral, and it really is all rather a blur to me even now. I know many do have a gathering after the funeral, but I think it is a barbarous practice,' says Elisabeth more than forty years later.

Although she had rejoiced at her husband's happy appraisal of the family fortunes on that Saturday night just before he died, Elisabeth knew that Keith had, in fact, died before many of his plans for his family's future had reached fruition. There was no chance of maintaining Keith's rather lavish lifestyle in a Toorak mansion – even if she had wished to. But before she turned her attention to such pressing matters, Elisabeth had to console her son who arrived home after his three-day flight exhausted and understandably upset at missing his father's funeral.

One of her early concerns, as advisors began to prepare a full assessment of her real financial standing, was the role of Pentecost, the chauffeur. On the day after the funeral she called him in to say: '"Pentecost, we've got to think of your future, and I just wonder if chauffeuring is really for you."

'He said "I know, My Lady, it's my eyes. They have never really been any good since I was blown up in Italy during the war."

'And I said "Well, I am going to ask *The Herald* to see what they can do for you."'

The next day, Elisabeth was able to tell her loyal British chauffeur that *The Herald* had agreed he could have a job as commissionaire at their Flinders Street office. So the uniformed Pentecost became the polite, helpful man behind the desk in *The Herald*'s front hall for several years before he retired and went to live contentedly in Queensland on a *Herald* pension until his death at seventy-eight.

Back at Cruden Farm with Rupert and her daughters, Elisabeth, knowing that her son must soon return to Oxford, sat down at the familiar round table in the cosy 'schoolroom' to discuss the future without Keith. Rupert already had a clear understanding – unlike many of the men and women at *The Herald* at that time – that he would not be moving in as his father's anointed successor to take over the growing Herald and Weekly Times empire. At his death, Keith had scarcely any financial interest left in the papers he had made a force in the land.

Rupert was aware too of the debts and yet-to-be-calculated death duties incurred by the estate, but not prepared for his mother's firm insistence that all debts must be paid and everything in Sir Keith's estate must be in perfect order before the detailed terms of his will and later codicils could be carried out.

'On the night that he died, Keith told me as we walked in the garden that he really did plan to make Cruden Farm our home in his retirement, so after he died I had no hesitation in making the decision to sell Albany Road,' says Elisabeth. 'You know, before he died, Keith was buying more and more glass, which was, of course, all meant to be a secret from me, because I was always wanting literally threadbare carpets to be replaced, although I never pressured Keith about that side of housekeeping because I knew how much pleasure he got out of his beautiful bits of glass and silver.

'He collected early English and Irish glass and, of course, there was his collection of Oriental ceramics. At Albany Road, we had built a glass cabinet right along the mid passage to house his treasures,' says Elisabeth. 'It amuses me when the young in this affluent society think it is necessary to change the curtains and furnishings after a few years. I know that they don't last as they used to, but some of my curtains at Cruden Farm are original.

'In his will he said that we really would need to have a sale and he had always said to me, "When I die take our best things to London and sell them," but, of course, I couldn't do that. So we began to plan for the sale here. Of course, Rupert knew all about how we thought we should straighten our affairs, but he did think that we were being unnecessarily anxious and that we could have maintained the interests that he would have liked to retain,' says Elisabeth thinking back to those schoolroom family discussions.

'I was the chairman and Rupert and the girls, who have all got good heads, were there too, which was a comfort because I haven't got a good financial head at all. I mean I am not a fool but my head reels at modern high finance, and I felt we had to be absolutely beyond reproach with Keith's estate. Maybe I was over-anxious, maybe we did more things than we should have done, but I just felt it was the right thing to do. I didn't want there to be any suggestion that things had been shaped for our benefit,' says Elisabeth.

Also in the back of Elisabeth's mind and clearly influencing her judgment were her childhood memories of sojourns in boarding houses when, faced with unpaid bills, her mother had been forced to let Pemberley. Debt was a factor Elisabeth had grown up with and was not prepared to pass on to her own children.

At the suggestion of Harry Giddy, one of Keith's executors who had succeeded him as chairman at *The Herald*, Jack Kennedy was included in the family discussion at that time. 'So Jack came on the scene as a very young man and has been a very helpful and supportive friend ever since,' says Elisabeth, whose own firm influence at that time was to play a key role in the fortunes of Cruden Investments, the family company, in the future.

'Rupert was twenty-one at the time and I think it would have been quite wrong for us to have left a situation of great complexity and a good deal of risk to the family, in his hands. I had to be guided, I think, by perhaps more mature minds. We didn't have any reproachful discussions, or fuss or conflict or unhappiness about it, but Rupert did feel, I think then, and as he went on to become successful, that we had made unnecessary sacrifices at that time.'

And then Elisabeth reveals the thought that has always given her the comfort of believing that she was right in taking the tough decisions she did. 'Maybe Rupert would have been quite different if we hadn't done what we did then. Perhaps he wouldn't have faced the challenges he had to as a young man. I think that it was much better that he had that challenge. It helped him to become what he is today,' Elisabeth insists.

The real nub of the family crisis was that while the gross assets of Sir Keith's estate stood at around £600,000 there were the debts that Elisabeth wanted paid off as soon as possible and they amounted to £190,000. Added to that, there were still harsh death duties to be accounted for.

Before his death, Sir Keith had sold *Herald* shares and mortgaged his properties in order to strengthen his personal hold on his newspapers in Queensland and South Australia. Since the previous year, he had held clear control of News Ltd and its little paper in Adelaide. Elisabeth, supported by both Jack Kennedy and Harry Giddy, was prepared to put Booromba, Wantabadgery and the Albany Road house on the market, but her view was that the Brisbane papers had to go too if Rupert was to be left with an unencumbered Adelaide *News*. Not surprisingly, Rupert wanted to retain all his father's own newspapers and the Southdown Press operation as well.

A New Life Begins

In the end, Elisabeth's views prevailed and Rupert left to return to Oxford to finish his degree. Before he flew out, he went to Sydney and then Brisbane to visit the *Courier Mail*, believing that he had lost it forever – although one day it was to be his again anyway. 'Rupert did think that it was very unfortunate that the Brisbane *Courier Mail* had to be sacrificed. That is what he really regretted at the time,' says the mother of the man who is today the world's most powerful media magnate. 'He realised that it was a tremendous property and thought it would have been a very good property for the family and him to spring off from.'

With Rupert heading back to Oxford, Elisabeth began to make the move to Cruden Farm, leaving a caretaker at Albany Road while art experts Joshua and Joan McClelland undertook the arduous task of preparing for the sale. At peace surrounded by her garden, Elisabeth began replying to the thousands of personal messages of sympathy she had received after Keith's death.

Some of Elisabeth's favourite things – the piano Keith gave her on their wedding day, the much-loved paintings and pewter, copper and other pieces that are still in place today – were moved to the farm in time for the subdued but lovingly supportive family Christmas that Elisabeth and her daughters spent together. Looking back at that first Christmas without her Keith, Elisabeth Murdoch says: 'It had been such a wonderful marriage. Well, I thought it was, and I only hope he thought it was as wonderful as I did. We were blessed in so many, many ways.'

For Elisabeth, in the New Year of 1953, one fascinating, fulfilling life was at an end – but another, even more memorable, was to begin.

CHAPTER NINETEEN

In the Beginning

As RUPERT SADLY prepared to return to Worcester College, Oxford, to complete the final six months of studies for his PPE – Politics, Philosophy and Economics – degree, Elisabeth was calmly taking stock of her own position. 'For a while my situation was very different from what Keith would have thought it would be,' she says. 'I knew that it was not going to be plain sailing and that I would have to be careful until gradually things became easier.

'I knew that this sort of thing happens to lots of people all the time, but really I was quite ignorant about finance and now I was wishing I had a good training in accountancy. I hate balance sheets, I just don't feel confident about them although Keith had often discussed business matters with me.

'I don't know if I ever gave him advice, but I think I was often a bit repressive when he discussed his grand schemes. I didn't have Keith's big outlook. And now I look at Rupert and I think "Dear,

dear. Rupert has got such a big mind too." He is absolutely meticulous in his business dealings. Although at times he might do unwise things, he's always straight down the line in business, as was his father.

'It was really always a mystery to me how Keith made his money at first, perhaps he put it into good shares. Certainly he had a very good financial brain – although, it was said, it wasn't as good as his brother Frank's. Frank was the manager of Gibbs Bright. He was a serious man whom I could never like as much as Keith's other brothers. He was the one person in the Murdoch family I didn't feel had the softness of the others,' Elisabeth says.

By 25 October 1952, Rupert was aboard a BCPA airline flight back to London and, as he still does today, using the flying time to write letters and plan future moves. One letter written then on Cruden Farm letterhead with, in the top corner, his father's train and telephone symbols – designed to show visitors at which station to leave the train, and the telephone number to ring on arrival – was to Harry Giddy.

For a twenty-one-year-old student certainly under a great deal of emotional pressure, it was an amazingly mature letter, especially as Rupert was undoubtedly determined to resist the decision taken by his mother and Harry Giddy to clear all the debts – even if that meant selling off the valuable Queensland Newspapers holdings. Rupert posted the letter back to Melbourne when his plane stopped over at Canton Island. In it he wrote:

Dear Mr Giddy,

This is just a short note to tell you again how very much I appreciate all you have done and are doing for my mother and myself – and the whole family.

I find it terribly hard to adequately express my feelings but I think that you already know what they are! At any rate it is a tremendous relief to me going off now as I am and knowing that you are there to help guide my mother.

Thankyou also for the delightful evening you gave us both on Thursday. I only hope that I didn't talk too much!

My conversations in Sydney with Alan Murdoch [Keith's brother and then President of the National Council of Wool Selling Brokers of Australia] and Colin Bednall [then a Brisbane *Courier Mail* director] were most encouraging. I tried only to find out all I could from them without letting out any secrets.

I was particularly careful with Colin, but he must at least have realised that we were pretty short of cash!

However, it seems that Booroomba, with stock, and Paddy's River, *should* fetch at least £125,000. It is certainly worth that.

Colin assures me that the total Murdoch holding in Queensland [Newspapers] is worth roughly half a million. Of course, this may prove to be a bit too high a figure, but if we were to sell, and I still hope that we can avoid this, then presumably we would not consider any offer under £450,000.

Also if we don't sell Queensland, we would not be paying probate on anything like this figure.

Apologies for bothering you with all this un-expert thinking, but I will write again in detail in one or two days giving my final hopes of what might be done.

Again many many thanks for everything and with the kindest regards to Mrs Giddy, John and Elizabeth.

Yours very sincerely, Rupert.

PS Apparently the electric typewriter in Dad's office belongs to

Queensland – according to the books! Apologies if you already knew this! R.

Other letters followed as Rupert gave more thought to the future and by December, Harry Giddy was able to send him a complex and finely detailed assessment of the family's financial position, researched by Jack Kennedy. Rupert also received an Assets and Liabilities statement on which the application for probate was to be based and this showed that the net assets were £358,852. In Giddy's 22 December letter he valued Booroomba, including livestock and plant at £136,265 – although this was 'rather on the high side' he thought. The estate's interest in Wantabadgery was valued at £34,040, while the beautiful Albany Road home, now estimated to be worth in excess of $3.5 million, was valued at £35,000.

Southdown Press, which became the heart of Rupert's profitable Australian magazine publishing empire, was listed as having a land value of £25,000 – but Giddy pointed out that there was a mortgage of £28,418 outstanding. Other assets readily available added up to a total of £214,482. Giddy estimated the amount of State and Federal probate duty owed by Keith's estate at approximately £200,000, and this figure together with existing liabilities resulted in a deficiency of £125,000.

'It becomes imperative to realise further assets to meet this position,' Harry Giddy stressed in a letter which must have seriously distracted Rupert from his studies. Giddy also added: 'It is therefore imperative to consider the sale of either the News Ltd shares or the Queensland Newspapers shares.'

Giddy gave urgency to his letter by revealing that he had just arranged with the National Bank for a temporary overdraft of £100,000 to enable him to pay immediate debts. And in a passage which probably put paid to Rupert's hopes of saving the Queensland

Newspapers shares, Giddy added: 'I do not think it is feasible to suggest that we should borrow against the security of Queensland Newspapers shares in order to hold them and leave the estate saddled with a more or less permanent load of debt.'

This assessment was clearly supported by Elisabeth, but while Rupert finally accepted the wishes of his mother and her advisors, she knows that Rupert was deeply disappointed at the loss of his father's Queensland interests. There was also concern that Giddy, now the chairman of *The Herald*, could be facing a conflict of interest in orchestrating the sale of the Queensland Newspapers interests to *The Herald*. This conflict of interest came to light years later when the cheeky News Ltd made a takeover bid for the powerful *Advertiser*. But *The Herald* held an option over all the Queensland shares, part of the deal going back to the acquisition of the News Ltd shares from *The Advertiser*. Jack Kennedy recalls that Harry Giddy came into his office early one Monday morning 'absolutely livid'.

'At that stage, he was a trustee of the estate and a director and chairman of the family company, Cruden Investments, but he was also, of course, the chairman of *The Herald* and on *The Advertiser* board. Well, on my desk landed this piece of paper resigning as a director of Cruden Investments Pty Ltd – such resignation to take effect immediately. He was clearly in a very embarrassing position and that was the end of that,' Jack Kennedy says.

In the end Queensland Newspapers were disposed of to *The Herald*, Keith's debts were cleared and Rupert was assured of only a modest inheritance from which to forge a great media business.

Rupert spent Christmas in London with Douglas Brass, later to be the gifted editor-in-chief of his newspapers, and his wife Joan, an old childhood friend of Elisabeth's. With a caretaker in residence at Albany Road, Elisabeth was now making Cruden Farm her home, selecting the few choice and favourite pieces from her life as Lady Murdoch to keep herself and share with her children.

In 1980, Max Harris, the peppery and erudite Adelaide author and columnist in Rupert's *Australian* newspaper, examined the catalogue for the sale of the Keith Murdoch Collection of Antiques held at 39 Albany Road, on 11, 12 and 13 March 1953.

Harris reported: 'Keith Murdoch's intense commitment to the arts was well known enough. For twenty years he had been associated with loan exhibitions all over Australia and he had been president of the Trustees of the National Gallery of Victoria and a member of the Oriental Ceramic Society of London.

'What is not known is how the man is revealed as possessed of an intensity of personal feeling toward works of art. The 636 items up for sale don't read like the kind of items that accrue to the rich mass attempting to add cultural status to affluence.

'It is all highly idiosyncratic. The buying was, in some areas, totally out of kilter with fashionable trends. The Murdoch acquisitions were often remarkably out of step with the accepted taste of the times.

'Murdoch's ability to sense aesthetic worth against the taste of the times is quite fascinatingly evident in the collection of European and Australian moderns,' Harris said before pointing to paintings that brought as little as 'a pitiful $84' – for a Paul Nash watercolour today worth thousands of dollars.

Harris lists the Bloomsbury School paintings avidly collected by Keith – and Elisabeth – and then writes about the Arthur Boyd oil which 'went for – wait for it – $11'. An early 'lyrical' Streeton, which could today fetch up to $1 million, was auctioned for only $115 in those unaware days. Paintings by E. Phillips Fox and the wonderful Rupert Bunny brought even less.

Max Harris wrote: 'Although I understand quite a large number of the finest pieces and paintings were withheld from the auction and remain with the family, it was the impost of death duties which brought about the dispersal of this historically important collection.'

And in a passage which today causes Elisabeth not a moment of regret, Max Harris says: 'If the 1953 collection, which brought a total of £68,000 were to be sold today, all the Murdoch descendants could split up the odd million dollars each and have a bit left over for good works.

'If the collection had been held together, unsold for the interest of posterity, it would have provided a permanent insight into the total personality of a most interesting Australian. There, the guilty secret is out.

'Beneath the implacable toughie who put newspapers together there was the mind of a lyric poet, a gentle and elegant sensibility,' says Harris, who began his examination of the Murdoch art collection with the statement: 'Keith Murdoch was a gritty, ink-stained newspaperman.'

The family's future was now based firmly on one debt-free newspaper, *The News*, in Adelaide. But Lady Murdoch needn't have worried too much about Rupert's future, and now was the time to prepare for the family trip to the Coronation to which Keith had been looking forward immediately before his death.

Elisabeth decided to take Anne and one of her closest friends, Helen Manifold, to London with her and together they flew to Rome where they picked up a car, a small Austin A40, left there for them by Rupert. With Elisabeth confidently behind the wheel in the fast and furious Italian traffic, the trio had a wonderful sightseeing trip, revisiting the special places Keith had taken Elisabeth to on their previous visit.

On the drive from Florence to Venice, Elisabeth was invited to lunch at the home of explorer and writer Freya Stark. They were joined by author and botanist Julian Huxley, whose book *Heredity, East and West* had just been published, and his wife. The two distinguished authors and Mrs Huxley were able to tell Elisabeth and the girls of the fascinating expedition they had just made to Asia Minor in search of new plants. After the delights of Venice, the three travellers began a never-to-be-forgotten six-week tour of the Continent with Elisabeth showing her daughter and Helen Manifold all the wonders she knew Keith had been planning to reveal to his family that year.

In London the decorations were already up and the city was preparing for the splendour of the Coronation when Elisabeth drove up to their rented apartment in Whitehall Court overlooking the River Thames. Keith's experienced and devoted chief correspondent in London, Trevor Smith, had already arranged to lease the apartment and somehow secured precious seats for Sir Keith and Lady Murdoch in the Abbey. Now only one was needed.

Early on Coronation day, with excited throngs already lining the route of the procession and people clinging to every vantage point, Elisabeth delivered the two girls to the home of Lord Camrose overlooking the Mall, and set off for the Abbey escorted by a former Lord Mayor of London. 'I sat next to a High Sheriff, a charming and kind man,' Elisabeth recalls forty years after that day. 'There was such a long wait, and I had a stomach upset which meant I had to keep getting up and leaving my seat, but he was so nice and understanding about it.'

Elisabeth had invited a number of friends and relatives to the apartment to watch the spectacular fireworks display on the Thames and have supper after the Coronation, and soon she was running out into the steady drizzle to buy food from a nearby delicatessen to feed the growing numbers. 'Marie and Johnny Durnford, who had been watching the procession from a vantage point at Admiralty

Arch, arrived soaking wet, and I rushed Marie off to have a hot bath. But Sylvia, the ardent monarchist, didn't turn up until nearly 1 a.m. She had headed for Buckingham Palace to see the Queen appear on the balcony, but had been swept along by the throng in the Mall and had lost a shoe. She arrived at Whitehall Court soaking and dishevelled with only one shoe, but she wouldn't have missed it for the world.'

The Coronation over, Elisabeth took the wheel of Rupert's Austin for a tour of the British Isles and a visit to her son swotting hard in Oxford for his final exams. 'We had a wonderful dinner with Rupert at his digs, but I was so disappointed that he didn't produce a selection of eligible young men for his sister and her friend to meet – but that's not Rupert,' says Dame Elisabeth.

But it was a happy trip and Elisabeth knew she had done what Keith would have expected her to do – carry on with the journey as he had planned it. Elisabeth met many of Keith's old friends who had been shocked at his death and were keen to see how Rupert would follow in the impressive strides of his famous father. They wouldn't have very long to wait. Rupert graduated a Master of Arts with an economics major and briefly joined Beaverbrook's *Daily Express*, then the mecca of all English speaking journalists, to learn about newspaper production from some of the masters the Canadian press baron had collected from around the world. After a few months as a down-table sub-editor in the *Express*'s famous Fleet Street black 'Glass House', he was anxious to fly back to Adelaide and take control of his inheritance.

When Rupert arrived in Adelaide in September, 1953, his friend and editor, Rohan Rivett, had already been in charge of the paper with a circulation of just 75,000 for two years. Rupert immediately decided that the course to be set for his father's old newspaper must take him into direct conflict with the much larger Adelaide Advertiser Group solidly backed by the Adelaide Establishment – and the Herald and Weekly Times.

By the mid-fifties, News was making enough money for Rupert to expand his interest in Southdown Press in Melbourne into total ownership. Then, in what was to become part of the Murdoch mystique, he bought an ailing newspaper – *The Sunday Times* – in Perth, Western Australia, and began regular long flights across the great Australian deserts every weekend to personally turn it into a runaway success.

Although the Murdoch family always remains close and supportive in any situation, there was concern in 1956 when Rupert announced that he was to marry Patricia Booker, an attractive Adelaide girl. Elisabeth felt that perhaps Rupert's loneliness in Adelaide may have influenced the marriage of two young and not particularly compatible people. In 1959, their daughter, Prudence, was born, but soon they were drifting apart as more and more of Rupert's time was consumed by his growing newspaper interests. Elisabeth says: 'There were all sorts of sad domestic complications which nobody could ever be judgmental about now, least of all Rupert. He always said he was entirely responsible for the breakup. His way of life was impossible for her and her handling of life was impossible for him. It was very sad. We keep in touch with Pat, and Rupert has supported her through many, many difficult times.

'Rupert's got his critics. We know this. We probably know his weaknesses too. But he has always had a marvellous band of people simply devoted to him, and that's a terrific comfort to a mother, because in those early days Rupert had to be out on his own. I think that there are people who thought I should have gone to Adelaide to look after him and make life better for him, but I thought it essential that Rupert should not have that sort of over-mothering.'

However, as the fledgling Murdoch empire expanded, Rupert never neglected to keep Elisabeth and his sisters completely in the picture. There were regular meetings around the family table in the old schoolroom at Cruden Farm or more formal annual meetings in the Southdown Press boardroom as Rupert reported on his gains and ambitions for the future. With less frequency, as international demands on Rupert's time increased, these family meetings have been held ever since.

On her return from the Coronation trip, Anne took up her Commonwealth scholarship at Janet Clarke Hall, University of Melbourne, and began three years of study towards attaining a Bachelor of Arts degree. 'Anne was a naughty girl, because she met Milan in her final year and failed one subject – which she has more than made up for since,' Elisabeth says with a smile now. But at the time Elisabeth, without Keith for support, was deeply worried. 'They wanted to get engaged and married and I wouldn't hear of it. Milan was doing his law course for the second time round and I was concerned that they were rushing things,' Elisabeth says.

Anne's suitor was Milan Kantor, son of a distinguished Czechoslovakian barrister and Doctor of Law who during the war had heroically led the Czech minority in Vienna against Hitler. Milan's mother was the daughter of a Greek Orthodox priest who saved her husband after he had been taken away by the Nazis as they marched into Austria. 'Somehow, she managed to have him released by signing away everything they owned and promising to return to Prague,' Elisabeth explains. 'Milan had managed to go to university in Prague and take his law degree and, after the war, some organisation in Australia nominated him to come out here and he left carrying a suitcase and took a job in Melbourne as a door-to-door salesman selling paint, while he waited for his parents to follow him to Australia.'

In the Beginning

While working and studying for his second law degree at Melbourne University, Milan Kantor met Anne Murdoch and they fell in love. 'It was very sad because Dr Kantor died the same week as Keith so the two fathers never met. Milan graduated, of course, and he married Anne. I'm devoted to Milan. He has a very good brain and he's brought a lot of charm and interest to our family,' Elisabeth says of her Czech son-in-law.

CHAPTER TWENTY

The Hospital Years

WHILE KEITH WAS alive there was a long-running joke in the Murdoch home. He would say 'Your hospital means more to you than I do,' and Elisabeth would reply: 'Now come off it, you'll get your gallery before I get my hospital!'

'Of course, unfortunately, Keith didn't live to see the hospital, but I have lived to see the wonderful Victorian National Gallery he fought and planned for. It was a family joke, but there was nothing jocular about our determination to see the hospital and the gallery completed,' says Elisabeth.

As tempting as it might have seemed after Keith's death, with Rupert soon back in Australia and quickly taking control of the Adelaide *News*, Elisabeth did not stay home and tend her wonderful garden at Cruden Farm. Instead she increased her already heavy workload at the Children's Hospital, driving almost daily to Melbourne and often returning to her lonely home late in the evenings.

The Hospital Years

The Royal Children's Hospital in Melbourne is unique among public hospitals in Australia. Not only was it founded by women, but it was administered and developed by outstanding Australian women volunteers for its first hundred years.

Located from 1876 at the former Carlton home of Sir Redmond Barry, the judge who sentenced Ned Kelly to death by hanging, the hospital was founded in 1870 as a charitable institution for sick children with needy parents, and was known as 'The Melbourne Hospital for Sick Children'. When the hospital first opened, 'Marvellous Melbourne' with its gas lights, shops and mansions in Toorak still had another, darker, side – slums as bad as any to be found in the British Midlands or the capitals of old Europe. In these slums such diseases as diphtheria and typhoid were endemic and taking a terrible toll of young, usually malnourished, children. Another scourge was the 'hip disease', or TB of the hip, which killed or crippled thousands of children. Without modern drugs there was little that could be done to save life or limbs – and even though the nursing was as dedicated as it is today, the prognosis for the survivors about to be sent back to the same unsewered slums was grim indeed. At the time of Elisabeth's first visit to the hospital as a Clyde schoolgirl observing babies being brought out of surgery, there had been many improvements in medical practice since the hospital was first opened, but the child mortality rate was still pitifully high.

But in 1933, Ella, Lady Latham had been unanimously elected as President of the hospital's all-female Committee of Management. In 1954, just as she had long planned, the distinguished Lady Latham stepped down after twenty-one years of outstanding service to the hospital, and Australia. Her chosen successor was Lady Murdoch. In the darkest days of the war in 1942, with some strong urging from Elisabeth, Keith's *Sporting Globe* newspaper and 3DB radio station, had helped launch a Good Friday appeal for the Children's Hospital

– an appeal which soon became a national institution raising millions for the hospital over the years.

When TV came to Australia in time for the Melbourne Olympic Games in 1956, Elisabeth was soon using the new medium to raise more money for her hospital, and at the same time launching schemes like Mrs Vi Greenhalf's Victorian Girl of the Year quest and seeking aid from the loyal Uncle Bob's Club – a club founded by four men who encouraged thousands of others to put in one 'bob', a shilling, a week into a fund to aid the hospital. Then there was the Children's Hospital's week-long Summer Festival in bayside St Kilda skilfully organised by the tireless Mrs Vi Greenhalf to add to Elisabeth's growing hospital nest egg. With the new four hundred bed hospital in the planning stage, the need for funds was now even more urgent, and Elisabeth knew that in order to get the six million pounds she needed from the State Government to complete the project, she would have to raise a substantial sum from public subscription. This appeal was magnificently supported by the ever loyal, hard-working Children's Hospital auxiliaries and so many other enthusiastic organisations and which soon became a national institution raising millions.

'Lady Latham said to me when she retired: "Now it's up to you, Elisabeth, to carry this rebuilding programme forward." I thought it was a marvellous thing that she appeared to have so much confidence in me. I loved it, and was really deeply involved in it, and had great affection for so many people working there. I felt I was in touch with everything. In those days it was possible to be more closely involved with the personnel of the hospital. Today, in many ways, hospitals may be more efficiently run – but, perhaps, not quite so happily.'

Lady Latham was then in very poor health. She had done marvels for the hospital and was in fact the architect for the new concepts of paediatric services with the great assistance of Vernon Collins, the first full-time medical director and, later, Professor of Child Health.

'The Children's Hospital had moved from being benevolent to needing a large number of professional doctors, anaesthetists and surgeons. We had to look at getting paid service. I think that the first of our salaried ancillary services was introduced when we appointed Dr Margaret McClelland as the head of our department of anaesthetics. From these early steps the whole development of paediatric services improved so we owe a great deal to Lady Latham's leadership and foresight,' says Elisabeth, who points out that it would have never entered Lady Latham's head to put her decision to appoint Elisabeth as her successor to a vote.

Elisabeth inherited an excellent committee and from time to time added more. She says: 'Not all of them had tertiary education – including myself – but they had other things to offer, a great deal of good sense and experience and respect in the community and certainly dedication.' Dame Elisabeth was fortunate also to have several very able and supportive men including Mr Donald Ferguson, Mr Peter Johns and Mr Barney Bitcon, whose advice on financial matters was very important.

'When you became a member of the Children's Hospital Committee, you knew that when the bell rang, you had to answer it! At that time there was a lot more opportunity to move around the hospital and get to know various people's requirements and their problems. There was much closer liaison with the nursing staff too. I don't know quite why but I suppose the nursing profession has changed a lot. But when I first joined the Committe of Management, Matron Hilda Walsh ruled the staff with a rod of iron and there was no question of the rights of nurses or being in any way militant.

'Patsy Mackinnon was a wonderful woman who later inherited the presidency from me during the period when people were beginning to become militant. Doctors were becoming much more demanding – and nurses too. She certainly came to that position when there was a great industrial relations stir on and the trade unions were becoming very difficult. I always thought how lucky I had been, because I was president when we were building the hospital and I was out among people urging them to support us and getting that support and having a marvellous communication with the whole community,' Elisabeth says. 'That was a great privilege because I met people throughout Victoria and in a way it was a golden time for volunteer workers and fundraisers, because if you really believed in something and knew it was needed, you could really get people in.

'That's how we got the hospital. The Government saw that this was what the public wanted and got behind us to give their support. Of course, you must realise that we were lucky too that the wonderful Good Friday Appeal continued to grow. I don't think the community can ever be grateful enough for what that Good Friday Appeal did over the years.

'There were a lot of difficulties, of course. Planning, delayed by the war, had gone on for so long and when a few of the people who had been consulted earlier saw what had actually come into being they weren't pleased. There were even people who, when the time came to move to the new complex, decided that they were very attached to the old, overcrowded hospital in Carlton. There had been a spirit there that was hard to introduce into the new hospital with its vast areas to cover. We always knew that, like any big business, we could have these problems when we moved.

'I remember Keith saying late in his life: "Oh dear, I just feel so badly. I used to know all the people at *The Herald*, and their families, and could talk to them and be interested, but now I sometimes get into the lift and I don't know who I'm in the lift with." That's what happens to any small business growing from a small

The Hospital Years

intimate operation to a very large one. We had what you could call growing pains but we had foreseen that possibility. We had help from a remarkable woman, Carmen Winter, an exceptional character who started our great volunteer service at the Children's Hospital. Of course there were suspicions that the volunteers were going to come in and perhaps even take jobs from the paid people. But it was all skilfully managed by Carmen who soon had trained volunteers meeting parents at the doors and taking them up to different departments.

'The volunteers would only go into the departments they were invited into and soon the suspicion dispersed. In fact, I don't think the hospital could possibly have run as well as it did without those volunteers. They ran messages from department to department and acted as interpreters – we even had a cab driver who could come in and interpret for us at night. Some had typing skills and proved their worth in several departments and soon we had staff asking for their services. They ran a splendid childminding service. They didn't do anything in the wards though – that was strictly for the nurses,' says Elisabeth who, after her retirement from the presidency of the hospital, became an Honorary Visitor – a role she still happily performs from time to time.

In his detailed history of the hospital, *From Charity to Teaching Hospital*, Howard Williams, AO, the distinguished paediatrician who served the hospital as Resident, in 1937, until he ended his term as Executive Chairman of the Hospital's Research Foundation in 1970, contrasts the style of Lady Latham's stiffly formal committee meetings: 'The women always wore hats and gloves – new and junior members were advised not to speak ...' to the meetings chaired by Elisabeth: 'She ran meetings where they all sat around a table and stayed afterwards for lunch so that they all felt they were more part of decision making,' he wrote.

Elisabeth explains that when she took over, the hospital was smaller in many respects than it is today. 'It didn't have quite as many auxiliary paediatric services outside the hospital. Back then, we didn't have to cope so constantly with adolescents drinking, drugs and unwanted pregnancies – all horrors that are so prevalent these days. It was a much simpler life and I think in the thirties, forties and fifties there was much more emphasis on the idea that presidents and vice-presidents should be really hands-on in the day-to-day running of the hospital,' says Elisabeth, who soon became a familiar figure known to doctors, nurses, cleaners, engineers, and the young patients, as she moved through every department of the hospital.

Elisabeth soon had another responsibility too – the Chairmanship of the Hospital's Interim Planning Committee charged with building a vast new hospital complex to take what had been the Hospital for Sick Children into the twenty-first century. 'I remember so well when the plans were open for inspection. The nurses were horrified. They didn't approve of what was then considered to be the most modern accommodation for them. A great deal of time was spent meeting with them to get their agreement for what was finally built ... but since then, of course, as the new technology came in with new medical treatment and techniques, things have had to be changed. We put so much thought into planning that hospital, but there have been changes since and one thing that shocked me so much was what happened to the nurses' home.

'We built it first to take the nurses out of what had been our old home, Heathfield. Well now, I'm told, it's no longer needed for nurses because nurses don't want to live in hospitals – and they don't have to! We did build flats for nurses and they still rent them, but the whole pattern of nurses' life has changed. Today, the doctors marry very young too and they're paid so much better. It's a very different hospital world today. Our nurses' home, more recently, was not even considered to be suitable for reconstruction and use by the hospital. But, in fact, it now has a role to play,' says Elisabeth.

But in so many other ways, the hospital, which has become an internationally recognised centre of paediatric care and research, is a triumph for the women of Melbourne whose vision made it possible. But in the mid-forties, in the aftermath of the war, and into the fifties, Elisabeth's abiding concern was obtaining the final site for the new hospital, and then raising the funds to build it. 'From the start, the site was always a source of contention for us all. It soon became very political too and Lady Latham had her husband, Sir John, a former High Court judge and Federal Attorney General, behind her, but it was still not finally signed and sealed when I took over. Really we considered it so important to get the land we had chosen on Royal Park, at Parkville, on the outskirts of the city, because we regarded it as vital for the health of the children to have fresh open air around them, and remember this was before fears of air pollution.

'On that fateful day when we met with the Premier, Henry Bolte, he said: "Well, Lady Murdoch, there is a strong opinion that we should rebuild on your present site in Carlton."' Elisabeth, those who were present still recall, didn't hesitate. She looked directly at the man regarded as Victoria's toughest and most successful Premier and said firmly: 'Well, then, Mr Premier, you will have to ask someone else to do it.' It was a tense moment, but Henry Bolte knew he had met his match as he quickly asked Elisabeth to put forward her proposal for the Royal Park site with its vast expanse of native trees and grassland close to other hospital, research and nursing complexes.

'Apparently my firm attitude was the punchline,' Elisabeth says with a smile. 'I think Henry saw we were determined. We had a pretty strong case as to why it should be built where it is now on public land and stressed how much the public needed it and were behind us. I added that as the public were contributing so much to its construction I thought it was only right and proper that they should get what they needed and where they wanted it. Now Henry began to see it as a political issue and we pressed the point that a new children's hospital would be very popular with the electorate. In the end, we got the wonderful site that we wanted. It had all begun with Lady Latham back in 1936, but it did fall to me as president to clinch the deal with Henry,' says Elisabeth.

'Of course, I didn't draw up the plans but I had to be in on them all and discuss every detail with the architects and that took up a lot of my time. The architect, Sir Arthur Stevenson, was a very strong and powerful man. I recall one fierce argument we had with him when Lady Latham was still in the chair and how horrified we all were when he actually addressed Lady Latham as "My Good Woman". It was a very challenging, very educational experience for me. I had to put my untrained mind to understanding all the details. We also had a regular senior medical committee meeting and I had to chair those meetings attended by medical people with very strong intellects. That really kept me on my toes. It came naturally to Lady Latham because she had a very, very good brain. But at first it was a very testing time for me. I think I gained and was given so much during my years at the hospital.

'While we finally got the land we asked for, there was still an argument about the need for underground parking. We wanted it very much, but we didn't have the money for it, so we asked for more land for parking, but they wouldn't allow that so we had to cut back our plans quite a lot before they were finally accepted and even then we had to cut back on theatre space and room for other facilities we knew we should have.

'Now everyone knows that it was very false economy, and they have had to go underground for vital parking space which is so much

39 Anne recuperating in the garden at Heathfield in 1939

40 Davey's Bay, Mt Eliza. Nanny with Anne (running in front), and Helen (far right) in the late 1930s

41 Elisabeth, with Helen and Rupert, in his Adwalton school uniform, at Heathfield in the late 1930s

42 Albany Road, Toorak, the Murdochs' home from 1946 to 1952

43 Helen's wedding day - with her parents at Albany Road in 1949

44 Ready for school, Rupert, in Geelong Grammar uniform, with his father in the early 1940s

45 A favourite photo - Sir Keith and Lady Murdoch on the steps at Cruden Farm in the late 1940s

46 Keith Murdoch and Winston Churchill at the Empire Press Union in the late 1940s

47 Elisabeth coming home from her overseas trip with Keith Murdoch in 1950 to a 'lovely welcome from my daughters'. From left Helen, Janet and Anne

48 Rupert as a young man with Elisabeth in the early 1950s

49 Elisabeth says 'thank you' to 3DB listeners for their donations to the Royal Children's Hospital Good Friday Appeal in the 1950s

50 Rupert Murdoch, now 29, holds the first edition of his recently purchased Sydney *Daily Mirror* in June, 1960

51 Elisabeth meets the Queen at the Royal Children's Hospital, 1963, with the Premier, Sir Henry Bolte and Prince Philip

52 Dame Elisabeth watches the proceedings at the 1963 Royal opening ceremony of the Children's Hospital with Prince Philip and Henry Bolte

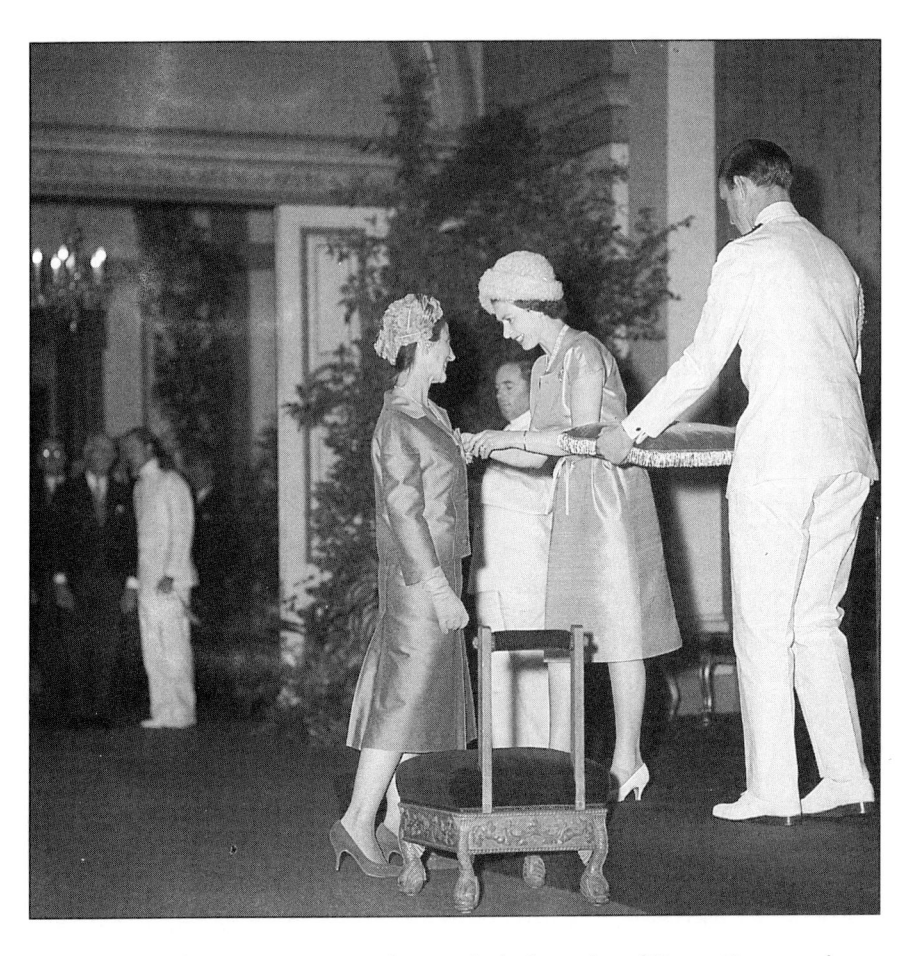

53 The Queen bestowing upon Lady Murdoch the order of Dame Commander of the Most Excellent Order of the British Empire in 1963

54 A galaxy of Dames at Dame Merlyn Myer's eightieth birthday at the National Gallery of Victoria: from left, Dame Elisabeth, Dame Hilda Stevenson, Dame Merlyn Myer, Dame Peggy van Praagh and Dame Margaret Scott

55 A critical eye. Elisabeth at an art exhibition

more expensive to provide these days anyway. It was very trying at the time because we knew what we should have had and we knew that we were right. I was so confident because I had some wonderful people beside me. I was heading up a marvellous team,' says Elisabeth. 'I think that one of the main reasons why Henry Bolte allowed his political horse sense to come to bear was that we had put in so much preliminary work to gain support for building a new hospital. Of course, I had to give him a little push. It was my natural reaction. You know, we were fired up and so convinced that we were going to build this new hospital that it had become almost a religion with us.

'I was very fond of Henry Bolte and knew that the public were behind us and had done so much already. It was really only a fair thing that we went ahead. I wrote a lot of letters to a great number of private citizens and corporations and I had a very good reaction to that because they knew I was doing it personally. We did not employ a paid organiser, although there was quite a bit of feeling that it was too big for us and we should put it in the hands of a professional. I said that I felt that people would respond more generously if they knew we were putting our own tremendous effort into it. And I had wonderful letters back. When I wrote to thank them personally in my own hand some of them came up with a second donation. So you know it worked. It was really, I suppose, a very homemade effort on my part.

'I was told we raised half a million pounds but I think we raised a good deal more,' says Elisabeth, who was vice-president for many years before beginning her eleven-year term as president.

While Elisabeth was playing a leading role in the construction of the great Australian hospital for children, Rupert was spreading his newspaper wings and making his first move on Sydney, the headquarters of the Fairfax and Packer media empires. In a convoluted spoiling operation that soon backfired disastrously on the imperious Fairfax family, the Fairfax group decided to sell Rupert the down-market *Mirror* papers – a deal which included a bureau office in New York – to prevent either Packer or the Melbourne *Herald* getting a larger foothold in Australia's biggest city.

And soon Rupert was to head off a bid by London's by then ailing Express Newspaper group to buy Sir Frank Packer's Sydney *Daily* and *Sunday Telegraphs*. Television, his first national daily, *The Australian*, and Fleet Street soon followed and Rupert's amazing international media odyssey was now well under way.

In Melbourne, Rupert's proud mother was just as busy and dedicated as her son. Some of her duties may have been a little less exciting, although they were certainly equally 'hands on': 'We used to do the hospital furnishing in the old days. We would tramp up and down Chapel Street and Bourke Street buying furniture and curtain materials for the nurses' home. We had a good relationship with the architects too. I got on well with Arthur Stevenson but in the early days of planning I was always pouring oil on troubled waters between him and Lady Latham. He was a notable hospital architect but he was also very opinionated and Lady Latham didn't like that,' Elisabeth recalls.

Climbing trees in the Pemberley garden as a child was good training for Elisabeth who now made regular inspections of the hospital building site. Wearing a hard hat and sensible shoes she scrambled over girders and concrete slabs as the great building began to rise. 'I was fascinated by it all, but so happy when it was reaching the final stages of construction,' she says. But while work on the hospital continued, Elisabeth decided to take a few weeks' break. 'Helen had her trip before Keith died and I took Anne to the Coronation so I felt Janet, who was dux of the school and head prefect, should be taken to Europe too,' Elisabeth says. 'So, before she went to university, I decided she must see the world. We went forth and flew to New York.

'The one thing Janet wanted was to see *My Fair Lady* on Broadway and we just couldn't get seats. Then we were told that if we went first thing in the morning and queued up we might just get some standing room. It was awfully cold, nearly freezing, when we got there at 5 a.m. – and the box office didn't open until 9 a.m.!' Elisabeth recalls with a shudder. As it was, the Murdochs were numbers 31 and 32 in the queue and were able to take turns to go away and get hot cups of coffee, until the box office finally opened and they secured the last two tickets allowing them to stand at the back of the stalls. 'It was wonderful, absolutely wonderful,' Elisabeth can still say with enthusiasm.

'So we arrived in London and my sister Marie had lent her flat to the parents of John Calvert-Jones – a young officer cadet from the Royal Military Academy at Sandhurst – for a party for his sister, Judy. It was that evening that Janet and John first met. Janet and Judy were the same age and became good friends. Janet was invited to stay with John and Judy's parents, Major General and Mrs Calvert-Jones at their lovely home in Somerset.' While in Britain, Elisabeth and Janet drove to Suffolk to stay with Lady Jackson, later Baroness Jackson of Lodsworth, the acclaimed academic who as, Barbara Ward, had become a renowned British economist and author. Together they visited the Earl of Albemarle and his Countess, Dame Diana. Elisabeth was enchanted when the Earl produced the orb and sceptre once carried by his kinswoman Elizabeth Stuart, the tragic and beautiful Queen of Bohemia known as 'The Queen of Hearts'. They dined with the ancient Royal regalia of the Queen, whose favourite son had been Prince Rupert, resting on the table in front of them.

'Janet continued to see John intermittently while she spent several months staying with Marie and Johnnie, her godparents, and visited

Paris to study French while staying with a French family. Elisabeth left her daughter in good hands and returned home to her hospital. Janet returned home early in 1958, but was not keen to go to university and chose instead to take a business course and work in the offices of Mr Fred Ballantyne, a noted architect. Later that year, Janet heard that John was to join his regiment, the 13th/18th Royal Hussars, at a time when the communists were still in active conflict on the Malay Peninsula. For his first leave John accepted Janet's invitation to her twenty-first birthday party at Cruden Farm and flew to Australia. After a month staying with the Murdoch family, John had clearly developed a special relationship with Janet, and when he returned to Malaya he was soon followed by Elisabeth chaperoning Janet. 'We flew up because apparently Janet wanted to see more of John, and I left her staying with a charming couple.'

Soon they wanted to become engaged but Janet's doubt was that she could not bear to leave Australia and it wasn't until the following April, 1961, when John was stationed in West Germany that Janet decided to visit him and they became engaged. John and Janet were married at the Toorak Presbyterian Church in February, 1962, with Rupert giving the bride away. John's friend Captain David Lewis of the Royal Tank Regiment, then aide-de-campe to the Governor of South Australia, was best man while Rupert's daughter, Prudence, was a bridesmaid with two of Janet's other nieces, Julie Kantor and Judy Handbury. After the wedding, the guests drove to Cruden Farm for lunch. The wedding over, Elisabeth gave her undivided attention to the hospital, due to be opened by the Queen just a year later.

But just before Christmas 1962, Bairnie, who was ailing and staying at Cruden Farm, had a bad stroke and doctors advised that she would no longer be able to return to Pemberley to live alone. Elisabeth insisted that her mother should be looked after at Cruden Farm although, in the last few days of preparation for the Royal

The Hospital Years

opening of the hospital, this added considerably to her many concerns. Now began Elisabeth's years of devoted care for her mother – especially after a second stroke which left her partially paralysed and confined to a wheel chair, with Elisabeth waking every two or three hours through the night to turn her over and tend to her needs. 'Those years were a big strain, but I never regretted being able to do something in return for all my mother had done for me,' Elisabeth insists. 'Mother was here at Cruden Farm during the years I was working practically full time at the hospital so we had trained nurses during the day.' At the time of her stroke, Bairnie was eighty-five. She died at Cruden Farm seven years later.

Added to her other distractions that year, Elisabeth was sent for by an old friend, the Victorian Lieutenant-Governor, Sir Edmund Herring, and asked if she would accept the DBE – Dame Commander of the Most Excellent Order of the British Empire. 'I said, "Ned, I feel awful about this. I have got the CBE, and I would prefer it if someone else got this honour." I wanted Vernon Collins to be honoured because I felt he had played such an important role in the new hospital and I thought it would be wonderful for him. But Ned Herring said: "Elisabeth, my dear, I'm afraid you will disappoint a great number of people and it would hardly be gracious."' So, convinced that any such honour really belonged to the whole team of people responsible for the construction of the great hospital, Elisabeth reluctantly accepted the DBE although, as she says now, she had long been comfortable with the Lady Murdoch title which became hers when Keith received his KB.

Elisabeth could not bring herself to break the terms of secrecy that applied to the award until the official announcement on New Year's Eve – not even to tell her mother. 'I felt I ought to tell her in case she died. I knew that it would give her pleasure, but I couldn't tell her because it was secret,' says Elisabeth. 'Opening the hospital was a gala event planned down to the last detail. Anybody who had anything to do with the raising of the money or planning was invited along. I felt that so many people had contributed that it was up to us to make it a wonderful occasion and one in which as many as possible of the people who had helped were involved. And that took a lot of organisation. We had an enormous number of auxiliaries and so many others who had helped us over the years.

'We chose the roof of the casualty department for the Royal opening ceremony but we still had to have a ballot for guests to be fitted in. I couldn't ask any of my close personal friends, but the children did come along. The nurses, doctors, patients and many of our supporters were able to watch the proceedings from balconies and windows. Weeks before the opening I had to walk over the route we would take with the protocol officer, Geoffrey Smith, and tell him about what was going to be shown to the Queen. I was asked to let Buckingham Palace see my speech – three months before it had to be delivered! I was so shy about it. No one saw it or knew what I had written and, of course, I had to remember it and be sure that I didn't have to read it from notes on the day, that was a big strain.'

But finally all the detailed preparations for the opening of the hospital were made and approved, and Elisabeth says: 'When the day came I had to be steely calm about it. And, of course, the awful thing was that when we met Her Majesty she wasn't very well or perhaps she had had a disagreement with Philip or something unsettling. But she was met outside and we had to walk past the lines of nurses who had gone to enormous trouble. They had bought themselves white gloves to go with their blue-grey uniforms, white aprons and caps, and they had sent wonderful orchids down to the Royal yacht and we walked by and the Queen was hardly looking at them, so I said:

"Ma'am, these are our nurses," and she said: "Yes, you seem to have a great number of them,"' recalls Elisabeth.

At Elisabeth's insistence, the hospital's fifty voluntary helpers dressed in their cherry red uniforms were also there as ushers for the day. Elisabeth had brought baskets of flowers from Cruden Farm to decorate the new boardroom, where official guests were to have afternoon tea after the ceremony, and she had supervised the floral decorations of native flowers throughout the hospital. But two days before the Royal arrival she had taken Mr Feint, the hospital manager, aside and said 'There is one thing I beg of you. That lift to the roof where the official opening takes place has got to work.'

'Well, on the day, we got into the lift and the lift wouldn't work, wouldn't move. And Philip saved my life because he made some marvellous joke and said: "It's just as well I'm a good mechanic" and banged the panel with his fist and finally up we went. But oh, for a moment it was just too awful for words – stuck in a lift that wouldn't work with Prince Philip and Her Majesty!

'And then, of course, we had another anxiety because the roof was open and we were having this terrible unsettled February weather, hot and thundery, and we thought it was going to rain. What to do? Well, we asked the government – for really it was their great show-off day to the public – and we thought we'd ask them to put up a small temporary roof. But they wouldn't, although they did have two rather elaborate umbrellas made so that Her Majesty wouldn't get wet. Thank God, it didn't rain. But oh dear, it was a close shave!

'Nearly all the people were seated – I think I allocated all those seats myself and there were one thousand of them – and it was a very tense occasion. I think I managed to get over fairly well because I didn't read my speech. But I was so disappointed that the Queen read hers – and it wasn't very long at all.'

Elisabeth had been awarded the CBE for services to the hospital in Sir Robert Menzies' Federal Honours list in 1961 – an award which temporarily short-circuited Henry Bolte's longstanding plan to recommend that the Queen award her the DBE on his Victorian State New Year's Honours list. As usual, the Victorian Premier finally got his way. On 25 February 1963, the day of the hospital opening, Elisabeth was spending her last hours as Lady Murdoch and, as protocol proclaimed, had the CBE in her handbag to return to an aide-de-camp immediately the Queen made her a Dame Commander of the Most Excellent Order of the British Empire.

But before that, there was the Royal progress through the hospital to be followed at a polite distance. 'It went pretty well around the ward but again it was Philip who saved the day because he kept a few paces behind making a joke or sort of relieving the tension. Really he did go up a long way in my estimation that day,' Elisabeth remembers.

Finally, the pomp and circumstance of the opening of the great new hospital over, Elisabeth and officials saw the Queen and Philip to their car and then Elisabeth took a seat in her car that was to follow the Royal progress through the crowded streets of Melbourne and deliver her to Government House for the Royal Investiture. Elisabeth recalls with a chuckle that she did venture a wave or two to the throngs of excited people who had just cheered the Queen as she passed by.

At Government House more than sixty other recipients of Imperial honours were waiting to have their awards bestowed on them by the Queen, and Elisabeth remembers that by the time her turn came the Queen had regained her good humour and was friendly and charming – both then, and later when she chatted informally to the new Dame Elisabeth Murdoch. Elisabeth had been able to invite her children to the opening of the hospital as her only personal guests, and it was decided that Rupert, his wife, Pat, and Helen should accompany her to the Royal Investiture. 'I recall coming home to Cruden Farm that night with this great decoration the Queen had given me. I must say that it was easier being Lady Murdoch than a Dame – much more comfortable. I really was very sad to give up my husband's honour and I remember I couldn't go with him when he received his KB in Melbourne, because I was pregnant with Anne – Aunt Lizzie Murdoch went with him to Government House and was inordinately proud. It didn't take long to get used to being a Dame though, and, of course, most of the staff were English and called me "M'lady" anyway. No one in Australia would dream of calling me – or anyone else – M'lady these days.'

CHAPTER TWENTY-ONE

The Dame at Delphi

IN MAY, 1963, with the hospital royally opened and running smoothly, Dame Elisabeth decided on a really good break in the UK where Janet and John were now living. But first she called on sculptor Tina Wentcher to thank her for the beautiful bronze bas relief of mother and child she had sculpted to be placed in the hospital's entrance hall. Elisabeth says: 'I had decided to indulge myself by stopping over in Greece on the way to see Janet and my two new grandchildren. I saw Tina just as I was getting ready to leave and told her of my plans and she said: "I have just had an invitation from dear friends to visit them in Athens, but I am afraid that my eyes and ears are not up to it," and I said: "Tina, you must come with me."

'In some trepidation as to what my family and friends would say about my impulsive invitation I went ahead and was delighted to receive a letter from her well-known and greatly respected oculist saying that Tina had consulted him and adding: "If you were able to look after her on a trip abroad, I assure you that you will be richly rewarded." So the die was cast and plans for the great trip were made after I was given three months leave of absence from the Royal Children's Hospital.

'Travelling with Tina had its moments,' Elisabeth chuckles. 'The batteries of her hearing aid were constantly falling out under aircraft seats, her contact lenses were often mislaid, but we were able to laugh. Arriving in Athens, we were met by her old and enchanting friend, Mrs Despina Geroulanos, daughter of a distinguished German Professor of Paediatrics, who made us very welcome at her home near Athens. There were 500 or 600 acres of land, 100 of which were given over to growing roses and carnations. The day we arrived in Athens, garlands of roses were attached to every door celebrating the annual Festival of the Roses. At the entrance to the Geroulanos property stood a fourteenth-century gatehouse and when we entered the charming house we were greeted by twenty-eight vases of the most beautiful roses – a different variety in each vase. They were enchanting.'

The Geroulanoses, a distinguished family, were charming hosts and soon found an excellent driver to take Tina and Elisabeth around Greece with a young German architect to share the costs. There were a few days of sightseeing in Athens, seeing the Acropolis by moonlight, the national museum and being shown Greek sculpture by her friend Tina. They voyaged to Hydra and Delphi, and lay on their backs looking up at mosaics on the ceilings of churches. There were visits to remote fishing villages where the blue waters of the Aegean lapped their hotels. And always Elisabeth and Tina were running into Australians they knew. There was a wonderful voyage around the Greek Islands with a visit to Rhodes and Crete. Then, after a farewell lunch the good friends flew to Rome where Elisabeth watched as, with minutes to spare, Tina overcome by the noise and crush, was handed over the heads of the milling throng at the airport to catch her flight to visit her sister in Sicily.

For the next two months, Elisabeth spent time visiting old friends in Britain and staying with John and Janet at their thatched cottage in Dorset near the Royal Tank School at Bovington where John was then stationed. Besides getting to know her grandchildren, Elisabeth also did the rounds of the opera, concerts, theatre, ballet and art galleries – delights she had missed during her strenuous hospital years. There was also a passing out parade at Bovington taken by General Sir John Hackett DSO and bar, a distinguished Australian soldier in the British Army who greatly impressed Elisabeth with his dignity and bearing. Born in Perth, Sir John had commanded Britain's 4th Parachute Regiment and had risen to become Deputy Chief of the Imperial General Staff. Elisabeth was delighted to see the high regard which the troops had for the Australian soldier.

Over the years Elisabeth managed to make many visits to her sister, Marie Durnford, in London. 'Marie opened many very interesting doors for me and I remember how I was inveigled into doing the wedding flowers for her brother-in-law's daughter. Her mother, Meg Durnford, was a friend of the Duke of Wellington. Meg had been promised flowers from the Duke's wonderful garden at Stratfield Saye House, in Hampshire, so off I was sent with secateurs and baskets. His Grace seemed rather anxious and unwelcoming and followed me around rather menacingly, but he soon retired muttering that I seemed to know what I was doing and he would leave me to pick anything I fancied. Later, he was more friendly and showed me some fascinating memorabilia of his kinsman, the great Duke, including a chest in which were stored clothing, false teeth and things like that.

'To express the bride's mother's appreciation of my flower

The Dame at Delphi

arrangements, she urged me to take her place with her husband, at a special traditional dinner at King's College, Cambridge. Well, that was a memorable occasion for me – sitting at the high table in the company of notable academics, surrounded by the beautiful college silver and enchanted by magical vocal music. I was in a very unaccustomed world and to complete the treat we attended Divine Service next morning in King's College Chapel,' says Elisabeth.

Then for Elisabeth it was back to work with a vengeance in Australia with the Royal Children's Hospital, her garden at Cruden Farm, and a host of other projects to attend to. In 1947, the Children's Hospital had formed a Research Committee with the object of developing active research into child ailments and care at the hospital. Elisabeth was later instrumental in establishing the Research Committee as a Research Foundation with an autonomous board and strong representation from the Hospital Committee of Management, senior medical staff, University of Melbourne and advisors from the scientific and business community. Elisabeth says that this was the goal her committee had been working towards for many years.

In fact, from small beginnings with one doctor and one biochemist, by 1967, twenty years later, the foundation was a research powerhouse with twenty doctors, a team of science graduates and eleven technicians internationally recognised for their studies of a wide range of children's disorders. Dr Howard Williams was in charge of the Clinical Research Unit doing pioneer investigation into asthma and other respiratory disorders in young infants. Dr David Danks was Senior Research Worker doing major work in the field of genetics, and Mr Douglas Stephens, head of the Surgical Research Unit, was studying renal tract diseases – research that would lead to progress towards the successful transplantation of kidneys. 'In those days, the president of the hospital was also chairman of the Research Board and Lady Latham had been very keen and Howard Williams very effective. From that Research Board emerged the Research Foundation – later our specific Murdoch Institute concentrating on research into birth defects on the genetic side,' Elisabeth explains.

Elisabeth was founding Chairman of the Research Foundation. 'One had to really learn so much. It was quite hard work to become reasonably familiar with what people were talking about and why they wanted to do what they intended doing,' she explains. 'We did have independent outside scientific advisers, and I was always very keen about several main thrusts of our work. Gastroenterology was one of our great strengths and research into upper respiratory problems was also going strong. I was, of course, always very keen on genetics – had been ever since Keith bought cattle.

'At that time, David Danks was becoming a very interested and certainly well respected young researcher into genetics. He was paid partly by the hospital and partly by the university and its cancer research people. He always shone out as having a very good mind, and he was anxious to pursue his line of research into genetics. In 1967, he had accepted a Readership in Human Genetics at the University of Melbourne. I used to constantly ask: "Why can't we get down to the root cause of why these awful things happen to children?" I remember being told I was quite right, but genetics was such an immense subject, and it took enormous funding. Of course, research into genetics is now a worldwide interest and a very important aspect of science, so finally I was to see something I always dreamt about coming into being, and the Royal Children's Hospital was leading the way in Australia.'

There were, of course, some difficulties in establishing such a major foundation but Dr John Colebatch was soon doing pioneer work in his Haematology Research Clinic carrying out excellent studies into the newer drugs used in the treatment of the then normally fatal childhood disorder, leukaemia. The busy doctor also played a major role in establishing the groundwork for the foundation's many operations. Elisabeth knew at the time that there was a great deal of pressure being exerted from the university for the Royal Children's Hospital's research work to be included in the research undertaken by a Chair of Child Health. 'But I think it would be fair to say that particularly Charlotte Anderson, Douglas Stephens and myself thought it was better to continue as a separate organisation, linked with the university, linked with their Chair of Child Health but under the control of our Board of Management,' Elisabeth says firmly.

Soon, as the work of the foundation progressed, Elisabeth and her committee were faced with the search for a director. The post was advertised and Dr Donald Cheek was appointed. 'Dame Hilda Stevenson, charged with the disposal of $100,000 held in trust, was preparing to hand it to the University of Melbourne when I said to her: "You know we need the Chair of Child Health at our hospital, don't you?" – and that's how we got it,' says Elisabeth. 'It was really no credit to me, but what extraordinary things can happen! Because Dame Hilda had been worried and didn't know what the university was planning to do with the money, she decided to state her wishes about its use. It is extraordinary, isn't it, how paper-thin the margins are between things you have and have not accomplished, because that money allowed the University of Melbourne to establish the Chair of Child Health – and we were lucky, very lucky to get it,' Elisabeth admits.

Guiding the new hospital was now almost a full-time task for Elisabeth, who saw as her duty the need to regularly visit every department, sit in on a number of committees, and get to know doctors and nurses. 'I have always loved people and there were many occasions when I had the opportunity to communicate with distressed patients and parents. It's marvellous when you can supply people with a little moral courage or that extra bit of friendship and understanding. Somehow a lot of people have remembered me for that. Perhaps it is larger in their memories than mine, but sometimes it's the little things that mean so much to people in times of stress,' she says.

In 1965, just two years after the triumphant opening of the new hospital, Elisabeth announced her resignation from a post that hand made her the woman with one of the highest public profiles in Australia; certainly it happened years before she became perhaps better known as Rupert Murdoch's mother. 'I have no firm philosophy about retirement but I feel professionals must step aside when the time is right,' Elisabeth still insists. 'There was no sort of rule or accepted retirement age at the hospital but I felt when it was built and running, well I would know when to retire, and I did.' When she did announce her retirement, Elisabeth described the day on which she had persuaded Henry Bolte to accept the plans for the new six million pound hospital as 'the biggest moment of my career'.

Another proud moment, she said, was the day on which she had seen the first ambulance leave the inadequate old hospital and drive to the new complex. After thirty-three years on the board, Elisabeth admitted on that day in September, 1965, that a great deal of her life had been tied up in the hospital. Her reason for retirement? 'It was time for a change, particularly as Mrs Alistair Mackinnon – Patsy – was such an outstandingly able and suitable successor, who after many years of service to the hospital was popular and greatly respected,' she said. Proudly, Elisabeth pointed out that the new hospital could at last supply services that would be able to treat the whole child. 'Not only are the physical disabilities treated, but also the emotional problems of the children and social backgrounds of the parents are examined as well,' she said. She forecast the introduction of a residential psychiatric unit and listed departments already operating in this field – psychiatric social work, speech therapy and others. And she listed as one of the most valuable advances made possible by the new hospital, her old hobby horse – unrestricted visits to the young patients. Looking out over Royal Park, the retiring Dame Elisabeth said: 'The whole of the park gives an extra dimension to our hospital. We had the windows lowered from the original plan, so that children could look out over the park from their beds.'

'I was involved with the hospital for such a long time and it was very enriching for me,' Elisabeth says now. 'I suppose it's a part of my great feeling for family too. Of course, the most rewarding thing I ever did was to marry my husband because from that all else came. I know that, I do – I never would have been involved in the Children's Hospital if I hadn't been Keith's wife, I know I wouldn't. My marriage really did open up so many other opportunities.' In fact, Elisabeth did not end her contact with Royal Children's Hospital on her retirement. She was persuaded to continue her work as Chairman of the Research Board.

CHAPTER TWENTY-TWO

The National Gallery Years

ELISABETH COULD have remained on as President of the Royal Children's Hospital for many more years. Instead, at fifty-six, she chose to step down and move to another of the great interests in life she had shared with Keith – the Arts.

Looking back at her decision to step down from the hospital that had become such an important part of her life, Elisabeth says: 'Everyone in those days seemed to hang on until they were in their seventies, but I thought that was wrong. Later I took the same view at the National Gallery. I believe that with any great public institution you must not hang on to your office like grim death,' says Elisabeth. 'There was no rule or accepted time at the hospital but I had always felt that when the Children's Hospital was built and running well I would retire, and I did.'

In July, 1964, Elisabeth was delighted when her son launched his finest newspaper to that date. *The Australian*, a 'quality' national broadsheet, was to cost him a fortune over the years until new technology enabled it to conquer Australia's vast distances and parochial interests, and establish loyal readership. Then, in 1967, his marriage to Pat at an end, Rupert married beautiful and talented Anna Torv, a young cadet on the *Mirror* in Sydney who, as editor of the cadet newspaper, had asked for an interview with the 'boss'.

Elisabeth and the family attended the quiet wedding in Sydney. But the exciting sixties were far from over for Elisabeth. She recalls: 'I was invited in 1968 at very short notice — in fact, twenty-four hours before the official opening of the great new National Gallery of Victoria — to become a trustee. Of course, I had been invited to the grand opening dinner, but then this invitation came out of the blue. It was a very difficult decision for me to make because it was the first time that a woman had been invited to be a trustee and I was very reluctant when Henry Bolte phoned me.

'He said "We want you to be our first woman trustee of the National Gallery" and I said I was very honoured but was reluctant to accept unless I could be sure the Board of Trustees would welcome me because I had a feeling that they had not been consulted. I was right — they hadn't! Clearly Henry had suddenly thought that this was a great moment for his government and it was time to heed the rising feeling in the community that women should take more prominent places. I'm sure he had respect for what I had done at the hospital and thought I could fulfill the requirements, and I think that he thought it would be a popular move to appoint a woman.

'Overnight he must have checked around and he rang me the next morning to say the trustees were all very happy at the move. I had worried all night and had phoned Sir Clive Fitts, who was then Consulting Physician at the Children's Hospital and Chairman of the Felton Bequest Committee to seek his sound advice. He advised me to accept.

'They announced my appointment at the dinner that night in 1968,' recalls Elisabeth. Sitting next to her in the Great Hall of the National Gallery when her appointment was announced was Federal opposition leader Gough Whitlam – a politician Rupert was to first support, and then drop, as the Labor Government brought Australia to the brink of Constitutional crisis in the early seventies. 'The night wasn't altogether a comfortable experience for me,' Elisabeth says now.

'I must say I had a very interesting and happy eight years in the gallery Keith had done so much to make possible, and I could have been there until I was seventy-two, but I had helped to prove that there was a place for a woman on the board and I felt I ought to step down and give other women the opportunity to play a role. I think it is always a good idea to go before you have to, and I was proud to have been there as the first woman trustee. It was a very privileged position to be a trustee of the National Gallery and proved my point that a woman could be useful there.

'I had been the convenor of the art library sub-committee and my colleagues thought it would be a good idea to form a Friends of the Gallery Library, so I worked very hard at that for ten years too. I hope I did my bit for the National Gallery of Victoria,' Elisabeth says.

But one National Gallery project that should have had Elisabeth's enthusiastic support had turned out to be 'a tremendous disappointment'. It was the 'Murdoch Courtyard' about which Elisabeth says: 'No disrespect, but I always said it was like an exercise yard in a penitentiary. It was meant, of course, for theatre, but Roy Grounds, the gallery architect, didn't plan for any dressing-room or support facilities so when they opened the gallery and put on a Shakespearean play it was mayhem and they soon realised that it was quite impossible for drama.

'They then began to use it as a display for outdoor sculpture, until one day I was horrified to see that one of the exhibits was cracking the bluestone paving. Different directors and curators looked at the space over the years and there was a great campaign from the trustees to get the Government to provide some money and to utilise it for a better purpose. There were all sorts of schemes put forward – including one to just put a roof over it. But fortunately good sense prevailed, and a very innovative plan was drawn up. Patrick McCaughey had a great deal to do with that, and the courtyard was transformed. But until then it was a dead loss and a great disappointment for all of us,' says Elisabeth.

'Keith's name was there, which was a great honour, and the Lindsay Courtyard was in the middle and the Coles Courtyard was at the other end, and we always thought Keith would have been rather sad because he had a great eye for beauty and I don't think he would have approved of that rather grim rock austerity, apart from the fact that it was simply not effective.

'I think it was extremely generous of the trustees to call it the Keith and Elisabeth Murdoch Courtyard, but when this was put to me by Patrick at a foundation meeting, it was very embarrassing. I said I would ask that it be called the Keith Murdoch Courtyard, but they seemed to want it to be called the Keith and Elisabeth Murdoch Courtyard. So I felt obliged to accept this honour. Having established the Keith and Elisabeth Murdoch Travelling Scholarship for the Art School students, I am very proud to have these two associations with the National Gallery of Victoria.'

During much of Elisabeth's active interest in the National Gallery, the flamboyant and talented Patrick McCaughey was the Gallery Director. 'He was very colourful, personable and nice and I liked him,' she says. And despite the pressures he often brought to bear on her, Elisabeth says: 'I still have warm affection for Patrick McCaughey and great admiration. He is a very endearing creature.'

Sadly Patrick McCaughey's talents have been lost to Australia. He is now a gallery director in the USA.

Looking back with much pleasure on her National Gallery days, Elisabeth recalls the congenial meetings of the trustees with Dick Seddon as Chairman and Baillieu Myer and Dick Downing as affable fellow trustees with Lenton Parr, Robin Boyd, Brian Stonier, Dr Ursula Hoff and Professor Margaret Manion, who was later to become the much admired Professor of *The Herald* Chair of Fine Arts at the University of Melbourne.

With its brilliant collections and stunning international exhibitions, the National Gallery, at the gateway to Melbourne, quickly earned its reputation of being one of the world's great art galleries, and Elisabeth was a key figure in moves to keep the gallery abreast of world trends, while preserving its heritage of fine Australian art. Sir Andrew Grimwade replaced Dick Seddon, and Elisabeth remembers Andrew as: 'a very active and effective chairman. Today I am still treated very nicely at the National Gallery – as I am at the Children's Hospital. I still get invitations from them both, but now I've got a lot of other irons in the fire,' Elisabeth can say at eighty-five.

As her hospital days had become her gallery days, Elisabeth continued to look after her mother, who now required constant nursing. Bairnie, whose mind remained alert and sharp, insisted on being given her daily baths, a task that Elisabeth found increasingly difficult, but somehow she managed and, with a wonderful nurse, continued to go to her mother's room through the night and take her an early morning cup of tea. Bairnie never saw the Children's Hospital or visited the new National Gallery, but she delighted in being wheeled out into the sun at Cruden Farm whenever Elisabeth found time to do some gardening.

At the same time, Elisabeth was convenor of the garden committee at Como, a grand Victorian mansion in Melbourne preserved by the National Trust, and a member of the Maud Gibson Trust. Elisabeth says she was very pleased and honoured to be invited to become a member of this trust established in recognition of wonderful help that Maud Gibson had given to Melbourne's Royal Botanic Gardens and the National Herbarium.

Maud Gibson, 'The Quiet Philanthropist', who died in Switzerland in 1970, was the daughter of William Gibson, a partner in the the giant Foy and Gibson retail store and knitting mills company. Believing that her family had greatly benefited from its close association with the Melbourne community, Miss Gibson set aside 20,000 shares in the very profitable family company to establish a trust to help the work of her beloved Botanic Gardens.

The administration of this trust was left in the hands of Maud's nephew, Peter Howson, later a Federal MP, and a committee was formed which included the Director of the Botanic Gardens and Professors of Botany and Agriculture at the University of Melbourne, and 'three other persons selected for their interest in landscape gardening or in plants and trees'. Anxious to establish an outlying botanic garden dedicated to Australian native trees, shrubs and plants, the committee soon had its eye on the Langwarrin Reserve, a stretch of native bushland adjoining Cruden Farm. This land had been set aside by the Commonwealth Government in the First World War as a camp and nursing station for returning diggers suffering from VD and other then incurable ailments.

It still belonged to the Defence Department and, as it was believed that Elisabeth might have some influence with Premier Bolte, she was invited to try and persuade him to secure the land as a site for the planned Maud Gibson Garden. But this time the Federal Government would not let the valuable, but no longer used, land go, so the committee had to look elsewhere. Meanwhile the committee helped the cause of horticulture in Melbourne in many ways, publishing books which went on sale as textbooks for university students and establishing a research committee.

At this stage, Miss Gibson gave another £10,000 to aid Melbourne's National Herbarium, then in grave danger of losing its priceless collection of botanical specimens, because of deterioration and lack of funds. Soon after this, the persistent members of the committee, aided by the redoubtable Henry Bolte, secured 450 acres of wonderful bushland, also owned by the Commonwealth, at Cranbourne. 'He paid the Federal Government something like £30,000 for the land and gave it to the Botanic Gardens for a native plant annex. He also gave us £5000 to fence the land but said: "Don't come near me for any more money for at least five years,"' Elisabeth recalls.

'Not enough is known about the work of Maud Gibson,' Elisabeth says. 'She established a chair of Otolaryngology at the Eye and Ear Hospital and her trust fund helped us acquire this wonderful land.' At first there weren't even enough funds for a resident ranger and trailbikes roared through the beautiful virgin bushland every weekend but today, after gradually buying adjacent land, the garden is gaining a reputation as one of the finest areas dedicated to native vegetation in Australia. Elisabeth and her committee members raised money and personally guaranteed loans which gave the gardens added financial stability. 'We also had to lobby the State Government many times to give us bridging finance. It was a very long, hard and dedicated operation,' Elisabeth says.

Elisabeth was on the Maud Gibson Garden committee for twenty-seven years before she thought it was time to retire. Today, the garden is flourishing, with permanent staff and a network of roads and paths. The intense planting programme bringing Australian plants from every state into one beautiful area continues, and a watchtower has been erected on the highest point. 'It will be a great garden of

Australiana, and is already open to visitors and attracting tourists from all over the world,' says Elisabeth.

Elisabeth's activities, including the presidency of Melbourne's Alexandra Club for two years in 1968 and 1970, all required a great number of appearances in town. 'One might perhaps put too much importance on one's attendance, but if you are filling a position I think you really ought to be there,' says Elisabeth, who at that time was often making two trips a day between the city and Cruden Farm. 'I was very fortunate in these consuming interests and constant activities because they've been very interesting ones but it hasn't left a great deal of time for me to enjoy too much leisure. I'm very lucky I go occasionally to the opera and the ballet but I used to go a great deal to orchestral concerts and loved anything to do with music.

'But you can't do it all so you have to get your priorities right and be grateful for the interesting things you can do,' says Elisabeth, whose collection of crowded little red leather diaries is a source of constant amazement to her family and friends. 'There are so many interesting things going on. I'm a Fellow of the local chapter of the Royal Society of the Arts and they have dinners with interesting speakers about four times a year,' says Elisabeth, who is also Patron and constant supporter of the Victoria State Opera.

CHAPTER TWENTY-THREE

Vintage Years

IF THE SIXTIES had been a happy decade of dedicated hard work and, at times, severe stress for Elisabeth, the seventies were to be, if anything, even more rewarding as she paid attention to achieving some of the personal goals she had long cherished. A portrait by the acclaimed Australian artist Judy Cassab painted in 1970 and now hanging in Rupert's home high above Beverly Hills and the Los Angeles smog, shows her as a relaxed and contented sixty-one-year-old.

Although only forty-three when widowed, Elisabeth says that she never thought about remarriage – however, the possibility was thoughtfully allowed for in Keith's comprehensive will when he wrote: 'I declare it is no wish of mine that my wife should not remarry.' With close and distinguished male and female friends around the world, Elisabeth's busy life was dedicated to her family, her garden and the overwhelming list of charities, institutions and causes she supported – and still supports – financially and in person.

In 1970, spurred by the fact that her grandson, James Calvert-Jones, had been born with impaired hearing as a result of rubella, Elisabeth became Vice-President of the Advisory Council for Children with Impaired Hearing. Janet had been a powerful force behind the establishment of the council with much help and advice from Mrs Nancy John, Mrs Whitney King and Mrs Frances Derham.

With Elisabeth's continuing financial and personal support, Janet Calvert-Jones, now the dedicated hands-on Chairman of the Herald and Weekly Times in Melbourne, had been the moving force behind the establishment of Taralye, an early intervention pre-school centre in Melbourne which has earned worldwide acclaim for its work providing early help for young children with hearing difficulties as well as advanced research into the problem and back-up for the children and their families.

But in the early seventies, after years of climbing to dizzy heights in trees, Elisabeth had a fall while pruning and gashed her leg badly enough to accept the advice that she really did need a holiday. Leaving Bairnie in the hands of the nurses who would tend to her needs around the clock, Elisabeth followed the Kantors' advice and set off again with her friend Tina Wentcher, then in her late seventies, for a short and adventurous holiday on the French Pacific islands of New Caledonia.

Back home, plans were under way which would lead to a project which continues to be one of Elisabeth's joys in life. When a near-neighbour of the Murdochs, Annie McClelland, died, she had left a will directing her trustees to build an art gallery and craft workshops that would involve the local community on her forty-acre property, less than a mile from Cruden Farm. The new gallery was to be built in memory of her brother, Harry.

Looking around for someone to head a committee, the trustees chose Elisabeth's friend and neighbour, Daryl Lindsay, artist and director of the National Gallery of Victoria from 1942 until 1955, who set about selecting an art advisory board. He invited Elisabeth, a current trustee of the National Gallery of Victoria, to be a member. Carl Andrew, a budding curator with overseas experience, was appointed the first director. 'He was very artistic and gifted but maybe not always sternly practical when it came to calculating what it cost to put on really good exhibitions. But he had great taste and distinct flair for mounting interesting and notable exhibitions,' was Elisabeth's assessment of the man she was to work with for some years.

The McClelland Gallery became an enduring interest for Dame Elisabeth, whose generosity and sound judgment has made it one of the most admired regional art galleries in Australia today. Before Elisabeth joined the Art Advisory Board at the McClelland, the founding trustees, Mr and Mrs Jim Graham and Mr William Harrison, had done a wonderful job in carrying out Miss McClelland's wishes, she recalls. But something had to be done about the size of the property which was impossible to maintain. Half the area covered in thick bush was offered to the local Cranbourne Council while the board waited for the bequest capital to grow through interest until there was sufficient money to have plans drawn up. Soil samples were even sent to London so that the carpet maker could provide a good, tough, hard-wearing floor covering of complementary colour. It is still in place and looking good today.

Before the new gallery building was completed, a development committee was formed with teams of local people helping to establish the grounds. 'They were marvellous. There were working bees every weekend.' But it soon became apparent that there would not be enough financial support from the McClelland estate for the fledgling gallery to carry on. So, knowing that the gallery was twenty-five miles from Melbourne, just a fraction inside the limit placed on government funding for regional galleries, the trustees applied to the Ministry for the Arts and were granted classification as a regional gallery. They received a small government grant which, Elisabeth points out, barely pays the salaries of the director and curator.

'We now have a little money to spend on acquisitions. There are one or two valuable bequests and we are very good housekeepers – although maintenance is difficult,' says Elisabeth, who was later appointed a Trustee of the Gallery and, following Sir William Dargie, Chairman of Trustees from 1980 until her 'retirement' in 1991 when she was succeeded by Lenton Parr. Friends of the delightful Australian gallery among the gum trees, which is in constant use for exhibitions, music recitals and other functions, point to the courtyards and other improvements that Elisabeth has funded over the years, including the Elisabeth Murdoch Sculpture Foundation.

Without ever seeing the gallery, Bairnie died peacefully in February, 1971, at the age of ninety-two. 'Mother had resented having to give up living at Pemberley and for a long time she was difficult to manage. She was such a stong-minded woman and it was not easy for us, although over the eight years she spent with us it was really a joy to be able to make her life as comfortable and bearable as possible. Gradually she became entirely dependent on us and it was hard for her to talk – but she "spoke" beautifully with her eyes and I understood perfectly what she was trying to say,' Elisabeth says. 'The grandchildren came often to see her and she loved their visits, and at one stage my sister Marie came out to look after her while I had a short break.'

When it had become obvious that her mother could never return to Pemberley, Elisabeth had reluctantly decided that the family home would have to be sold. Rupert had objected, but as Elisabeth says now: 'I know that it would have brought millions today but Marie, whose husband Vice-Admiral John Durnford had died in 1967 after serving a term as Mayor of London's Chelsea, needed money and this was our way of ensuring it.' With Bairnie's death, the old adopted family Christian name of de Lancey ceased to exist in the Australian branches of the family, although it is proudly carried on in Britain and France.

Finding she now had more time, Elisabeth plunged into new pursuits. 'I helped to get the Noah's Ark Toy Library going. I was an original founding trustee with two doctors. We started off to help parents with handicapped children who constantly wrecked their toys and had a miserable time. Over the years, two remarkable women, Annetine Forell and Nancy Glue, organised a band of devoted helpers both professional and voluntary.

'Toys help with play therapy for children. The library started in a small way in a tiny cottage in the back streets of Prahran, a Melbourne inner suburb, and before long larger premises were needed and a house in The Avenue in Windsor was found and from there they went out all over the state. Now there is a travelling library and over the years they have experimented with the design of special toys that are hard to destroy.

'We were helped a lot originally by private funding and I took a keen interest in it. I am still a regular subscriber and they do splendid work. I think anything to do with helping parents with handicapped children is so worthwhile because they have such a terrible, demanding life and you can't help feeling thankful that you didn't have to cope with that yourself,' says Elisabeth, who later became Patron of the library.

Then there was her interest in SPELD, the organisation that helped children with early learning difficulties. But for the first half of the 1970s, the two galleries were Elisabeth's consuming interest. In 1976, she stepped down as a Trustee of the National Gallery of Victoria and was immediately honoured with the rare appointment of Emeritus Trustee. Her interest in the gallery and the great Arts Centre complex of which it is now part, has never waned, especially as on her retirement Elisabeth was asked to form a Friends of the Gallery Art Library. 'I headed this up for ten years with tremendous help from Lady Coates and a splendid supporting committee,' she says. At about the same time, the popularity and influence of the McClelland Gallery was growing and Elisabeth was now Chairman of its Arts Advisory Board.

At an age when even the most public spirited of philanthropists would have been slowing down, Elisabeth Murdoch was at the height of her extraordinary power and influence in the community. People needing support for a variety of good works all over Australia were constantly seeking Elisabeth's financial assistance and know-how and, as tough and discerning as she could be, Elisabeth always provided a sympathetic ear.

In 1975, Australia was facing a constitutional crisis when the Governor-General, Sir John Kerr, found it necessary to sack the Whitlam Labor Government and appoint Malcolm Fraser as caretaker Prime Minister until a general election could be held – an election which Fraser's Liberals subsequently won by a landslide.

Accepting that what they believed was Kerr's constitutionally correct action had left deep divisions in the community, Fraser and his ministers began looking for a replacement Governor-General soon after Kerr had sworn them in. As Tony Staley, a former Fraser minister who was appointed President of the Liberal Party in August, 1993, recalls, a front runner in the list of candidates for the post of Governor-General was Elisabeth Murdoch.

As Staley reveals – and Malcolm Fraser confirms – the Fraser Cabinet agreed that Elisabeth would have the standing in the community and the qualifications and ability to be an excellent Governor-General at a critical time in Australia's history. This was a time for healing and uniting a divided nation and Elisabeth, as Australia's first woman Governor-General, could have been the one to do it, Fraser and his ministers argued. No immediate decision was taken but eventually, after much discussion, it was decided that Elisabeth could not be put forward to the Queen as the Fraser Government's choice for Governor-General. Tony Staley says: 'Although Dame Elisabeth would have been ideal for the job, we considered and decided that it would be impossible to make the mother of Rupert Murdoch, the powerful media tycoon, Governor-General.'

Despite the stature of the sources of these revelations, Elisabeth is today totally incredulous when told that the point was almost reached when she was to be approached to see if she would accept Australia's highest office. 'What a ridiculous story. It was never mentioned to me at the time,' Elisabeth says angrily. 'I am astounded. How could anyone be so irresponsible? How could anyone even suggest I should be Governor-General of Australia?

'The post of Governor-General is very important, requiring the sort of intelligence, education and experience that I haven't got. If that had been publicly suggested, there would have been an outcry suggesting that it was a purely political thing,' says Elisabeth. 'Could you imagine anyone in their right minds saying that it could be? Certainly there was no official approach and I would have been aghast if there had been. Never in a million years would I have said "Yes".

'You see, I'm ashamed when they invite me to be included in *Who's Who* and ask me to write down my academic degrees and qualifications and I can write down nothing except "home duties"! Really, I like to think that the position of Governor-General is very special to this nation and I cannot believe that they would have offered it to me,' says Elisabeth firmly.

However, despite Elisabeth's protests, there are still those on both sides of the Australian political fence who think that Elisabeth Murdoch, AC, DBE, and mother of Rupert Murdoch, would have made a wonderful Governor-General of Australia. But there were, and still are, many other interests in the life of Elisabeth Murdoch.

CHAPTER TWENTY-FOUR

A Rich Tapestry

IN ALL THE WORLD there are now just six tapestry workshops, and connoisseurs agree that Australia has one of the most notable, thanks largely to the skill and dedication of Sue Walker, Director of the Victorian Tapestry Workshop, and the men and women of Melbourne who support her.

Elisabeth was in at the beginning as a member of the Victorian Tapestry Workshop Interim Committee, which researched the workshop's viability in 1973, and she succeeded Lady Delacombe as Chairman of the Committee in 1975. She says today: 'Really, our tapestry workshop is the only one which is really weaving in an interpretive modern way which is still traditional. I think it's amazing what they achieve because they do seem to bring the pictures to life and capture extra dimension. That is so clever.

'The whole idea for the possibility and desirability of establishing the Victorian Tapestry Workshop came from Lady Delacombe, wife of the Victorian Governor, Sir Rohan Delacombe. In 1971, they were resident in Government House just across the King's Domain from the National Gallery of Victoria, and when she had free time in the mornings, Lady Delacombe used to walk across and enjoy the gallery.

'At that time, we had a beautiful exhibition of eighteenth-century French tapestries which were on loan from the Musée de Beaux Arts in Paris and they did so much for the rather austere walls of the Great Hall. I think the first time she mentioned it to anyone was to myself and Marion Fletcher who was in charge of costumes and textiles at the gallery. I was still a trustee and I remember Lady Delacombe saying: "Elisabeth, it seems such a shame that we can't have our own tapestries woven. Australian artists Arthur Boyd, John Coburn and others take their work overseas to Portugal, England, France and Japan to have them woven there. It would be wonderful if we could start a tapestry industry in Victoria and we could weave their designs here."

'It was a very simplistic point of view because I don't think any of us realised what conventional, traditional tapestry meant in the way of equipment and skilled people to carry out the work,' recalls Elisabeth. 'Lady Delacombe then spoke to Eric Westbrook, who was just relinquishing the directorship of the gallery and moving to the Ministry for the Arts as its Director. She told him she would like to get a committee going at Government House to discuss the idea.

'He was enthusiastic so she asked about eight people including Marion Fletcher, Baillieu Myer, Peter Rankin, the then Professor of Architecture at the University of Melbourne Professor Robertson, the Premier's wife April Hamer, and her very efficient private secretary Patricia Fisher, and myself.

'We had these little meetings at ten o'clock over morning coffee which was served by the butler out of silver coffee pots and, as is often the way when silver pots are used, the coffee was never very hot! But we had such interesting discussions and as our ideas developed it was decided that we should have a feasibility study made. To do this, it would be necessary to send someone abroad and, of course, this would require money,' says Elisabeth.

'We were very fortunate to be promised a Government grant of $15,000 and it was decided that the best way to find the most suitable person was to invite half a dozen to apply. When the applicants were being considered, I was in England. I was rather thankful to be away when these people were being interviewed because John Blanch, the successful applicant, had worked for Keith at *The Herald* and I would have been biased in his favour. John was also an honorary aide-de-camp to the Delacombes and all of us knew him to be a splendid character and he was chosen to go abroad and carry out a feasibility study, which he did extremely well.

'Lady Delacombe wanted John to go to Edinburgh where there was a smallish workshop called the Dovecote Studio where she had met two or three weavers who she thought might like to migrate to Australia if our scheme developed. The Director of Dovecote Studio was Archie Brennan, a very talented man who had developed this very successful workshop. He was very enthusiastic about the possiblity of establishing the tapestry industry in Australia as he was about to come out as a visiting artist and weaver in residence at the Australian National University. He gave John a lot of information and was very useful.

'John Blanch visited workshops in Portugal, France and England and made a very thorough study of tapestry and its production and then returned to make his report to our committee. We were delighted with the prospect of proceeding to achieve what had now become, we believed, a viable undertaking, but we had to build up a convincing case to ensure ongoing interest and support from the Government.

'We had to start modestly and we had to find a pool of weavers.

What we finally did was suggest to the ANU that if we paid half of Archie Brennan's fare, could we call on his services on weekends. He was happy to come down to Melbourne and gave us lots of advice.

'A gifted graduate from his Dovecote Studio, Belinda Ramson, was at the ANU and we were able to arrange with her to conduct courses in the traditional form of weaving. Such was the interest that ninety-two applied but, alas, only twenty-four could be fitted into the programme.

'Archie Brennan gave two illustrated lectures. We asked architects, artists, and anyone interested to hear him talk so that we might get them involved. The Arts Centre was being built and after Archie's second lecture I received a very encouraging note from Roy Grounds saying: "Get going girl, I'll commission six tapestries for the new Arts Centre."

'Then we had to find premises. John Blanch did an exhaustive tour in and around Melbourne looking for a building that was high enough, had good light and was accessible to public transport. This took a long time and it was almost two years before the Housing Commission would lease us a suitable building in Park Street, South Melbourne. By this time, the Delacombes had gone back to England and before leaving, Lady Delacombe said: "Elisabeth, you will have to take this on." The committee was very supportive. We carried on very happily although we missed her very much indeed.

'We used to meet in the Premier's office and dear April was a great help. She was, of course, very discreet and correct but her support was very helpful and I believe she nurtured her husband's interest in our project.

'So now with a pool of trained weavers and a building assured, we were able to go to the Premier just before Christmas, 1975, with a commonsense submission. Bails Myer and Peter Rankin were magnificently supportive and to our great joy Dick Hamer agreed to let us go ahead, providing financial support from the Ministry for the Arts who appointed ten members to the board.

'Now it was our job to appoint a chairman and Lenton Parr, the noted sculptor and outstanding administrator as founding Director of the Victorian College of the Arts, was unanimously elected. How fortunate we were that we had him to lead us on. The next move was to find a director and there was one whose submission was outstanding. She was Sue Walker, who has been a brilliant leader and is largely responsible for the great success of the Victorian Tapestry Workshop.

'Our headquarters had been a rather dilapidated but glorious old Victorian glove factory before we moved in to do it up. We had been given funds to renovate the wonderful old building and had to wait a little while for renovations to be carried out. We started with three weavers, the senior and most gifted being Merrill Dumbrell. They got their supplies in, and their looms, and we started. When the first tapestry, a design by Alun Leach-Jones, was completed, a marvellous stroke of luck came our way.

'We received a letter from an artist who had won a design competition for three tapestries in a new cultural centre in Saskatchewan in Canada. He was seeking estimates from tapestry workshops for his designs to be woven and he wanted us to submit samples of our work to see if we could interpret to his satisfaction. This was an enormous challenge and it was wonderful for an emerging Australian industry to have this opportunity.

'The weavers got to work, and we sent the woven samples and, with some temerity, the estimates for the work, and we won the commission from rivals all over the world. It was a very significant win for us because when the tapestries were completed they were such splendid promotional material they showed people here and around the world what we could do.

'Gradually more commissions came. The weavers were developing wonderful skills in understanding and interpreting the designs and we were helped and encouraged by the corporations and private patrons of the Arts who commissioned tapestries, as well as various universities and museums. Our tapestries are not just copies or duplication of works of art. There is often so much more depth in a tapestry than in a design and our weavers are respected very highly by artists for their interpretation.

'We are tremendously proud of what our weavers have achieved. The whole enterprise is one of the successes of artistic endeavour in Australia. No tapestry workshop can ever break even. The weavers earn their salaries and sometimes a margin but no tapestry workshop in the world can exist without subsidy.

'Rupert has an attitude, which I think is wrong, in that he doesn't understand the industry and its history throughout the ages,' says Elisabeth. 'He doesn't believe that it should be subsidised by government. If he knew a little more about it, he would know that no tapestry workshop in the world has ever been able to completely pay its way because the work is so very demanding and time consuming. It is impossible to be able to earn enough from the tapestries themselves to cover the overhead of the administration as well as the weavers' salaries.

'Compared with the French Tapestry Workshop, our subsidy is slight. In France, the workshops are considered national assets and are worthy of substantial assistance. I believe it will never be possible to produce the finest tapestries unless there is some sort of assistance. In spite of Rupert's opinion, he and Anna are full of admiration for our work and have commissioned several beautiful tapestries.'

Among the stunning tapestries undertaken by the workshop is

the wonderful work now hanging in Parliament House, Canberra and other tapestries in the National Gallery of Victoria and the Arts Centre. Then there is the finely detailed woven aerial map of the Melbourne suburb of Ivanhoe – with the clarity of a satellite spy camera shot – now hanging behind the altar of the Ivanhoe Grammar School chapel.

Tapestries hanging in the World Trade Centre in Melbourne appear to be enlarged photographs of old dockyard scenes until closer inspection reveals the myriad of woven stitches. Banks, galleries and business enterprises have commissioned large tapestries which are used to brighten and cover walls rather as they were used in cold medieval castles. And from all over the world, artists have commissioned the Victorian Tapestry Workshop to bring their designs and paintings to life.

CHAPTER TWENTY-FIVE

Well-Used Opportunities

JUST AS the Fairfax family's alarm bells had failed to sound when Rupert was allowed to purchase the tabloid *Mirror* in Sydney, Fleet Street was content to be mildly amused when he bought first the *News of the World* and then the London Daily Mirror group's ailing tabloid *Sun*. Yet today most of Rupert Murdoch's growing band of biographers agree that his bold entry into Fleet Street was the real launching pad for the extraordinary development of his media empire.

In Britain, they called him 'The Dirty Digger' – because of his use of circulation-boosting topless page three 'birds' – and hooted with rage when he eventually took over the moribund *Times*. But then, and through the tough days which followed as he took on the Luddite British print unions and won, Rupert always kept his mother informed of his plans, his hopes, triumphs – and reverses.

While never doubting and seldom complaining, Elisabeth did share a moment of sympathy with her old friend Una Fraser, mother of Malcolm, then the embattled Prime Minister of Australia. 'The newspapers write such terrible, untrue things about Malcolm,' complained Una Fraser. 'I know, dear, they do that with Rupert too,' replied Elisabeth soothingly.

By the 1970s, Rupert's sights were firmly set on the US and soon he told Elisabeth that he was bringing a party of prominent American bankers to Australia to show them the growing News Limited operations. While in Melbourne, Rupert told his mother, he would like to bring the party 'home to dinner'. But while driving home to Cruden Farm on the afternoon her guests were due, Elisabeth was dazzled by the sun and drove into the path of a taxi truck crossing an intersection near the Melbourne office of *The Australian*.

Startled reporters ran into the office saying that Dame Elisabeth's Peugeot, with its VIC 12 numberplate, was damaged, a truck was on its side and an ambulance had just rushed her off to the Royal Melbourne Hospital. Rupert, who was nearby visiting his father's old colleague, Sir John Williams, was first to arrive in the casualty department and by that time Elisabeth was sitting on a trolley as a doctor inserted stitches in a bleeding head wound. 'Oh, please hurry,' Elisabeth was heard to say. 'I have to get home and serve dinner for twenty guests.'

On the previous day, Elisabeth had been named 'Woman of the Year' by the Australian Quota Club for her work aiding research into deafness. It had been a busy week with Rupert in town. But until 11 p.m. that night, the injured Elisabeth was the life and soul of the party around the long oak refectory table as her daughters watched anxiously. Then, when blood began seeping through the silk scarf she had tied over her head, Janet finally successfully insisted that her mother was going to bed.

Now, despite his growing interests overseas, Rupert was still hoping to spend more time in Australia. Ignoring his own less than happy time at Geelong Grammar, he had put down the names of his children as boarders and Elisabeth was looking forward to having Rupert and his family back home.

In 1978, at the height of a disastrous and long-running drought, Rupert made a move that would have delighted his father. He bought the vast historic Boonoke sheep station in the Riverina for $A3.5 million dollars. In what Elisabeth describes gleefully as 'Murdoch's luck', the rains came to break the drought soon after the purchase and the price of wool moved up, with the first season's wool clip helping to meet the purchase price. Today, it is worth far in excess of the price Rupert paid.

Elisabeth has made a number of visits to Boonoke since News Limited took over and has suggested changes to the Boonoke gardens and approved of the renovation of the stately colonial homestead. 'I was so pleased when Rupert and the family bought Boonoke because I was always keen on the country and the wool industry. People were faltering in their faith in the wool industry and Rupert's decision to buy did give it a boost. Boonoke was so well known, as were the Falkiners who had owned it.

'My interest was increased by the fact that my father had been involved in the wool industry for so long. Dad was instrumental in helping many people buy their properties, and he had a lot of friends on the land. So when the rains came we were very thrilled – not only thrilled for our sakes but for all the splendid people who worked there. They deserved a break after that long drought,' Elisabeth says.

'I really love that country, and we are very fortunate because the homestead is so beautifully watered by Billabong Creek. I love those endless plains, going right away, over the edge of the world. To me that is the real Australia. Boonoke has the typical rural image I have of the whole country. Really marvellous.'

Recalling the happy family visits to Wantabadgery with Keith,

Elisabeth delights in visiting Cavan when Rupert and his family spend rare holidays there. Rupert still makes flying visits to Boonoke with overseas guests but really regards Cavan, his property among the hills that overlook the meandering course of the Murrumbidgee River an hour's drive from Canberra, as his Australian retreat.

By now, Elisabeth knew her son did have designs on the stagnating Herald and Weekly Times Group which included radio and TV outlets as well as newspapers, but she also knew that Rupert never let sentiment influence sound business moves. As it turned out, Rupert did bid for the group in 1979, but made a strategic withdrawal taking a big sharemarket profit and leaving the H&WT more vulnerable than ever.

Reporters attending a press conference with *Herald* executives announcing Rupert's 'defeat', found installed in the panelled room an elderly black and white TV set and a wireless set – with valves – a fair indication of the state of the company that would soon fall to Rupert. Elisabeth was disappointed that Keith's *Herald* had not returned to family control, but happy to bide her time until Rupert decided to move again.

Meanwhile, Dame Elisabeth decided to move ahead with a long-cherished plan to initiate a Chair of Landscape Architecture for the University of Melbourne. 'It started because a few of my friends whom I admired very much were very interested in the formation of such a chair, and the person at the core of it was the very gifted, attractive and accomplished George Seddon,' Elisabeth says. 'He was the Director of the Centre for Environmental Planning and he was intent on getting such a project going in Melbourne. I began by helping with the fundraising and the family put in the remaining half, or quarter, or whatever it was,' Elisabeth says, with a dismissive wave of her hands.

Announcing the endowment of the new chair, the Dean of the

Faculty of Architecture and Planning at the University of Melbourne, Professor Seddon, said that Cruden Farm was a good example of how farming techniques could be used to conserve and enhance the natural landscape. 'Landscape architecture is a profession with at least one hundred years of history, and is highly developed in all countries but Australia, which is rather late on the scene,' Professor Seddon said.

Elisabeth recalls: 'Then the university had to advertise throughout the world for a first-class landscape architect and what we had to offer was chickenfeed. When we looked, there were thirty-eight chairs of landscape architecture in the USA alone. Finally the university in its wisdom elected an American, Michael McCarthy. Certainly, he had great gifts and they thought a lot of him. He was there for five years, and did a lot of good work – including help with the restoration of Mount Macedon and its historic gardens after the Ash Wednesday bushfires swept through in 1983, just as he was coming to the end of his five-year term.

'Then he was offered a post at the University of Texas where he would be the head dean of six different faculties and his yearly budget would be six million dollars. So where do you get a replacement? The biggest people would not look at the sort of fees the University of Melbourne could pay and the only person they really thought could fit the bill was David Yencken who, though very talented, was not a landscape architect. However, he had a lot of experience in government departments and environmental planning, so eventually he was elected.

'The university is very courteous in keeping me informed with what is going on in the department. The Australian Institute of Landscape Architecture made me an Honorary Fellow. When I can get along to something I go but I can't very often. In my eighties, I think it's lovely to be remembered and occasionally go to meetings but you can't always be part of the furniture. David Yencken has always tried to keep in touch and try and involve me in things, which is nice,' says Elisabeth whose contribution to the Australian landscape goes far beyond the university chair named in her honour.

'I've been very lucky, very very fortunate with my family and with my life. You might call it a well-used opportunity. Our opportunities are really gifts, and if one is able to make the greatest use of those gifts, then the path is always easier,' says Elisabeth Murdoch.

CHAPTER TWENTY-SIX

Cap and Gown

IN 1982, the University of Melbourne paid Elisabeth a rare honour when it conferred on her the Degree of Doctor of Laws – *honoris causa* – an honorary degree. Elisabeth was somewhat amazed on learning that the university she had never attended but with whom she had been closely involved over the years had decided that the honour was due to her: 'as a person distinguished by eminent public service'.

'I didn't know how these things worked. I was so non-academic and thought it rather peculiar but I realised later that it was awarded for things done for the community so finally I said "Yes". Then the Vice-Chancellor, David Derham, asked me to give an oration and I didn't really fully know what that meant either,' laughs Elisabeth. 'I thought about it a long time and believed that I would just have to talk to students and their parents, you see, so I really worked on my speech. I worked like mad and every night and early every morning trying to get something into shape. Finally, about ten days before the date I had been given I felt it was as good as it could ever be.

'I went to see somebody who was dying down here in the local hospital and when I got back, I was feeling very drained and I thought I'd get myself a cup of tea in my little teapot. Well, I had a darling dog the Kantors had passed on, their lovely old airedale, who was the colour of the rugs and, after making the tea, I was bringing it along the passage on a tray and the next thing I knew I had tripped over the dog and boiling, literally boiling, tea went all over my wrist. I was lucky the car was at the door because I had just come in, and I was able to get into the car and go straight across to the doctor. It was a very painful burn, and it was just ten days before that oration, but the great piece of luck was that I had done my speech. But it was ghastly – it couldn't have happened at a worse time.'

Then the full meaning of what she was about to undergo – all the pomp and circumstance of a university graduation ceremony – was brought home to Elisabeth by Margaret Blackwood, the Chairman of the Council of Janet Clarke Hall. A few days before the event, Margaret Blackwood asked Elisabeth if she would like to come and practise her speech in the university's great Wilson Hall: 'She told me the sound was difficult and offered to stand at the back of the hall and tell me if I could be heard. I could, and that did inspire me with a little confidence, but I knew then that I would be addressing a hall packed with professors, doctors and all the other academics, as well as graduates and their parents,' Elisabeth recalls. 'Of course, I knew too that I would have to read my speech although I had been trying to memorise it until then.

'So the day came and my arm was still bandaged up and painful and it really was a terrific challenge. I suppose I had to tell myself that I couldn't afford the self-indulgence of being silly and nervous and just had to remember that if this was to be a great ordeal, I had to meet it. You felt you had to be worthy of the occasion...

'I didn't have a cap or gown so I was given the ones the Queen Mother had worn, and left behind, when they conferred a degree on her some years previously. Anyway, it came to my turn and the Chancellor, Professor Roy Wright, presented the degree and then I had to get up and get on with it... Somehow it went down well and I was absolutely thrilled when they gave me a standing ovation. I suppose they were sorry for the poor creature who was doing it. I wasn't pompous or prudish, but it was one of the hurdles in life I got over with great relief. It was quite a formidable occasion for me.'

In fact, the oration Elisabeth gave on 31 July 1982 was, many people who were there agree, memorable. Wilson Hall was on her side from the moment she began: 'Knowing very little of the mysteries of how university councils honour non-academics, the idea that I should ever reach the dizzy heights to which you, Mr Chancellor, have today elevated me would never have entered my mind...' said Elisabeth, a tiny figure at the rostrum in the great hall wearing her floppy academic cap and gown with the gold brooch presented to her by the Royal Children's Hospital Committee of Management and senior medical staff pinned to her dress.

Elisabeth's favourite gold brooch bears the RCH's pelican emblem floating on a sea of tiny diamonds; a pelican, Elisabeth explains, because they are the symbols of mother love, charity and self sacrifice, who, according to legend, tore their breasts to feed their young with their own blood when food was scarce: 'Very appropriate for the Royal Children's Hospital.'

But on the Wilson Hall stage Elisabeth continued: 'To be sharing in this ceremony with you, the graduates, who have really earned your academic distinctions, is a great honour. This is a very special day for you, your parents, families and friends, the atmosphere in this famous Wilson Hall, charged as it is with pride and affection on this great occasion of celebration, is uplifting and reassuring.

'In congratulating you, I have the sincerest admiration for your strength of purpose and intellectual ability, and rejoice for you in your achievement. To receive your tertiary education at this great university must be a happy experience, and a considerable privilege which, of course, brings its obligations.

'As students, you have, no doubt, met those obligations by your involvement in the life of your campus, and whatever course your life now takes, you will have a special feeling for your alma mater and will, I am sure, want to show your appreciation and loyalty by keeping in touch and supporting her in every way possible ...'

Dame Elisabeth ended her speech on an inspirational note: 'In my experience, if you expect the best from your fellow men, more often than not you get it because your trust and faith prime them with that extra steam needed to generate their best performance – I've received a lot of that sort of steam myself. It is very helpful and I truly believe in its value as I do in the value of family life in which loving understanding, intelligent discipline, mutual respect and loyalty give so much strength to its members and to a community.

'We have very much to admire and be thankful for in our society, but we also have some serious defects and difficult issues. If we are to do anything about them – and we must – we will have to stand up and be counted, and try to tackle them constructively, at the same time endeavouring to build on all that is good in our nation. Good, the more communicated, more abundant grows ...

'To you Mr Chancellor, my academic friends and sponsors, I extend my profound gratitude for the generosity of spirit which prompted you and your colleagues to confer on me this truly wonderful honour,' said Elisabeth as the students and academics rose in their gowns and colours to applaud.

Looking back to that great day in her life, Elisabeth says: 'I never had much to do with academic circles although I have since made a lot of friends at the University of Melbourne. I enjoy very much just a sniff of academia. They are very interesting people. It was quite a revelation to me. And my oration went down well and I was, of course, absolutely thrilled.'

CHAPTER TWENTY-SEVEN

The Murdoch Institute

IT WAS at the glittering dinner in the Great Hall of the National Gallery of Victoria that Jim Leslie issued his invitation to Elisabeth Murdoch. Mr Leslie, as Chairman of Australia's Qantas Airways, was co-sponsor with *The Australian* of a stunning exhibition of the works of Picasso. Beneath the towering vases of Australian native flowers, Elisabeth and Jim were having dinner when he asked her if she would care to join the official Australian party on a pioneering Qantas flight to China.

Today Jim Leslie, now the Chancellor of Deakin University, explains that while observing airline protocol, the Chinese had said that they would be including 'an ancient widow' in their reciprocal official party and asked if the Australians had a similar candidate. 'I didn't tell Dame Elisabeth that when I asked her if she would like to join us,' chuckles Jim Leslie.

As it was, the Chinese widow was forced to withdraw because of her advanced age and the Leslies have an album of official Chinese photographs showing Elisabeth striding out with Alison Leslie in front of officials on a hot trek over the Great Wall of China, smiling out of official group photographs and joyfully surrounded by Chinese schoolchildren. The Chinese were amazed at the energy and enthusiam of our 'ancient widow', laughs Jim Leslie.

While revelling in the Picasso exhibition and her trip to China, Elisabeth had another preoccupation in 1984 – the Murdoch Institute for Research into Birth Defects. Elisabeth says today: 'I don't know really whose idea and resolve it was to approach me to find the money for the Murdoch Institute. Patsy (Dame Patricia Mackinnon) first came up with the proposition to me but it was so big that I said I really couldn't approach Rupert about it . . . it was just so colossal.

'Then my daughter, Helen, who is so wise, said: "Mum, don't you turn that down out of hand. Give Rupert the opportunity. Let him look at it, there's no harm done." I could easily have said: "It's much too much for us . . . love to do it but haven't got the wherewithal." I certainly didn't have it. But then I did go to work on Rupert . . . that's how it happened really. It was the whole family, but we didn't have a family meeting. Rupert decided and they all agreed. They knew it was my one great ambition.'

The family contribution to Elisabeth's ambition was an initial $A5 million towards a targeted $A10 million. The Murdoch gift was one of the largest private family contributions to research in Australia's medical history. And on the day the new research institute was unveiled, Professor Danks was able to announce that a further $A1 million had been donated by Sir Jack Brockhoff, with further funds from the Brockhoff Foundation being channelled into the Jack Brockhoff Laboratories within the Murdoch Institute.

Professor Danks pointed out that serious birth defects afflicted two per cent of all babies born in Australia each year: 'devastating the lives of 5000 children born each year and their families at a cost of $A2500 million a year'. A proud Elisabeth told a press conference: 'My family, like every other family with children blessed from birth with good health, is very conscious of our good fortune and deeply concerned for those others who suffer the misfortune, tragic consequences and sorrow of birth defects.' Professor Danks said: 'The aim of the Murdoch Institute will be to hasten the day when every child will be born healthy and with normal abilities.'

But later, away from the cameras in the boardroom where the Murdoch donation had been announced, Elisabeth resumed a familiar role as she visited the wards and chatted with mothers and their child patients. 'You know, every new mother's first question is always: "Is my baby all right?"' said the caring great-grandmother who had long hoped to help remove that lingering doubt. Then she was shown the $105,000 atomic absorption spectrophotometer and the other scientific marvels already being used in research.

Nearly ten years later, the institute on the top floors of the Royal Children's Hospital under the directorship of Professor David Danks, is often described as the best such unit in the world, as it continues its wide-ranging pioneering work into birth defects. Elisabeth's interest in genetics, first roused by Keith's enthusiasm for stud cattle, has not waned since she first worked to help establish the Chair of Child Health at the Children's Hospital.

In the ten years since its inception, the institute, with its sixty scientists engaged in research and thirty scientists and clinicians engaged in technical and clinical services, has opened new frontiers in research into birth defects. Outlining the highlights of the institute's recent work, Professor Danks points to the progressive development of a rapid method of identifying faults or mutations in genes which cause genetic diseases.

'That's an ongoing operation, but we are in the front row, among the best in the world in that area,' he says. 'Another major research breakthrough at the institute has been the identification of the gene at fault in Menkes' Disease, a rare disorder of the utilisation of copper in the human body which causes rapid and progressive brain damage and arterial degeneration, with death by the age of two years.

'The importance of this discovery is not so much to save the baby born in Australia with this disorder once every two years or so, but that we are identifying for the first time one of the components of the mechanism of using copper in the human body.

'If it weren't for the fact that organisms had learnt to use the elements iron and copper, there would be no life on earth,' says the professor, stressing the importance of the pioneering Australian research. 'Life on earth depends on being able to extract energy out of oxygen without killing oneself in the process. We carry on all day every day using the technology of a hydrogen fusion bomb. We've learnt to do that in a gentle way without blowing ourselves up, and the elements that enable us to do that are the elements of iron and copper.

'Understanding how the body uses iron and copper is pretty important, and this rare genetic disease we are working on enables us to recognise one of the processes. Copper is very essential but very toxic. It's as though copper has an armed bodyguard wherever it goes in our body. Now for the first time we have identified one of the team of armed bodyguards, and that has very wide implications,' says Professor Danks, who, like Elisabeth, tends to understate achievements.

Then, the professor reveals, there is the work which has resulted in the institute's 'contribution to understanding the way in which body cells make the energy they need for survival and work.' And: 'another big one going on in Melbourne has us as one of the world leaders in working out how the pairing of chromosomes takes place during cell division – how it works, how it is controlled. Faults in that control lead to things like Down syndrome where a baby receives two doses of a particular chromosome from one parent rather than the two normal doses.'

Clearly, if the name of Murdoch was not already firmly established in the realms of mass media, the work going on at the Murdoch Institute in Melbourne will ensure that Elisabeth's family name is associated with great strides in medical science in the years ahead.

CHAPTER TWENTY-EIGHT

The Garden that Grew

IT'S A MAGIC alchemy of nature, blending, as it does, the trees, shrubs and plants of Britain, Asia, the USA, and other lands with the ancient sun-soaked natives of Australia. That is why the Cruden Farm garden is a delight throughout the seasons, with leaves turning and flowers blooming in unique disciplined arrays, as if controlled by a master gardener . . . as indeed they are.

Yet Elisabeth insists: 'I am certainly not a great gardener. That's not right. I think I'm a reasonable gardener. I have an eye for colour, space and form. It is, people say, unusual to combine Australian and European plants in the same garden as we have done here. Generally speaking, I notice that experts like Professor George Seddon single out the fact that Cruden Farm's garden manages to bring the landscape into the garden and the garden out into the landscape.

'There have been some good things written about my garden but, no, I'm not a great gardener although I think I might be a sensitive and felicitous one,' says Elisabeth, who gives her elder sister, Sylvia Ritchie, credit for the example which, she says, encouraged her to be more ambitious with her own gardening. She points to Sylvia's wonderful garden at Delatite, overlooking the Australian Alps, and recalls the small cottage garden Sylvia created when she was first married, before she and her husband moved into the big old homestead. 'She is a keen and gifted gardener,' says Elisabeth.

Michael Morrison, Elisabeth's dedicated and knowledgeable gardener at Cruden Farm, disagrees with Elisabeth's modest assessment of her own prowess. 'Dame Elisabeth is a great gardener in her own right and she has created a wonderful garden here at Cruden Farm, and done so much of it herself,' he insists, after visiting some of the world's great and famous gardens with Elisabeth.

After twenty-one years at Cruden Farm, Michael Morrison knows the love, understanding and foresight that Elisabeth puts into her ever-expanding garden ... a garden in which scarcely a tree, shrub or brick path remain from the original plans outlined by the legendary Edna Walling, when Elisabeth and Keith were first married.

On her eightieth birthday, the family gave their mother a gift which has given Elisabeth – and her friends and visitors – much joy: a powerful golf buggy which Elisabeth uses winter and summer to reach far corners of her garden and take privileged guests on conducted tours. With the same skill she always brought to driving her cars, Elisabeth whips the electric buggy along the familiar pathways, beneath overhanging trees and down gentle steps, around the lake and past the islands covered in daffodils, over the bridge to her magnificent picking garden.

But for the visitor to Cruden Farm the first delight is the long lines of stately lemon-scented gums that survived the fire to become one of the most spectacular avenues of native trees in Australia. The driveway leads from the front gate where drivers take their lives in their hands entering from busy Cranbourne Road. But then the drive opens up to the circle of lawn outside the front door where two massive elms, planted nearly sixty years ago, are now reaching their full glory. Since Michael discovered, and began treating, traces of elm leaf beetle, Elisabeth, as usual thinking well ahead, has planted a young linden tree that could one day help fill the gap if one of the two giant elms was tragically lost.

Beside the elms grow one of the two Quercus firthii oaks propagated at Mount Macedon and now regarded as very important trees by dendrologists – tree experts. One has been classified by the National Trust as a 'significant' tree. Elisabeth's sixty-year-old oaks could be mistaken for ancient giants as they tower over smaller vegetation.

Even before Keith brought Elisabeth to see the farm that was to become her wedding present, there was a garden around the little country cottage long ago transformed into Elisabeth's stately home. Says Elisabeth: 'Originally along a curved drive there was Spanish broom, a very strong smelling yellow. There was a ti-tree hedge along one side of the house and it was a very little, very undistinguished garden – a sort of cottagey garden, rather suburban with a lawn in the middle and three little beds planted with annuals.

'My first impression? Well, I was thrilled at this little cottage with a pergola with roses and climbers, and honeysuckle over the verandah and wisteria on the corner. It was very pretty, and wonderful to be able to pick the flowers. I couldn't change much at first because Duell, the devoted gardener, worked from daylight to dark and kept the little farm going as well. It was an escape for Keith but I tell you it was jolly hard work for me,' recalls Elisabeth.

Then Edna Walling was called in to supervise the garden of young Mrs Murdoch. 'She was a terrifically close planter. She always had twice as many plants as you needed in the garden because that was accepted in those days and, as time went on, there were big things growing far too close to each other. Added to that the walled gardens were rather too small, because it gets very hot in the summer and there wasn't enough air getting to the gardens she had designed. Today, people who build walled gardens leave an open side to them. If we'd made it a few years later I would have known that. However, we battled on and did all this,' says Elisabeth, as we set off around the garden on her golf buggy for another lap. 'I didn't really care for this part of the garden,' she says, as she skilfully steers past what was once the front door of the farm cottage onto the last surviving brick pathway.

'There were an awful lot of brick paths, and it was more or less all annuals, and I didn't feel we had the right balance until the fire swept through and we were able to take it all out. So the fire was a blessing for me because it gave me the opportunity to develop the garden according to my own taste. I think I was able to achieve quite a lot after that. And because I had learned a bit, and I had a feeling for it, I had my own ideas. I was able to go ahead.

'There was a little old stunted red-flowering eucalyptus at the front of the house and Edna Walling left it there. It certainly had character but it was out of place. About thirty years ago I took it out,' says Elisabeth. 'It's remarkable to think that those two oaks were brought down from Macedon in two little pots by the Hon. W. L. Baillieu who helped us to plant them. It's maddening to think that I tended some of the Edna Walling trees for ten or fifteen years and then decided that they were completely out of scale and had to come out. Edna Walling was at a very significant stage in her career when she did this garden. She was just working through her "English phase" and she had become rather intense. I found her a difficult person and once this garden was planted she never came here again. Strange!

The Garden that Grew

'I don't know whether it was me. We never had any confrontation but, looking back on it, we never had a sympathetic relationship either. Yet she was the pioneer of landscape gardening here and she must hold a very special place in the history of gardening in Australia,' Elisabeth insists.

The first blue blooms of the ceanothus are out as the buds burst on the contrasting white broom in the garden outside Elisabeth's sitting room. Camellias are flowering and the first leaves are appearing on the hydrangeas. The beautiful hosta lilies from the foothills of the Himalayas are sprouting up through the rich compost. The copper beech planted after Keith's death is already displaying its spring finery, but Elisabeth points out that only a camphor laurel remains from the original cottage garden.

Elisabeth's garden design provides an exciting new vista at every turn she makes in her golf buggy. There are regular stops at points which give a distant view of the house or a special tree and always there is a surprise around the next corner. Says Elisabeth: 'Every year I say I'm not going to plant any more garden but somehow I am always tempted to make room for yet another tree or shrub.' Elisabeth points proudly to a small ginkgo tree – a botanical survivor of some prehistoric age – which she planted for her American granddaughter, Elisabeth. 'Ginkgos are very slow growing so I planted one for Elisabeth on her twenty-first birthday and sent her a cable which said: "Have today planted a beautiful ginkgo for my namesake Elisabeth. May you both flourish and have very happy lives." She was thrilled,' says Elisabeth Murdoch.

Looking back at the tennis court, the scene of many energetic tennis matches between Rupert and his nephews, Elisabeth says: 'Once the court had a beautiful net around it but after about thirty years it was almost beyond repair so now it is only surrounded by grassy banks – not many balls are hit over them these days.'

ELISABETH MURDOCH

A controlled buggy descent down some garden steps brings you to Elisabeth's lake. 'To call it a lake is perhaps rather pretentious,' she insists. But Elisabeth greatly admires and loves her waterscape with its stately weeping willows and many young oak trees as well as ducks and waterfowl swimming among the lilies and rushes. In spring, daffodils cover the islands and banks.

Michael Morrison tells of the construction of the Cruden Farm lake: 'It was all Dame Elisabeth's idea. We had a deep dam in the paddock for the stock and used water from it during the drought in the eighties,' he says. With housing estates getting closer to Cruden Farm, Elisabeth was concerned about the dwindling wildlife and decided to put in a haven for the birdlife that once flourished in the area.

With Dame Elisabeth watching closely, a gifted contractor Austin Bastow, along with his son Derek, was brought in with a bulldozer and a mountain of earth was moved leaving two islands. Finally a small stone bridge, similar to one Michael had photographed at Cranbourne Manor in Britain, was added when the lake was extended. Today, the lake with ducks and water hen swimming among the waterlilies, is one of the highlights of the garden and a cool retreat for family picnics in the summer.

Elisabeth's walled gardens are today completely in harmony with the rest of Cruden Farm. Above the stone gateway leading to the larger of the two walled gardens is a bronze dancing brolga much loved by Elisabeth. 'An old friend, Colin Anderson, who was very sensitive and very artistic, came here on his honeymoon and said "Why don't you have a brolga there?"' Elisabeth recalls. 'Keith and I had just been been to Queensland on our honeymoon, and we'd been to see the wonderful dance of the brolgas outside Townsville at sunset, so we commissioned Leslie Bowles, a fine sculptor, to go out to the zoo and this was the brilliant result,' Elisabeth says.

The Garden that Grew

Michael Morrison explains that Edna Walling had originally planted the walled garden with standard crab-apple trees down the middle, plus apple trees and stone fruit trees espaliered along the walls. 'It looked a dream for about three weeks at apple blossom time, but apart from that it was all grass with flagstones down the middle,' Michael laughs. Elisabeth's solution was to remove the standard crab-apples, the espaliered fruit trees and the flagstones and then plant perennial borders. A fine pin oak growing near a bad crack in the wall seemed to be in danger, so Elisabeth brought in a crane and replanted it at a safe distance, giving it weeks of care and attention as it recovered.

Michael recalls that in the summer, early-rising Elisabeth's first hour was invariably taken up with cutting the dead heads from roses baked by the sun in Edna Walling's adjacent walled rose garden. Again Elisabeth found the solution. She removed the roses to a new picking garden, now overlooking the lake, and had a swimming pool installed 'for the grandchildren' in its place. Now Murdoch great grandchildren often swim in the pool under Elisabeth's watchful eye. In summer, Elisabeth regularly takes a swim at dawn before beginning work in her garden. 'I do try to wear gloves when I'm out in the garden, but rough hands don't bother me. I know my time in the garden has made me weatherbeaten which is not particularly attractive, but think of the time it saves me,' laughs Elisabeth.

Near the walled garden on the site of Rupert's well-publicised 'hut' – in later years it even became a shelter for gardeners – Elisabeth has placed a statue of bronze dolphins by Douglas Stephen. They are the symbol of Pisces, Rupert's birth sign, and mark a spot often visited by his mother as she inspects her garden.

Elisabeth Murdoch's remarkable picking garden is a constant source of joy to her many friends as well as the hospitals, churches and other organisations that regularly receive wonderful arrangements of the flowers that grow there. Recently, Elisabeth supervised the construction of bluestone steps leading from the picking garden to the drive in front of the stone stables. 'We spent hours getting it right, because Dame Elisabeth didn't want the steps seen from the front garden, but hoped they would invite visitors using them into other parts of the garden,' explains Michael Morrison. 'Of course, the garden is getting older now and the wonderful trees are reaching their full height so Dame Elisabeth has effectively enlarged the garden.

'I think that the lake is a wonderful addition, but I know we would have been pushing to get it just for aesthetics. It's principally there for the wildlife, and don't forget that this is still very much a working farm,' says Michael Morrison. Indeed, Elisabeth frequently puts her garden to work for charity too. There are open days, twilight concerts and other charity gatherings. Staff members have family weddings in the beautiful gardens; gardening clubs and international visitors are often given conducted tours by Elisabeth.

In a tribute to the Cruden Farm Garden, published in *Landscape Australia* before the lake was in place, Professor Seddon wrote: Cruden Farm, Langwarrin, is indeed a farm, as its name suggests. It is also a profoundly satisfying landscape; in its effects, it is simple, direct and unselfconscious, but art and skill have gone into its making, using the common elements of the Australian farm landscape in subtle composition. The skill, subtlety and simplicity are all eloquently expressed in the driveway.

'There is no grand entrance – just a gap in the trees that line the boundary along the Frankston–Cranbourne Road. Through the gap, there is a long, gently curving driveway, surfaced with crushed stone, lined with a fairly close planted crescent of lemon-scented gums (Eucalyptus citriodora) on each side, meeting above in an interlaced

56 Dame Elisabeth at the Victorian Tapestry Workshop

57 A recent photograph of Dame Elisabeth and Rupert Murdoch

58 The new honorary Doctor of Laws in 1982

59 Walking along the Great Wall of China with Alison Leslie in 1984

60 Elisabeth and Michael Morrison with Douglas Stephen's sculpture, *Pisces*, at Cruden Farm

61 Dame Elisabeth, her golf buggy and Lily the dog

62 Cruden Farm's driveway with the beautiful lemon-scented gums

63 The lake at Cruden Farm

64 Cruden Farm in bloom

65 The picking garden at Cruden Farm

66 Rupert Murdoch outside the Herald and Weekly Times in Flinders Street, Melbourne, in the late 1980s

67 A face in the crowd - Elisabeth beams her approval at the press conference as the Herald and Weekly Times returns to the family in 1987

68 The Governor-General, Bill Hayden, bestowing upon Dame Elisabeth the Companion of the Order of Australia in 1991

69 Elisabeth and Inge King supervise the placement of the sculptor's work beside the lake at McClelland Gallery in the early 1990s

70 Dame Elisabeth at home in the sitting room, the 'soul' of Cruden Farm, in 1993

71 Dame Elisabeth and her son, Rupert, in the 1990s

72 Rupert Murdoch and his daughter, Elisabeth, at her wedding in 1993

73 Elisabeth Murdoch's marriage to Elkin Pianim in Los Angeles

74 Family photo taken in 1989 on Dame Elisabeth's eightieth birthday

From left standing:
Rowley Paterson, Elisabeth Murdoch, Grant Fowler, Lachlan Murdoch,
John Calvert-Jones, Janet Calvert-Jones, David Calvert-Jones, Rupert Murdoch,
Anna Murdoch, James Murdoch, Dame Elisabeth, Geoffrey Handbury,
Helen Handbury, Tom Kantor (behind Helen), Milan Kantor, Anne Kantor,
Eve Kantor, James Calvert-Jones (at back), Martin Kantor,
Mrs Paddy Handbury (in front of Martin), Mark Wooton, Paddy Handbury
holding baby Jack, Robyn Handbury, Paul Handbury

In front:
Sarah Paterson, Debbie Handbury, Penny Fowler holding Stephanie,
Prudence Macleod, with Robert Handbury and Helen Paterson in front of her,
Judy Paterson holding baby Nicholas, Christine Handbury and Julie Kantor

Absent:
Matthew, Fiona, Kenneth, Jessie and Elisa Handbury

75 Helen Handbury

76 Rupert Murdoch

77 Anne Kantor

78 Janet Calvert-Jones

canopy. On the right (west) side there is a curved, rough-clipped hedge of dark-leaved hawthorn. On the left is a traditional post and rail fence, and beyond it, farm paddocks of green or straw-coloured grass.

'I don't know of any visual sequence that I like more than this, the rhythm of approach is so good, the pattern of sunlight and shadow from the trees so pleasing, the succession of smooth trunks both sensuous and strong – and magical at night as headlights flood them in succession ... At the end of the drive there is – not unexpectedly – a two-storey house and around it there is a garden. The garden is one of the most notable gardens of Australia and is much admired for itself, but I admire it most for its setting. One can always look out from the garden to the undulating farm landscape to which it relates so well,' wrote Professor Seddon.

Writing of Elisabeth's walled garden, the professor described it as: 'A rectangular enclosure with a broad lawn path down the middle and a deep herbaceous border on each side. At its peak, there are tall spikes of delphinium, Thalictrum glaucum and Thalictrum dipterocarpum, Nicotiana, perennial phlox, asters, Anemone japonica, bordered by the invaluable Anthemis tinctoria "Mrs E. C. Buxton", penstemons, verbena, the smaller cactus-flowering dahlias and the lime-green Alchemilla mollis (Ladies Mantle to an older generation). All are grouped with that muted colour and informal sculpturing that look so natural and demand such judgement and hard work to create.'

Describing Elisabeth's 'front lawn' garden, the professor wrote: 'The plant material is rich, and although there is little that is botanically rare, there is much that is uncommon in Australia, and a tour with a group of knowledgeable gardeners is rewarding: exclamations, recognitions, delight and coveteousness are all expressed within a few minutes.'

And the house: 'The house is mostly white-painted wood – clapboard, the Americans call it – and the character is that of a Louisiana plantation mansion, with its theatrical portico. The rest of the house speaks of warmth, comfort and good craftsmanship, with no hint of Tennessee Williams. House, garden and farm are a unity, integrated by the creative imagination and practical competence of their mistress.

'Maintenance of the property is handled by a farm manager working five days per week, one gardener working four days per week with additional help for two days per week. This is, of course, in addition to the considerable work of the lady of the house.'

'The Lady of the House' was delighted with Professor Seddon's overview of her garden.

Although Elisabeth has a wide circle of gardening friends who are frequent visitors to Cruden Farm, her interest in other gardens in Australia and around the world is unabated and she was the original Patron of the Australian Garden History Society founded in 1979. As Jocelyn Mitchell, speaking as chairman of the Society in 1988, said: 'Dame Elisabeth Murdoch, who is known to most of us for her many contributions to our community, is a talented and indefatigable gardener. Without her enthusiasm and patronage, there probably would not be a Garden History Society of Australia.'

Giving an opening address to the enthusiastic ninth annual conference of the society in Melbourne, Elisabeth said: 'I look back to the early beginnings of our society and remember with admiration and gratitude how Peter Watts persuaded a handful of men and women, amateurs and professionals, to work for the establishment of a society. And, owing to his persistence and dedication, it did finally get off the ground and stimulated enough interest to attract a number of enthusiastic and capable members. With their ardent pursuits of horticultural knowledge and history of our gardens and the garden pioneers of our country, they established the society's first journal and set about sharing and disseminating their knowledge to a wider membership.

'We must be grateful to those early contributors for the early growth of the society and for the programmes, interesting visits to historic gardens and lectures and activities which they arranged,' she said.

It was in 1992, with Elisabeth navigating and Michael Morrison driving, that the two gardeners set off on a journey of discovery around the gardens, great and small, of Britain. Staying at Britain's bed and breakfast establishments chosen by Elisabeth from a guidebook along the way, they saw the beauty of the mature gardens designed by some of the greatest landscape gardeners the world has known.

But first Elisabeth took her daughter-in-law, Anna Murdoch, to see Wisley, the superb Royal Horticultural Society gardens at Woking, Surrey, and Saville gardens. Elisabeth, Anna and Michael had a wonderful day at Hatfield House with the very hospitable Marquis and Marchioness of Salisbury. Elisabeth and Michael stayed with Rosemary Verey, the famous gardener, who took them to Essex House, the home of Mr and Mrs James Lees-Milne, and then on to lunch with the Duchess of Beaufort at Badminton. From there they went on to more than twenty other beautiful gardens, including Countess Fitzwilliams' glorious garden at Milton.

One of the highlights for Elisabeth was a conducted tour by the Prince of Wales of his much loved garden at Highgrove, after a fundraising meeting. In Somerset, Elisabeth and Michael visited Penelope Hobhouse's wonderful garden at Tintinhull, near Yeoville. In Sussex, they lunched with Christopher Lloyd at Great Dexter. Elisabeth and Michael were welcomed into the houses of many friends with beautiful gardens and Elisabeth was happy to see Sir

Rohan Delacombe and Lady Delacombe in their charming garden, not long before Sir Rohan died. They were entertained by Lord and Lady Carrington at Bleadlow Manor. Lord Carrington is a very keen and good gardener and Elisabeth was particularly interested in the sculpture garden he was making.

Elisabeth wrote at the end of Michael's itinerary: 'Thank you Michael for being such a perfect companion – and a splendid driver!'

Back in Australia, Elisabeth found work plans well under way on the Californian garden project at Melbourne's Royal Botanic Gardens which she had supported from the start. A garden lawn near the main entrance of the gardens was being transformed into a Californian garden with trees and shrubs from the West Coast. Then came a letter from the Royal Botanic Gardens' board telling Dame Elisabeth that the garden would be known as 'The Elisabeth Murdoch Californian Garden'.

Closer to home, Elisabeth had joined her friend and neighbour, Peter Chance, and a group of local residents to finally persuade the Government that the Langwarrin Reserve, the tract of splendid coastal bushland behind Cruden Farm, should be preserved. The land, once an army camp, had rare bush orchids, native flowers, shrubs – and animals – and had, over the years, been swept by bushfires as well as being used by shooters and trail-bike riders. Today, thanks to Peter Chance, Elisabeth, and hard-working local conservationists, it is a nature reserve, patrolled and protected for community use by the Department of Forests and Lands.

CHAPTER TWENTY-NINE

'Mothers are always right...'

IN MAY, 1985, as Rupert's media interests expanded in the US, it became necessary for him to seek US citizenship in order to meet legal requirements for the ownership of television stations. Much was made in the Australian press about Rupert's renunciation of his Australian citizenship – again a legal requirement before adopting US nationality.

Asked for her view, Elisabeth was unperturbed. 'It doesn't make any difference to our family. Our family relationships are exactly the same,' she said, adding that the whole affair had been 'blown out of all proportion'.

'Rupert's affection for his home country is in no way affected by this. He's still very fond of Australia and I very much hope one day he'll be back here. He loves this country and he has properties here,' Elisabeth said. 'Rupert is never happier than when he is here on short holidays and I don't think that is going to change. It's not the sort of criticism that really matters to me. If Rupert had not achieved so much, nobody would be taking any notice, would they?'

But before Elisabeth's busy decade ended, there was a sad family mission to London after Rupert flew from New York to visit his aunt, the widowed Marie Durnford, on her eightieth birthday and found that she was terminally ill with cancer in her Chelsea home. When Rupert told his mother, Elisabeth immediately flew to London to be with Marie. A skilled nursing sister was brought into the home and Elisabeth kept a sad vigil at Marie's bed until, five weeks later, she died.

As Elisabeth says now: 'Marie was the one who was the frailest of us all, but in some ways she was the strongest. She gave comfort and support to many people and was much loved far and wide by all who knew her. She had such courage and something which she gave out to people who would charge their batteries through her. It was a great happiness to me that I could be there until the end.'

In 1984, there had been a memorable party at Cruden Farm to mark Elisabeth's seventy-fifth birthday. In a great marquee enclosing the weeping elm, more than two hundred guests dined and danced to music played by a stringed orchestra or strolled in the floodlit garden. Early-arriving guests were startled to see Elisabeth high up a ladder twining ivy around the tent poles as friends below pleaded with her to be careful.

Three years later, Elisabeth arranged another splendid party at Cruden Farm for directors of the American Newspaper Publishers Association then visiting Australia. Leading the influential group was *New York Times* chairman and publisher, Arthur Sulzberger, and, as she happened to be in town, spectacular American country and western singer, Dolly Parton, was invited along too. It was a glorious summer evening in the garden of Cruden Farm and it was a joyous occasion for Elisabeth as Rupert was that night able to tell his

'Mothers are always right...'

American and Australian media colleagues that he had finally secured control of the Herald and Weekly Times.

As Rupert was congratulated by the Americans just a few paces from the site of his old hut, Elisabeth was looking after the guests. She was introduced to the charming Miss Parton who promptly took her hand and said 'Say, Dame Elisabeth, that's a big diamond ring.'

'Ah yes, Miss Parton but I believe yours is much bigger,' was Elisabeth's tactful reply.

For her eightieth birthday, the party was even more spectacular with more than six hundred guests gathered on another balmy summer evening around Elisabeth's lake. Dinner came in special hampers decorated with a colour picture of Cruden Farm with its gardens ablaze with blooms. Then Rupert Murdoch made a speech which delighted his mother's assembled family and friends.

To an audience that included the Lieutenant-Governor of Victoria, Sir John Young, Lady Young, and other dignitaries, along with family and the friends that Elisabeth has made during her working years at hospitals, galleries and charitable organisations, Rupert began: 'Your Excellencies, ladies and gentlemen, friends and family ... all fellow members of the Elisabeth Murdoch admiration society ...'

'Helen, Anne and Janet join me in welcoming you tonight to celebrate our wonderful mother's eightieth birthday. We only regret there are a mere 620 of us here – if we had allowed Mum to invite all those people she considered good friends there would have been standing room only for at least 2000.

'It is very difficult for a son to talk properly about his mother, and particularly this one ... All of us, her children and grandchildren, hold her in such respect and awe that telling enlightening or embarrassing tales does not come easily – quite apart from risking a pretty frosty reception.

'Of course, Mum's example of enthusiasm and energy and

achievement, all driven by the highest moral values, continues to inspire us all. Interestingly, her grandchildren particularly share their confidences with her as they seek her guidance. She is a person of many facets who projects different images, at once compassionate and sensitive as well as being ferociously strong, both physically and mentally. Perhaps this is not surprising when one considers her genes.

'Some of you have known her longer even than I, and remember her remarkable parents. Her mother, Mrs Greene, was the archetype Victorian matriarch, feared by some, and admired by all; her father, Rupert, the sportsman and gambler, loved by all and especially his youngest daughter whom, by all accounts, he indulged shamelessly.

'The day she was born he exuberantly announced to her sisters that she was to be named Joy, even though he later had to compromise with the name Elisabeth Joy. But Joy she was to him as both a bewitching little girl performing endless acrobatic feats for him and his friends, and later as his staunch defender and apologist against all criticism . . . Doubtless her elder sisters often found her a pain in the neck as well as being a handful to her devoted but strict mother.

'Indeed, just after Mum left school, Grandmother Greene heard that her Elisabeth had been seen being kissed at a dance – and in no uncertain terms expressed her terrible shame, only to be interrupted by "Pop" Greene, who exploded loudly: "Mrs Greene" – as he called his wife – "You had better make up your mind, Elisabeth is going to be kissed – and kissed many times."

'But from those wonderful and different parents and sisters, came a life to which most of us here tonight, are in some sort of debt. To our father, of course, she gave twenty-four years of happiness, stability, support and home-building without which he would never have achieved what he did. And to Mum he gave the opportunity to grow into the extraordinary woman she has become.

'Mothers are always right...'

'Of course, we've all had our difficult moments! When poor Geoffrey Handbury, after a seemingly endless courtship, asked Dad for permission to marry Helen, he feigned shock and said he must ask our mother at that second in the kitchen. Five minutes later Dad returned sheepishly with a bottle of champagne, reporting Mum as saying: "Keith you choose your sons-in-law. I only pick your ties."

'Now, forty years on and seeming to have retained all her youthful energy, she maintains an impossible pace – sleeping only four or five hours a night, gardening rabidly, occasionally revealing her gambling instincts at fairly excited sessions of bridge and tending to the whole family in good times and bad – between all this her constant work for others goes on as she practises her true noblesse oblige.

'We all know her great public activities over the last fifty years, but none of us, friends or family, know all the hundreds of less visible but important things she does for others. Mum's decades of work and leadership at the Children's Hospital, her support for the Victorian Tapestry Workshop, and her devotion to the McClelland Gallery around the corner, to name but a few, mask the countless efforts for other causes and people. She lives by the belief that the small things, whether money or a simple letter of encouragement to get individuals going, are as important as the grandest efforts.

'In other words, her priorities, as her life, are totally value driven. So, tonight, we celebrate the first eighty years of her life at once one of strength and love, of competitiveness and compassion and service to others. And as we can all see here around us, it is a life filled with love and care for the outdoors and a belief in the civilising potential of beauty in all things.

'So, ladies and gentlemen. I give you the toast –
'Elisabeth Murdoch.'

The response sent the ducks on the lake fluttering off into the gathering dusk.

Four months later, Elisabeth Murdoch was in Canberra to receive the insignia of a Companion of the Order of Australia from the Governor-General, Mr Bill Hayden. This time the honour was for her work as a patron of the arts and she told reporters: 'I'm not a feminist, but it's nice to show that women can be useful.'

As peace returned to the Cruden Farm garden and Elisabeth resumed life at an undiminished pace, she focused her attention on a favourite project – the Elisabeth Murdoch Sculpture Foundation – with its immediate aim to develop a sculpture park in the eight hectares of former bushland around the nearby McClelland Regional Gallery.

As she said: 'One of my great satisfactions in life has been the establishment of the Elisabeth Murdoch Sculpture Foundation, which was very generously established by my family because they knew how dedicated I was to developing the McClelland grounds as a sculpture park.' Already the McClelland had a notable collection of small and large sculptures but now the collection was to asssume national significance. 'I've been working for this for twenty years and now it has really come about. The family got in on it and now they've established the foundation. I'm a very lucky woman. Now we can go ahead and we've got much beautiful sculpture already.'

The stated purpose of the foundation, to which many supporters of the gallery have donated, was: 'To acknowledge Dame Elisabeth Murdoch's lifelong contribution to the cultural life of the Australian nation.' A few months later, Rupert was back in Australia and presenting an important work by Norma Redpath called *Desert Arch* to the foundation. Persuaded by his Editor-in-Chief, Douglas Brass, to purchase this work for the foyer of the News Limited office in

'Mothers are always right ...'

Sydney, Rupert now said he had been persuaded by his mother to hand over the 'very lovely and very Australian' work to the foundation. Rupert said: 'The gallery is making an enormous contribution to the quality of life here. Australia as you all know is a long way from almost everything, but it need not be isolated ...' He added: 'Mothers are always right, and I take much pleasure in handing over to you *Desert Arch*.'

Gallery Director, Simon Klose says: 'The whole idea of the foundation is to perpetuate Dame Elisabeth's support of sculpture here at the McClelland Gallery. Our first priority is to try to plot the path of sculptors in utilising sculpture as a medium of aesthetic expression. The whole establishment is at the service of the community and to some extent interprets and presents the concerns of artists. The most important work which the gallery has been able to acquire through the foundation is the Inge King work, *Island Sculpture*, which is displayed on the island in the lake that Dame Elisabeth created in the middle of the park.'

When Rupert and Anna moved into their new home in Los Angeles above Beverly Hills, Elisabeth paid them a visit and offered expert advice on their big Californian garden. Rupert also took his mother to Las Vegas: 'This splendid vulgarity like something out of *Arabian Nights* – unreal. I am sure there is a lot of human tragedy underneath the surface,' she said of her visit later. 'I didn't have a go at the pokies. I don't think I'd know what to do. But I did have a go at blackjack, although I'd never been in a casino before. It was fascinating. I loved it. Rupert gave me fifty dollars and said: "Here you are Mum, really enjoy yourself." Well, I was thrilled and I had a very entertaining three quarters of an hour and I gave him fifty-two dollars back – quite an achievement!'

There was another visit to the US in 1991 when Rupert chartered a luxury cruiser and took Anna, his mother, sisters and brothers-in-law on an exciting voyage around the beautiful Nantucket Sound, past Martha's Vineyard, and then around the Cape Cod coast to Boston – and the Independence Day celebrations. On the trip they went ashore at picturesque fishing villages and took Elisabeth to see some wonderful homes and gardens.

CHAPTER THIRTY

Visions of Splendour

WITH RUPERT's endeavours prospering around the world, Elisabeth says: 'He's always been very thoughtful and very caring to members of the family. Whenever there have been opportunities where money was needed, Rupert is always there.

'I think the Murdoch family will survive beyond the grandchildren and great-grandchildren. They will go their own way, but I think there will always be a close feeling and a concern for each other. One of Rupert's children will take his place one day and whoever it is will have the family's full support,' Elisabeth says firmly. 'You can be sure that the nature of our family relationship will remain very strong. I cannot imagine that one branch of the family would ever be competing against another.

'But occasionally I do worry that eventually there will be a horrifying amount of money available for the grandchildren and I do hope they will use it properly and wisely,' says Elisabeth. Although newspaper business sections and magazines which list the 'most wealthy' families in Australia, were estimating the family assets at more than $A5 billion at the end of 1993, Elisabeth says: 'I won't dwell on it. My views about so-called wealth are pretty old-fashioned but nevertheless I still hold them and I wish people weren't so very conscious about material things because they don't really mean a great deal.

'They don't bother me because I am fortunate enough not to have to worry about paying next week's bills and I never have had to worry. I think it's something in you and it's very much in my family too. I have always hoped that, like his father, Rupert would never own a Rolls Royce – although there was the "Christmas bonus".

'When he was in Adelaide at one stage, he knew that the employees had all been very well paid but a Christmas bonus would have put a big strain on the finances. So it was cut out that year. But at the same time Rupert, or the company, bought a rather handsome looking and large American car. Well, someone was heard to say: "There goes our Christmas bonus," so from then on Rupert's car was known as the "Christmas bonus".

'I had Keith's grey Daimler, which was an office car, and we did have a Cadillac towards the end of the thirties, but there have been no Jaguars, or Mercedes in my life ... goodness no! I think Keith did have a different vision of splendour, as I like to put it, to Rupert. I think Keith was a man of his time but I think his vision of splendour for his fellow men was naturally very different to that of his son.

'I don't remember taking very much notice when Keith turned sixty. I don't remember a sixtieth birthday party. But August 12 was always a great day, the opening of the grouse shooting season in Scotland – and Keith's birthday. I think that Rupert in his sixties is much more active physically than his father was. Keith, despite his various setbacks and illnesses, had a good constitution but by the time he was sixty his heart had to be considered when it came to physical exercise.

'Fortunately, so far, Rupert has not developed any tendency to heart trouble as he gets older. He's very fit and very sensible about his lifestyle. But he is not so sensible about the hours he works or the amount he travels, but that's all part of him. It's really part of his whole make-up,' says the mother of the world's most successful media chief.

'He values time for sleeping. I think he's quite pleased to sleep so little, but he's always been very much a master of time. It seems like an arrogant thing to say but the time on the clock never stands in the way when Rupert feels something has to be done or completed, or he sees an opportunity to do something he wishes to do or contacts he wishes to make. It's a twenty-four hour day which is sometimes very useful to him.

'Keith needed more sleep, but there were times when he worked right into the early hours of the morning ... which I didn't like because it didn't suit him. But I always knew when Keith did it he was desperately worried about something. He might have a terrible fibrillation of the heart, which occurred when he was worried. I'm sure that it was a nervous thing caused by anxiety, especially if things weren't very happy in the office or if there was someone he had to confront or move around.

'Keith was very sensitive and I think Rupert underneath it all is very sensitive too but, of course, he's had much more to do and covered a far wider field, and I suppose you get used to facing up to these awkward situations,' says Elisabeth. 'Rupert does delegate a lot. It's hard for me to recall how much Keith delegated but he didn't have as much to delegate as Rupert does. I'm amazed at what

Rupert keeps hold of in his brain. It's that kind of a mind. It's not a great intellectual brain, but it's a very capable and extremely expansive sort of a brain,' says Rupert's proud mother.

'I wouldn't say Rupert was a great reader. Keith read more and with his interest in art he set himself to learn about old glass, furniture, silver and pictures. It used to amaze me how Keith mastered the information, the know-how, about everything he was interested in. I think that Rupert and Keith do have a number of similarities. I think Rupert likes putting things together and working things out – Keith certainly had that too. But it was all on a much smaller scale in those days.

'You think how communications have developed. It's easier to widen one's operations these days. I think Rupert does puzzle and work things out a great deal. I never saw Keith play chess with his father, but he used to work out chess problems when he was worried. He used to take chess problems to hospital with him on paper. I don't remember seeing him with chessmen, just the problems on paper. I always knew he was worrying when he worked on his chess problems. It was a sort of antidote for him.

'I think Keith really had a great wish for people to have the opportunity in life to have a better education and a better understanding of art, and I think he had a very starry-eyed vision of what was possible amongst nations. He always thought the League of Nations was most impractical and he often thought the United Nations was a very flawed kind of solution to mankind's problems. He cared deeply about them.

'Of course, I was closer to Keith. I was with him all the time and therefore I probably saw very much more how his mind worked, but when I'm with Rupert I'm always very pleased to find the breadth of his concern for people and causes.'

Reading a recent newspaper article about Rupert which said 'Mr

Visions of Splendour

Murdoch is a man who did not know any simple love as a child,' Elisabeth displays rare anger: 'It is absolutely and totally untrue. That kind of thing maddens me, it really maddens me.'

There was anger too when a review of a biography of Kerry Packer run in Melbourne's *Age* newspaper contained the passage: '... it seemed to be a hallmark of Australian newspaper dynasties that the children should suffer ... for both Rupert Murdoch and the young James Fairfax had remote, overpowering fathers who made their sons' lives a misery in one way or another. Frank Packer was possibly the hardest father of the lot.' It is a charge that Elisabeth, her daughters, and family friends who knew the close, loving relationship between Keith and his children, strongly deny, on Rupert's behalf.

Then it's back to Keith: 'As a young man, Keith was thinking that he should go into the Church – as he said in those moving and touching letters he wrote to his father. I don't think my work in the community was an influence on him. In fact, Keith was a wonderful influence on me. I think possibly I may have passed on some of my innate desire to be a good citizen to the children. I think perhaps they gained a bit from me in that way but I think they gained a great deal more from their father. I think I was the minor partner really in the children's make-up ... I really do think that their good points come from their father.

'Rupert is very quick to respond to the needs of other people. He's always very generous. I'm not really a jetsetter. I love to visit but it's a question of time. It's not cheap to fly overseas and one has one's priorities about these things. By the time I haven't got things to do here in Australia I won't be fit enough to go,' says Elisabeth, who is already planning overseas trips well into the future.

To many of the grandchildren, Cruden Farm has become – and

will remain – a place of happy holiday memories, weddings, birthdays and family gatherings. For some it was a haven to escape mounting teenage problems or find peace for frantic examination cramming. Matt Handbury, Elisabeth's eldest grandson, and now managing director of Murdoch Magazines, recalls a rebellious period when he was growing up and staying in a Cruden Farm cottage.

'One Sunday, Granny invited me to lunch and I decided to shave off half the beard and moustache I had grown, leaving one side of my face clean shaven and the other covered in hair,' Matt remembers. 'Do you know, Granny didn't even notice, or, if she did, she didn't mention it at the table.' Elisabeth chuckles when reminded of that day: 'I had to steel myself to ignore it. He did it to get a rise out of me and I was determined to take no notice.'

Over the years Elisabeth has kept a close check on any apparent outbursts of extravagance in her family. 'We should be attempting to use our wealth properly. They really must understand what wealth's all about – it's really not some self-indulgent thing,' she insists.

What does Elisabeth expect of her growing family in the future? 'I would hope that they would lead useful, happy and concerned lives with a very responsible view of what they should and are able to do according to their circumstances.' Elisabeth is well aware of the pressures that can be brought to bear on younger members of a powerful family, and she is proud of the way her grandchildren have coped with the situation.

Elisabeth reels off the names, and details their pursuits and occupations, of the boys and girls in her family. One is a photographer, another was teaching in Botswana, another – 'an interesting girl' – studied fringe drama in Paris. One or two are showing an interest in media studies but none, so far, is playing a major role in News Corp. 'I do think it shouldn't be made too easy for the children to go into the company. They mustn't rely on it. But, of course, Rupert has always been very anxious to help. They don't get let off lightly. I think they have to be worthy of their hire.

'They have all, of course, been offered holiday jobs. But apparently they do feel a "pressure". It's all about power and money and you do try and use it for good but apparently if you do belong to what is known as a powerful family, you have problems. I get so sick of this because it is not something I'm really aware of.

'I'm just not conscious of it but apparently out in the marketplace it is a fact and it worries me that some of the children have found it very difficult,' says Elisabeth. 'Still I think mostly they are on the right track. Rupert made his own opportunity. He had to prove himself and it was a pretty tough go at times and I still think that in a way it was the making of him.

'Trusts were established so that an inheritance would go to grandchildren and we have been able to tailor those trusts to help them. We've had to keep to the letter of the law. Grandchildren have not had free access to wealth and all their parents have been very wise. They've all arranged that children do not have too much ... one day later on they will and they will all be a bit wiser as they get older,' says Elisabeth, who indignantly rejects any suggestion that she is the 'matriarch' of the Murdoch family, and adopts her vexed closed-eyes expression when any mention is made of a Murdoch 'dynasty'.

'The grandchildren are all comfortable. Rupert has seen to it that they've all had opportunities. They've been very fortunate. Some have done very well. Some have not done quite so well. Rupert's been very thoughtful and very caring to all the children. On a number of occasions the girls have said to me "Isn't he remarkable? He is thoughtful to everyone."

'Although Rupert had inherited a lot of his father's characteristics, I also see quite a bit of Greene in Rupert. Dad was a charming man. He was much better outside his house than he was in his home. Still you remember him with tremendous appreciation for what fun he was in so many ways and how maddening he was in others.

'I really think the Murdoch genes are dominant. I think all the children's better points come from their father. I have a strong feeling that our path in life is destined by what we are made up of. I'm very strong on the strength of the genetic strain, although I know there's a lot of difference in opinion about how strongly genetics influences us as opposed to environment.

'I'm not just saying it. I mean it. I really mean it sincerely. I know I'm fairly quick and intelligent but I think they've got their father's better brain,' says Elisabeth. Again it is a view that people who knew Keith and Elisabeth would dispute. Elisabeth's own feelings of concern for her family and others had remained unabated since she first began knitting singlets for babies under her desk at Clyde.

For many years Elisabeth has supported a bewildering selection of charities and good causes but as Rupert said in the speech marking his mother's eightieth birthday: 'None of us knows how much she really contributes to the community.' Certainly there are always letters and phone calls from people and organisations looking for help. Elisabeth carefully considers them all, often sending a cheque or a written explanation as to why there are others with a greater claim on her funds. But Elisabeth has a keen eye for any frivolous or extravagant requests and very few unworthy causes get in beneath her guard.

Elisabeth is extremely proud of the contributions her family have made in Australia and overseas. Rupert has provided generous funding to the Library at Worcester College, Oxford. Rupert also announced that News Corp. would give £3 million to fund the Murdoch Chair of Language and Communications at Oxford. The worldwide list of Murdoch-funded projects is long and varied.

CHAPTER THIRTY-ONE

That Wedding

DURING THE Australian spring, the gardens of Cruden Farm are a delight with sweet-smelling wisteria casting a blue haze on the western corner of the house. Daffodils are in full bloom on the islands and banks of Elisabeth's lake and the buds are bursting on the great elms and oaks in the front driveway.

Yet Elisabeth was happy to miss ten days of this spectacular rebirth of her garden to again take the long flight to Los Angeles – now very much Rupert's home and world headquarters. In late 1992, Elisabeth had finally decided to have a hip replacement operation and insisted on it being performed by a local Frankston orthopaedic surgeon at a local private hospital. The operation was a great success with Elisabeth soon walking on crutches, then sticks and returning home. Before long, Michael Morrison was taking her around the garden in a wheelchair, but that was soon abandoned and her walks became longer and longer and soon the golf buggy was returned to service for more distant inspections.

Overriding Elisabeth's objections, the children insisted on having a small lift installed to take their mother to her upstairs bedroom – one of the few concessions she has made to the modern progress in her comfortable but strictly non-ostentatious, and still unheated, home.

This time, Elisabeth's trip to LA was to attend the wedding of her granddaughter, Elisabeth Murdoch. And to make her trip more comfortable for her rapidly strengthening hip, the family insisted that she travel first class with Janet to allow more leg-room on the Qantas jet.

Rupert's daughter, said to have inherited all her grandmother's energy and determination, had met her husband-to-be, Elkin Pianim, at Vassar University some years before. After graduating, Elkin, son of a distinguished Ghanaian economist Dr Andrews Pianim, and his Dutch wife Cornelia, had begun a banking career in New York while young Elisabeth began training for a career in television.

Dr Pianim had been locked up as a political prisoner for nine long years by Ghanaian dictator Gerry Rawlings, as intense international pressure was mounted for his release. 'Elisabeth and Elkin had a long courtship before they were finally engaged by which time Elkin was working at a branch of Rothschilds in New York,' Elisabeth explains. 'They are both such level-headed and courageous young people and we all have faith in their ability to make a very happy marriage.'

After his release from imprisonment, Dr Pianim had visited Rupert and Anna in Los Angeles. Both wrote to Elisabeth to say how impressed they had been by the calm, dignified man held in high regard at the United Nations and other international forums. It was a view Elisabeth shared when she flew into Los Angeles after the long flight. 'It was obvious to us all that the Pianims shared our family values, and like all the Ghanaians we met at the wedding, they were such fine, highly educated people, and had achieved such a lot in their lives. They also have a quality of such goodness and simplicity and Dr Pianim is so very devoted to the welfare of his country. We all hope he will play some part in Ghana's future. He was actually Ghana's finance research officer at the UN for some years before he became a political prisoner.'

Completely unperturbed by the forthcoming mixed marriage, Elisabeth adds: 'When my children were young I would have found it difficult – no doubt I would have had to accept, but difficult. Now all that is changed, and I know that Elkin and Elisabeth can overcome any difficulties. You know, I think our family has been enriched by the marriage of Elisabeth and Elkin. We very quickly established a happy rapport with his delightful family.'

As Anna and Rupert prepared their home, 'Misty Mountain', on a peak overlooking Beverly Hills, for the reception, Elisabeth had booked into a hotel after flying to the US. The three daughters and their husbands were all in LA, as well as several of Elisabeth's grandchildren, cousins of the bride. After their arrival, Helen and Geoff Handbury arranged a dinner party for the Murdochs to meet the Pianims at the Peninsula Hotel.

The following evening, the Pianims invited Dame Elisabeth and her family to a dinner party to meet their relatives. 'It was quite a moving occasion – a splendid thing to do,' says Elisabeth. And then there was the wedding at the Spanish mission-style St Timothy's Catholic Church not far from Rupert's 20th Century Fox studios.

'Anna did think up a marvellous, lovely, lovely wedding, with beautiful music,' Elisabeth says. 'It was interesting to see the variety of guests. People came from all over the world.' Described in the glossy magazines as 'a dazzling blend of Hollywood glamour and

That Wedding

African colour,' the guest list at the wedding included Ronald and Nancy Reagan, movie moguls, media magnates and News executives as well as the Ghanaians – who outshone everyone except the bride in their colourful traditional costumes. Elisabeth and Anna drove up to the church together but Rupert risked a raised eyebrow from his mother by arriving with the bride in a gold Rolls Royce!

After the bride and groom left the floodlit church, the 360 guests drove up the narrow mountain road to the Murdoch estate and the reception held in a fairytale marquee erected on the tennis court. Where the guests could not see the spectacular view through the transparent sides of the marquee Anna had placed painted panels duplicating the distant hills and trees. Through the transparent roof of the marquee the Californian stars shone. Arriving guests crossed the courtyard where Anna had positioned a spectacular white birdcage. 'In the cage were white doves hired for the night. You can hire anything in Hollywood,' Elisabeth laughs.

And everywhere there were flowers – Australian native flowers, which Elisabeth had to explain were grown locally and had not been brought from Cruden Farm, and exotic orchids. Throughout the happy reception, musicians played gentle music until the wedding 'waltz' when the bridal couple whirled around the floor to the strains of Stevie Wonder's 'Ribbon in the Sky'. Then Broadway star Ben Harnay sang 'More I Cannot Wish You' from 'Guys and Dolls' – dedicated by Anna Murdoch to her daughter Elisabeth.

Less than a week later, Dame Elisabeth was flying alone back to Australia armed with colour photographs she had taken of the wedding and reception. 'It was beautiful. All so dignified and beautiful,' she said. Driving up the familiar curved driveway to the peace and beauty of Cruden Farm, Elisabeth was greeted by 'Queenie' – so called because her real name is Mrs Victoria Alexandra Smith. The delightful and dependable Queenie has been helping the Murdoch family for many years and now lives at Cruden Farm with Elisabeth. Some daffodils were still in bloom as was the wisteria, and the first of Elisabeth's roses were budding.

In the schoolroom, the mail was piling up and the diary, crammed with future engagements, was open near the phone. 'Back to work,' said Dame Elisabeth Murdoch.

Before she had flown off to her granddaughter's wedding, Elisabeth had dined with British commentator and author Paul Johnson. On his return to Britain, Johnson, author of *The Intellectuals*, a book which destroys many of the world's most idolised left-wing icons, wrote in *The New Statesman*: 'In assessing a famous man, it always helps to know his parents. Recently in Melbourne I spent much time in the company of Dame Elisabeth Murdoch, a vivacious old lady who radiates intelligence, charm and fun, who told me among other things that she has twenty-two great-grandchildren. She confirmed my impression, formed long ago, that Rupert Murdoch, far from being a monster, is essentially well-meaning, someone who wants to make the world a better, or at any rate, a more exciting place.' Amused to receive a faxed copy of the Johnson tribute, Elisabeth could only chuckle: 'Old lady indeed!' And Elisabeth Murdoch added: 'I don't think of myself as being young, but I can never relate exactly to what being eighty-five means. I can't really accept that I'm really old. I like to imagine I'm ageless.'

Life with Elisabeth

HELEN HANDBURY

Ours was a lovely, happy childhood. There was never a cross word. There was never any anger but I was conscious of Mum being over-anxious and a bit critical, I thought. Talk about genetics. I wasn't a very nice child, especially when I went to boarding school ... Rupert would fly off the handle and he was made to stand in the corner of the dining room a few times for swearing or getting a bit rebellious.

Now we sometimes wonder who is the family favourite. I don't think I am. And, in fact, Rupert and I always thought that Anne was the family favourite especially after she had that serious illness. Looking back it was so sad, because it turns out that Anne felt very deprived. She used to say that Mum never visited her in hospital, but poor Mum had been sitting out there absolutely agonising after they told her that she had to stay away because they wanted to handle it on their own and get her better. The doctors and nurses said Anne must not have any emotional upsets – how wrong they were in those days.

Mum was just twenty when I was born and I always thought that she was very anxious about me. When I became a mother I was about the same age and I realised what a difficult task motherhood could be.

I know Mum has ideas about who has the finest mind in the family, but, again, I don't believe it's me. The headmistress at Clyde where we all went said: 'You girls are so alike and so different.' It's funny because we had never thought of ourselves as different, except for Rupert being a boy, but Miss Hay said: 'Well, Helen, your head rules your heart, Anne's heart rules her head, and Janet does take some interest in her looks.'

I think position in the family makes a great difference. I had a wonderful time with Dad because I was the oldest and Rupert was always poor old Miss Kimpton's favourite. Miss Kimpton was absolutely magnificent. When we were children we loved our nanny and our governess. There was never the slightest disloyalty, no jealousy or possessiveness, and I think Mum handled it all very well. I've always admired Mum so much for marrying into a household where Dad had his bachelor staff, and then taking over and managing so magnificently. She never allowed the fights below stairs to enter into her enclave at all. Dad was a very balanced and big man. He took in our whole family and could have easily managed another ten.

But we were so young, Janet was only thirteen, when Dad died so sadly we didn't have a long association with him. Now, I was my grandfather's favourite – until I went to boarding school. But Nanny always told me the story of when Rupert was born and Pop came and said to Dad: 'Oh Helen's nose will be put out of joint,' and Dad said: 'Helen's nose will never be put out of joint' and Nanny told me that Dad thought that it was a very good thing too.

Life with Elisabeth

I was reading some letters Mum has kept of mine written from school and I must say that they all wrote to me at school – Granny Greene, Granny Forth and Granny Murdoch – but not Pop Greene. I'm afraid we didn't appreciate Granny Greene. When we were very small we believed that she was very cruel to Pop. But he was so naughty. We used to delight in it. He was so charming and spoilt us so. He did things we weren't allowed to do, gave us ice-creams and took us to the beach and then took us back to Great Granny Forth's for Sunday afternoon tea parties in our bathers with ice-cream all over us. But he paid for it once. I must have been under ten and he thought he'd teach me to drive and I backed into the fence opposite Heathfield. Of course, I was quite oblivious to the fact that poor Pop would have to pay for it. He didn't dare mention it to Mum or Dad and had to fork up himself.

Granny was obviously in love with him but it is extraordinary that she had married someone like my grandfather with his gambling and boisterous nature. She took him on. But poor Aunty Marie was the one he was really unkind to, who really suffered. She was very like the Forths in looks. She had buck teeth, of which she was very conscious and, of course, when you're told you're unattractive, it does affect you. But they always do pick on your weaknesses, don't they?

We always thought that Granny Greene retired into semi-invalidism as a weapon, or maybe a denial, but she did go on forever. We used to think she was ancient when we were young. And she used to stay in bed once a week. I think she stayed in bed at least until Pop got out of the house.

I did go with him to the races but I never saw him gambling. That was never talked about in the family, but we did go and watch him start the races and we were very proud of him. In our little world Pop was THE starter and he was such a good sport, and had such a good eye – which Mum reckons she's inherited, and she's probably right.

Like Mum as a child, Rupert and I spent our life in the garden, until we went to school – which was what we thought was a very normal childhood. Our parents' company was a treat. We were not deprived of it but our idea of heaven was to get on the bed with them in the morning, while they had their breakfast and read the papers – and we'd be in the bathroom when they were getting ready for dinner parties. We were with them every minute that we could be, but apart from that Rupert and I did lead a rather secluded life.

Mum and Dad always seemed to be talking about going out to social occasions, 'Oh we'll have to go,' they would say – and now we're behaving just like our mother and father used to. 'You'll enjoy it once you get there,' Dad would say.

I can remember coming in very late with Dad snoring, and Mum saying: 'Your father's been lying awake worrying.' I was guilt ridden about that. But Mum was really the one who was anxious, she worried that we would be spoilt. She was a bit more in tune than Dad about what was going on.

I must have been rather unkind one time and I was summoned by Granny Greene and I said 'The trouble with Mum is that she's such a snob.' And Granny said with her closed eyes as she always did: 'Oh I think the trouble is she's not quite snob enough, my dear.' Granny always closed her eyes when she said wise things like that – just like my dear mother.

One thing that made me cranky was being sent off to boarding school. I was no good at sport and when I went up there to Clyde there were reminders of Elisabeth Greene everywhere and everyone said 'Oh thank goodness she's in this house,' and I was so bad. I was terribly self-conscious and Mum of course was always so brave.

I remember we used to go to Davey's Bay and we were very

different because, unlike the other children, we were TAKEN down there and Kimpo would shout out in her English accent 'RUPERT, HELEN, IT'S TIME TO GO HOME!' and, of course, all the other kids would simply scream.

It's interesting how it affected Rupert one way and me the other because it really drove me more into myself. Mum, of course, used to come down and do the greasy pole. Most of the mothers were older and we used to think this was wonderful because Mum would dive and win the diving competitions. They were such agony for me that once I dropped an iron on my hand, deliberately, so I couldn't swim. I was really very, very self-conscious. I suppose I wanted to shine for them, but I didn't.

Mum was always so pretty and young and then she had to do so much work during the war and we used to get irritated by this, as children do. She had such a strong sense of duty. We always thought that she was a Calvinist and, you know, she actually seemed to grow much older than Dad as we grew up. It was her attitude. I think she was worried about his health and things financially, and she was just concerned about her children growing up, I suppose.

At Geoff's sixtieth birthday everyone was making lovely speeches about him until Rupert got up and said: 'I was very interested to hear all this, but it was not ever thus. I can remember Dad saying while he was shaving: "I don't like the shape of his head and there's not enough space between his ears."' Then three or four women responded and said my father was still going on like that on the way to the church. He was so very protective. Nobody would ever have been good enough for us. Yet later I can remember him saying: 'You're very lucky to get someone as nice as Geoff is, I suppose.'

Rupert always had all the drive and ambition of the Murdochs as we knew them. Dad had terrific determination and strength. I think we're all very dull compared to his generation.

We would stay with Granny Greene at Pemberley if Mum and Dad had a big party at home, and she was very kind to Kimpo and tried to launch her into her Victoria League circle. I suppose Granny Greene was leading a very narrow life by the time I knew her. When Geoff first went to meet her there were photos of Lord Fisher, the Archbishop of Canterbury, around and someone who went to the south pole, as well as a rear admiral, a knight and a pastoralist on the mantlepiece and he felt that the standard was going to be very high in our family.

When we were young, Granny Greene and the family all favoured the Ritchies, which was fair enough because they didn't see as much of them as they saw of us. We lived such a sheltered childhood. I remember worrying, for some reason, that perhaps Dad had been married before. We were never told anything about his fiancée or that side of his life before he met Mum.

We all came down every summer to Cruden Farm from the word go. A *Herald* truck used to move all the linen and things and the house in town used to be left in the care of one maid and a butler. I used to think the dust covers went over the furniture when we left, but they might not have been quite as old-fashioned as that.

Another childhood outing of the week when we lived in Kooyong Road was to go with the chauffeur to Armadale Station to meet the steam train coming in from Frankston with our big hamper of food from the farm. In those days it was almost like a country village at Armadale and there would not be another person in sight at the station.

Of course, we knew about Dad's failed bid to own a Rolls Royce and now I couldn't care less about cars and Rupert just hates cars. But as children we were always taught by Mum not to be ostentatious. We were always very careful never to be ostentatious at all. But only last year Janet's husband, John, turned up at the airport to

Life with Elisabeth

meet her with a bright red Mercedes sports car and Janet said 'For once in my life, that's just too much.' She was conscious, not out of inverted pride, but more out of concern for other people's feelings, really.

At home when we were children, we soon learnt that we must always show concern for our domestic staff and care for the feelings of other people. Mum's father, being so besotted with her, must have given her a lot of confidence when she was little. She had told me that she used to long for a burglar to come into her room so she could jump onto his back and overcome him.

When we were children, Rupert was the organiser of the manure collection and sales, and I was always keen on making a bob too. Certainly he sold the rabbits – I think he said it was for the Red Cross! He used to kill them and I used to stand by while he skinned them. I can kill a rabbit, just as Mum could. We used to muck around on the farm and we were always out there working with the men, rabbiting, and helping them kill the chooks. I suppose we were pretty beastly really, Rupert and I. We used to quite enjoy gutting rabbits and saying: 'Ooh, look at all the little baby rabbits inside.'

We used to make revolting lavender water too, and we used to ride our ponies into Frankston to have them shod. There were wonderful Sunday morning rides with Daryl and Joan Lindsay and pony cart trips too. It was a lovely life when Rupert and I were very young. I remember playing a little bit of tennis and there was always lots of family. Cruden Farm became the centre for both the Murdoch and the Greene families, rather than Pemberley.

Janet and Anne were still at school when Dad died. I was in Melbourne. Mum and Dad called on us the day before to have a play with my baby, Matthew. It is so very sad that our children didn't know a grandfather at all. It was such a terrible shock when Dad died and I feel we didn't support Mum as much as we should have.

I'm sure we tried, but she didn't seem to really want us to. It wasn't my place to interfere in the financial side. It was awful, awful, awful. We each had 10,000 Cruden shares. I can remember Dad explaining it to us and saying that he hoped we would always support Rupert ... and we took that very seriously.

One thing that embarrassed me was when Dad took us to the football and he'd have the binoculars and would be in the outer and say things out loud like: 'Magnificent, look at all those wonderful young Australians.' If he did it today it would be very suspect. He barracked for Melbourne; I barracked for Collingwood. He loved the football, but I don't think he was an MCC member.

Rupert had a bad time in Adelaide after Dad died. It was an unfortunate place for him to start off. Mum was in an awkward position. She didn't realise how lonely he was, over there. In those early days after Dad died we would have family conferences around the schoolroom table. There wouldn't be any disagreements with Mum sitting there with her beady eyes [laughs]. We really were the staunchest of families.

Of course, I haven't got a business head at all. Wealth means nothing to me. We go on living simply – that's a natural progression from our childhood really. We used to always live simply and I used to be so envious of my friends and the things they were allowed to do.

I used to believe I was very unkindly treated by Mum when it came to clothes. When she was little she used to wear hand-me-downs from her sisters so she wasn't conscious that my wardrobe was rather inadequate. And the girls from school used to wear silk stockings and I used to be so embarrassed because I didn't – and, of course, they'd pick on me. I only had one school uniform because all the family donated all the wartime clothing coupons for all the boring things like underclothes and sheets and towels and things. I remember standing on Flinders Street Station in the middle of the holidays and this girl being beastly to me and saying sarcastically: 'Oh, gosh I thought you were going back to school today. What a shock you gave me wearing your school uniform in the middle of the holidays.'

I think we led a very simple life. I've always said as far as personal lifestyle goes Rupert could go back to living in a tent without the slightest concern. The younger generations of our family do remain pretty Scottish on the whole. Anna King Murdoch, our cousin Keith's daughter, is the only one of the next generation in an interesting trade, the rest are pretty subdued – farmers and things like that. There is an early American connection from the past but we were never told anything about them.

Kimpo always wanted Rupert to get a bit more pocket money, after all he was the boy. I used to laugh because I'd get the handkerchiefs and he'd get the ten bob note. Granny Greene was almost regal, I remember, but Great Granny Forth was really the one that Mum adored and spent a lot of time with.

RUPERT MURDOCH

I WOULD SAY that my mother's two outstanding qualities are her moral values – which translate to her work for charity and a whole lot of other things – and her sheer physical energy ... which is much greater than mine. But if we're looking at genetic streams you would say that any physical energy I might have, I got from her. Yes, they are the qualities I will always remember about her, but then there is her affection, her very real love for her children.

Of course, she has given expression to that affection a lot more over the past twenty years than when we were young. My earliest memories of my mother really revolve around Cruden Farm where, although she was a very good mother to us all, a very interested mother, there was no question she put her job of supporting our father ahead of us. She could afford to have Kimpo to help look after us but she was always very interested in what we were doing ...

I can remember very vaguely being at Heathfield – which takes you back pre-war. I have vague flashes of memory about the garden and old Kline and Bob, the two gardeners. And I can remember the big house, but not much about it really, although I do remember when there were big parties on we would be allowed downstairs for ten minutes or so.

I can remember playing in the Heathfield garden with Helen, but it is Cruden Farm where my memories really start. There were the family picnics with the Lindsays. I was too young to ride so I went in the go-cart with Nanny sitting there with the hampers of food while Dad and Mum and all the grown-ups went on ahead.

I can remember our trip to England and certainly the voyage back across the Pacific because I clearly recall my mother throwing me in the ship's pool – the deep end – and not letting anyone rescue me. I had to dog paddle to the side and I was screaming. That was the way to teach you to swim in those days. That's how my mother was taught and it was certainly valuable experience for later life. Yes, I remember that very clearly.

On that trip to England our parents left the ship at Gibraltar and drove through Spain and Europe while we sailed on with Nanny. I remember getting off the ship at Southampton with Nanny, and a driver taking us to her family's home and living on a real English farm, in a farmhouse in Hampshire or somewhere further north.

For the first time I had Yorkshire pudding – as a main course, Yorkshire pudding and vinegar! We had a great time. There were older children there. Then when our parents arrived we went down to London and a largish apartment, Queen Anne's Mansions, near the Houses of Parliament. I think it was bombed out during the war.

I can remember Miss Kimpton being interviewed, by my mother, and perhaps just one other applicant. I was four, turning five and, yes, I do recall riding lessons in Hyde Park, with some horrible fellow teaching us to ride formal English-style. Riding with a straight back and even getting a couple of touches of the horse crop across my hands to help me to hold the reins properly ... and being dressed up to go riding – ridiculous ritual. Fancy riding clothes for a five-year-old!

I don't know how long we were in London but my father took long trips in those days, and he went off to the Olympics in Berlin and he was getting alarmed about Hitler. We were pretty much out of the way in London. My father was busy all day in Fleet Street and no doubt they were being entertained at night, and going away for weekends and not taking us. I know the English.

I do remember going in the train across the US and over the Rockies. Father flew off to New York and, I think, my mother came with us, and Nanny, and Miss Kimpton. We rented a very nice wooden cottage on this island in Seattle Harbor. I met someone from there the other day and I can imagine myself back where we had a very happy three weeks and saw a lot of my mother. Then my father turned up and we caught the ship and I learnt to swim.

We got back to Melbourne and settled in for my first memory of routine teaching – or learning anything – with a governess and Helen in the schoolroom at Heathfield. Helen went off to school after a couple of years leaving me with Miss Kimpton, a doting sweet lady, who spoilt me, and despite her claims to the contrary seventy years later, I'm sure taught me nothing. She wasn't unintelligent but I didn't learn much before I went off to preparatory school at Adwalton.

I can't remember being moved out of Heathfield in a hurry when the war came – but I have a suspicion I was just starting at Geelong Grammar and when I came home on holidays my parents had a charming little apartment in Wallace Avenue, Toorak, where I used to enjoy an occasional stay with them. It was fun then. It was just them, all to ourselves.

Life with Elisabeth

I was at school when the fire swept through Cruden Farm too. I don't remember how I heard about it except, I think, a letter arrived thirty-six hours later, a very warm letter from Daryl Lindsay, telling me how extraordinary my mother had been, how she arrived there and began rallying everyone and how she saved the house. I don't think they thought to call us and tell us there'd been a fire. I only got the letter from my godfather, who was not given to writing letters to me, and somehow I think it was the only letter he ever wrote to me, but I remember it very well, a thirteen-page letter!

Childhood memories of my mother really revolve around life at Cruden Farm and I can remember her playing cricket with us and, of course, swimming at Davey's Bay. She was the one who wanted me to go to Geelong Grammar. My father wanted me to go to Scotch College because he and his business friends all thought I'd get a better education there or at Melbourne Grammar. Geelong Grammar was mostly sons of graziers and Darling, the headmaster, was under some suspicion – I mean he was not seen perhaps as a serious educator. Experimental, perhaps, but he was not then held in the respect he is today, or towards the end of his reign.

But it was my mother who insisted. Because of the pressures of their life, my father and mother travelling a lot, it made sense for me to go to boarding school. They visited me a lot, whenever they were allowed, while I was there. It was always a great occasion – maybe because of the food they brought. You'd look forward immensely to them coming down, or to other parents coming down, and hoping you'd be invited to lunch with them. I remember the Myers. They had a son there and they'd take me out on picnics to the You Yangs [mountains] or the beach.

Mother was embarrassed because she thought they'd bring too much food and spoil us. We'd have a few hours playing around then Mum and Dad would call on the schoolteachers and ask how I was getting along. I do remember learning the rudiments of chess from my father and maybe discussing family finances with him. This would have been the time he was thinking of buying the Adelaide *News* and explaining that he didn't have any shares in *The Herald*. He used to talk to me a lot about those advertising newspaper wars and other things.

In his forties or fifties I guess, people would tell him that he'd got all his money – all his eggs in one basket and say: 'Look, old man, you really ought to spread investments around and get some land' ... which was, of course, the worst advice he ever took in his life. But he loved the land. He bought Wantabadgery as an investment, but I'm sure it was nothing more than an expensive hobby. He never got a penny out of it.

Yet Wantabadgery was like a second home to us. We loved it as children. Helen and I used to go there with Kimpo during the war – I remember early in the war, things were very desperate, and we were shunted up there with Kimpo for three weeks during the September holidays. We used to go rabbiting and catch hares and do all those things. Really, we all had a very happy childhood – the happiest of childhoods – and for people to say that we were somehow deprived of love is nonsense.

Certainly I didn't enjoy Geelong Grammar, although I'm sure I had some happy times there – I was there for long enough. I was a bit of a loner, I guess. I had a few friends but not a lot and I didn't enter into things easily. I was too lazy at sport and things like that so I spent a long time at the art school. I loved one or two of my teachers. But despite the claims that he had great influence over me, I never met Manning Clark. I remember going out collecting for a Red Cross appeal once, knocking on his door and being met by a nude Mrs Manning Clark who said 'Go away'. That is the only memory I have of the Manning Clarks at all. I was twelve years old at the time.

Murray-Smith (Stephen) did befriend me and was an influence on me. I liked Stephen. My sister Helen was the same. They were both wrapped up in social conscience. I was interested in politics, what was going on, but I don't remember the great issues of those days. I guess it was the beginning of the Cold War, but we never discussed that sort of thing down there – it was more Ben Chifley and Bob Menzies and all that Australian political stuff. Stephen had probably just graduated from university and was, perhaps, just a part-time student teacher. He was probably just a fashionable trendy lefty.

We used to spend the whole summer on Davey's Bay. They were wonderful holidays. We grew up there and when I was about sixteen or seventeen, Helen and I got a small sailing boat called a Sharpy. We used to race every Saturday or Sunday – with modest success. They were wonderful times with Mum and Dad at Davey's Bay. Father used to come down and sit on the beach or go for a swim, although it was pretty rocky. When we were much younger, Dad had bought a little boat with a small engine, and we used to go fishing in the bay for flathead, bags full of delicious flathead. Later he took to fly fishing, and loved practising casting. Anna is the same, she just loves fly fishing. I just fish for fish. Put a grasshopper on the hook if I can. I just like to catch the fish.

My hut? Yes, it was small with a bed and a little side cupboard. I've been trying to remember if it had a light. It was just ten yards from the side door, right beside a big tank stand, and there was a concrete track leading back to the house. I slept there very happily, summer after summer. It was never cold, and I never slept there during the winter – we used to go to Wantabadgery in winter, so I can't remember a single winter at Cruden Farm.

But I do know that if you still want to get really cold in winter, you go inside the house at Cruden Farm! People say that I was put out in the hut to toughen me up. I find that hard to believe. It might have been, but I think it was to create an extra bedroom as, in fact, there was usually an aunt or someone sleeping in my room inside. My mother always tries to avoid anything ostentatious. She planned a party for her eighty-fifth birthday, but I told her to put it off and have a proper party when she is ninety.

ANNE KANTOR

I WAS BORN on 20 September 1935 at Epworth Hospital in Richmond and, when I was only five-months-old, Helen, Rupert and I were taken to England by Mum and Dad. My mother had gone overseas with my father when Helen was a baby but hated leaving her and vowed that she would never do anything like that again. Next time, she said, she would take the family with them and that is why I had my first trip at such an early age.

Of course I remember nothing of the trip from Australia across the Pacific. Apparently on the outward trip we went across the Canadian Rockies on a train and I cried a lot. I do remember back in Australia in the summer that Janet was born. I was three and a bit, and I vaguely remember that Christmas and the next summer, 1940, when I became very ill at Cruden Farm with osteomyelitis – a bone marrow infection. Suddenly it seemed that there was something very seriously wrong with me.

Mum realised that she had to get the very best treatment available for me – quickly – and I was very fortunate that a Frankston doctor friend, whom she called in, directed her to a highly skilled orthopaedic surgeon who was holidaying on the Mornington Peninsula after just returning from the US with the latest knowledge and experience of the treatment of osteomyelitis. Until that time, the complaint had such a dreadful history and usually involved many operations over a long period. Often it was fatal.

I was rushed off to St Ives Private Hospital in Melbourne and, after the first operation, Mum was told by the special nursing sister that the next ten days would be very crucial and that the sister could do more to pull me through if she could be in sole charge. Mum felt very miserable about not being able to be with me but, as she was very impressed with this very determined young woman, she agreed to pay only very brief observational visits.

Sister Thake, who was a cousin of artist Eric Thake, apparently did a magnificent job and came home with me to Heathfield and helped build me up for the second operation which was performed six weeks later. After that I was taken to our Wantabadgery property with Mum and another exceptional nursing sister, Sister Buxton, so that I could recuperate in the warmer, sunny climate of the Riverina. But just as we settled in, Sister Buxton was called up for service abroad, and Mum was left to cope with my wounds herself, which she managed to do very effectively. I don't suppose I realised how very anxious she was at the time.

We were up there for five or six weeks before we returned home to Heathfield, and a long period of rehabilitation with my father's sister, Aunt Helen, a wonderful physiotherapist, helping me with my exercises. We all loved Aunt Helen, who was greatly respected in her profession.

I had to wear a caliper for almost two years but, eventually, I was able to walk well again and my main memory of that time was being in the Heathfield garden with my legs up on a long chair, and feeling very distressed that I could not play with other children. However, Mum, Kimpo, Nanny and everyone did all they could to keep me happy and occupied and, later on, I was able to ride and swim and be normally active.

It was not long after my recovery that we all moved down to Cruden Farm because my parents were asked to lend Heathfield to the US Air Force at very short notice. We loved Cruden Farm but did feel a bit isolated because Dad had to go up to town for most of the week and Mum went backwards and forwards to look after him. We had blackout paint on the windows in case the Japanese bombers came, and one of my memories of that time is of them talking about a proposed dugout and air raid shelter. Digging was commenced but never finished.

We stayed at Cruden Farm until the end of the war and then went back to our new home, 39 Albany Road. My final memories of Heathfield's garden dates back to then. We used to sneak through the Albany Road fence and run around Heathfield's gardens. Heathfield wasn't sold and cut up until I was married so we used the Heathfield tennis court too.

Probably because of my leg, I didn't go to day school before I went to boarding school. I think Mum thought I should be kept a bit quieter than the others. While we were at Cruden Farm it might have been quite good for us to go to the nearby Langwarrin State School, but our parents obviously didn't think so as we had lessons at home with Kimpo. I was finally sent to Clyde in 1947. Helen had been school captain the year before, which eased my way into the school, but I now realise that a lot of my difficulties in starting boarding school were due to my naiveté in relation to other girls. I had really not had much contact with many other children before then. I really enjoyed my years at Clyde and participated in many school activities. I wasn't very good at sport, but it was a great thrill to be in the hockey team.

Dad died in the October of my fourth year in school, just before my final exams. It didn't help my results, but I passed. Before he died, Dad had made splendid plans for another family trip overseas which would have meant that Mum and I were in London with him for the Coronation. So Mum and I carried out Dad's plan and I still remember the way Mum set herself to learn Italian before we left and how she introduced me to Italy and my interests in art. Although I had spent time with Dad in the National Gallery, I think it was Mum who introduced me to the Renaissance.

The following year, I started at university in Melbourne and was the only one of the girls who finished a university degree – a BA and a degree in Social Work. Still, I don't think I am highly academic and certainly don't regard myself as the brains of the family. Helen did a year at university and fell in love ... and that was the end of university for her. Janet enrolled but didn't go to university after she went abroad with Mum.

Helen is the one who really followed in Mum's footsteps. She met Geoff when she was very young. Mum and Dad felt that she ought to travel and meet more people before she decided on such an early marriage. But that idea didn't work at all. She came back having gained much from her trip but now even more determined, and she was allowed to marry Geoffrey ... and Helen proved to be so right.

But over the years my memories of Mum and Dad as a couple are very happy. My father was very good at switching off from work and making time for his family. We had wonderful picnics at Cape Schanck and Point Leo and lovely riding outings. I remember going along behind the rest of the family in the pony cart which was, I suppose, because of my restricted movements in those days. Dad

Life with Elisabeth

loved his billy tea and chops cooked on big forks made from gum tree branches. I will never forget those days – Mum, Dad, Helen and Rupert on horseback as we went off to picnics in the Langwarrin Reserve near Cruden Farm. We all loved billy tea into which Dad had put a few gum leaves.

Most of my memories of Dad come from later days though. I often used to go into *The Herald* office or the art gallery with him. Really, he was responsible for securing the present site of the National Gallery and Arts Centre, and started my interest in it. After his death, when the new National Gallery was built, I was a gallery guide for a number of years.

But before then I remember the wonderful benches stacked with papers at his office at *The Herald* and I remember the funny old *Herald* car park in East Melbourne. Because Dad would have spoilt us silly, Mum would always have to be the restraining one. Often she had to be a bit strict with us – and I know why – because Dad was so very indulgent.

I remember going into the garage with Dad whispering to me: 'I've got some lovely glass which has just arrived. Don't tell your mother, she'll make me send it back.' I loved those little secret rendezvous with my father. My main memory of my mother is of her amazing energy and strength. I swear, and she doesn't believe me, I can remember her mowing all the lawns down at Cruden Farm with the big old motor mower. In the early days at Cruden Farm there was only tank water and Mum was always watering the garden with hoses that had very little water pressure. None of us were very helpful in the garden, I must admit.

I have memories of long hot summers and of being sent to bed and hearing happy noises of talking and laughter in the dining room down below. Altogether, it was a very happy time in my life.

We actually had a frightening day at Cape Schanck once when

Mum and I were caught by the tide down on the rocks. I remember being scared, but Mum was there so nothing really could have happened.

I certainly remember the day of the big bushfire in 1944. Janet and I were hastily taken away from the farm and driven to Cranbourne a few miles away where we had to sit on the policeman's front lawn. But before we left, I remember Alice the maid saying to Kimpo: 'Miss Kimpton, shouldn't we go in now and pack the silver?' When it was safe, we were taken off to see the fire still burning at the end of the road. The story was that Mum came racing back from town and got everyone onto the tennis court and kept them calm as the fire swept towards them. Then she raced upstairs and removed the cash box from under her bed containing the funds of the Clyde Old Girls Association – of which she was Secretary.

There were a number of people there and Mum was soon hosing down the walls of the house. In the end, the wind changed and the house was saved. I can still remember being very disappointed because I wasn't big enough to be there. It was Miss Kimpton who took us off to Cranbourne, which was the right and proper thing to do, but I was still very put out. That was the trouble with being the third in the family. I always wanted to do what Rupert and Helen were doing.

Then there was the time that Dad fell off his horse and broke his ankle. It apparently happened under a big tree by the dam after Helen and he had ridden down a track and under a low branch. I know that Helen felt dreadful because she thought that Dad had followed her and that it was her fault.

There has been a lot of talk about Rupert sleeping outside in a hut but I remember Rupert also having a bedroom inside the house. But, yes, he did sleep out there as well. I think Rupert was much naughtier than I – and he got away with it too. I really wasn't ever

Life with Elisabeth

naughty, I was a painfully good child. I don't remember ever getting the slipper. I think that when you have people – such as a governess – in between the children and the parents as we had, it seems in a way you're naturally good to accommodate the governess, knowing that she is the one who will be criticised by parents if the children are unruly. There is a sort of hierarchy in the home.

I remember Janet and I wanted shorts and Kimpo fought and fought for us until we had shorts made for us and we wore them proudly on Christmas Day. They were brown corduroy shorts and you'd think we'd been given the earth we were so excited by those shorts. Still they were such happy times, although I can remember being lonely down at Cruden Farm during the war when Helen and Rupert were away at boarding school.

I have such fond memories of our family holidays and I loved it when Rupert and Helen came home from school and there was lots of fun and then, of course, there were those wonderful holidays at Wantabadgery. Up there I used to love to be Rupert's little helper and I used to go round all his rabbit traps with him. Then he would go back to school and he'd leave me to clear the traps and kill the rabbits, and skin them and sell them, and then he'd get the money. I was such a mug, but then Rupert was sixteen and I was only twelve.

I must say though that I was very good at pulling the rabbits' necks and skinning them, then stretching their skins on a wire. I can remember riding on the back of Rupert's bike down at Cruden Farm as we set off to catch rabbits and set traps. Then Rupert had me scooping up cow manure in the barn paddock. There I was getting bags and scooping up manure in the paddock ... for him to sell!

JANET CALVERT-JONES

If NOT MY earliest memories certainly my best were those holidays at Wantabadgery – experiences like the joy of driving with Mum in the old Cadillac with its wartime charcoal gas producer are unforgettable. They were wonderful times because we were all together so much and they really were holidays.

Always with me when I think of Mum during my childhood are the memories of her love of flowers and flower arranging. I will always have this vision of Mum arranging flowers. And then there are the memories of Mum and Dad. See, I was just thirteen when Dad died, but I will never forget those happy times spent at Cruden Farm, and Albany Road with them. Sadly, I don't remember Heathfield.

During the war, we lived at Cruden Farm. That was home, and we had a flat at Wallace Avenue ... and we had classes with the children of other families with the famous Kimpo. At Cruden Farm,

Life with Elisabeth

my earliest memories were of going in the pony cart on family outings with Mum, Dad, Helen and Rupert riding their horses and Anne and myself in the pony cart with Nanny.

Really now I just remember I had a very happy childhood with such wonderful times at Cruden Farm. Always there seemed to be lots of family there – Mum's family and Dad's family, old aunts and uncles and friends. Mum and Dad were obviously very considerate and I suppose it was what was done in those days. Sunday lunch with the grandparents or the great aunts was, I still recall, rather a formal time – much more formal than you would experience in many families these days.

Of course, when I was little we were usually confined to the nursery when eating. We'd have breakfast all together and then we had lunch with Mum if she was home, or with nanny. Certainly, we never went into the dining room – except on Sunday, and then not until I was nine or ten. I can't remember Dad reading his newspapers in the morning. I suspect he had breakfast and read the papers in bed before going off early.

I remember Mum as being stricter than my father. Mum was pretty strict, but I know she was always fair. I don't remember being smacked or punished or anything like that, but I suppose we must have been disciplined at times. I know now that Mum must have had a jolly difficult domestic scene to administer because there were so many people involved. There was Nanny, and Kimpo the governess, and there was the cook and the two maids and Dad's chauffeur. Talk about 'Upstairs, Downstairs'! In those days, it must have been jolly hard, yet any strict action that I can remember would always be aimed at making us be 'nice' to other people . . . Being nice to Kimpo, nice to Nanny – not that we had any reason not to be.

We simply adored my Grandfather Greene. He was such great fun. He was the naughty one. He was the one who would take us to

Luna Park or down to Sandringham Beach on a Sunday in his car. He'd come for lunch and he'd sometimes take Anne and myself to buy an ice-cream on the beach to escape all the formal sitting around of Sunday afternoon in the drawing room. He really was fun, great, great fun, and he always had such a wonderful glint in his eye. I'm certain he was quite impossible for my grandmother to live with. We used to call him Pop and we all adored him. In comparison, Granny seemed rather prim and proper.

I remember Granny as being stately and dignified. We were always told her health was 'frail' and she used to have a 'fruity' burgundy each day for lunch prescribed by her doctor to build her up. Come to think of it, I really never saw Granny doing anything strenuous. But Mum will tell you that Granny was terrific and did a tremendous amount during her younger days. Of course, Granny came to live at Cruden Farm for the last years of her life and then Mum was amazing. Granny used to write to me when I was first married and lived in England, but I can't say that we were really close until, perhaps, when she came to live at Cruden Farm.

I think I admired Mum for that more than anything in those days. She took on her widowhood, and looking after Granny and the children – as well as everything else she did. She was amazing the way she quickly became so independent and lived such an independent life. It was a very different life when we were children. As far as Mum and Dad were concerned, we had a lot of freedom and space. We weren't all on top of each other, the way most families were. It was just the way we were. Dad was extremely busy anyway and they went away a lot and entertained a lot and had an enormous amount of outside commitments.

Certainly, Mum did put Dad first, but not to our detriment. As children we had to fit into their lives, I suppose. I think it's often too much the other way nowadays. I believe that many parents spend their whole lives running after their children. Anne and I used to play together all the time. I remember Rupert always slept out in his hut. but it wasn't until the other day that I heard he was 'banished' there! I thought it was just a wonderful escape for him. I think they genuinely built the hut as a lovely sort of adventure for him. I've never heard Rupert complain about it.

But I know that Mum did say that in a house full of women it would toughen Rupert up. I felt very close to my father because I was the one left behind when Anne went off to boarding school. For three years I was the only child at home full time, and I was unashamedly spoilt rotten by both my father and my mother. In fact, I suspect I was spoilt rotten. I was always helped by my father to win any card game, and I remember he used to come home every night and have a game with me out in the garden.

I was mad on ball games and every night we'd play catchy, cricket or some other game. In those last couple of years, I usually dined with him – except on formal occasions. I can still remember how I dreaded the moment when I was produced to meet all the guests. Dad would say: 'Now dear, it's time to kiss everyone goodnight,' and then I'd be dismissed and everyone would go to dinner. At home I always felt very close to both Mum and Dad and I'd be in and out of their bedroom and Dad's dressing-room. I would always be there and Dad had all his gadgets, scissors and pens and penknives. Mum and Dad were clearly devoted to one another. The only arguments I ever remember, and I don't suppose that they were real arguments – but to me they seemed so serious – were the breakfast discussions on where to go for our picnics.

My parents were both very determined people and I suppose they did argue about more important things than picnics – but I can't remember anything now. Certainly, I don't remember Dad or Mum raising their voices to anybody and I don't remember Mum ever being in any way temperamental. I've never seen her in a bad mood, never known her to get cross with anyone. Yet she can voice her displeasure, I suppose.

There are still people here at *The Herald* who remember my father and mother and they all say how he knew everyone by name. How did he do it? I don't know how he did it. He must have had enormous capacity for remembering names – just as I know my mother still has.

Anne and I were at boarding school when Dad died, and Kimpo was dispatched to break the news and take us home. It was terrible and I think Anne understood it better than I did. Although I was thirteen I was naive and it was all so unexpected. I think it hit Anne more because it was her last year at school.

Rupert was away at university in England, of course. We went back to school very quickly after the funeral, which we went to. It was an enormous funeral at the Toorak Presbyterian Church, and the family all went back to Albany Road and stood at the windows and watched the cortege go by. At that terrible time, Mr Harry Giddy was the great support and advisor to my mother.

Looking back now, I remember my younger days as a big lovely happy blur, always centred round Mum and Dad and the nice regular life she was determined we should have. We adored Nanny. Kimpo was rather strict. She was a disciplinarian and taught us two and two makes four. She took on a lot of Mum's home responsibility when she was out a lot at the Children's Hospital and doing all the other things she did.

We didn't notice a change immediately after Dad died. There were ten years between Dad dying and my marrying but, immediately after the funeral, Anne and I went back to school while Mum had those terrible days, weeks and months shouldering the responsibility and adjusting to it all.

Life with Elisabeth

Helen was the clever one and was dux of the school twice. I was dux only because I did a second year's matric. I loved school. I was such a big fish in a small pool. I loved sport, and I believe I took after Mum in things like baseball. I loved knowing Mum had done it all before too. I wanted to emulate her because her name was on all the honour boards ... best all round sport and on the baseball team, the hockey and the tennis. We were all tree climbers in those days at Clyde ... just like Mum.

I left school at the end of 1956. Mum took me to England the following year via Honolulu and America. She was just the greatest fun to be with. She really went out of her way to make it interesting for me. We went to San Francisco and on the day we landed there was an awful earthquake. Then we went to New York where she had wonderful contacts. We saw *My Fair Lady* and then went on to London where she wanted me to be formally presented at court with her in tow. Oh dear! Specifically we were there to see my beloved godmother, Aunt Marie, and godfather, Uncle Johnnie Durnford.

I met John, my future husband, the first day I arrived in England. My aunt had lent their flat to his parents for a cocktail party and they were wonderfully hospitable to me while I was there. I had a terrific time in England but not a mad social time. Mum took me to France to better my French at a French school for English debs. Ghastly! Although through that time we met a nice French family who did everything to make me feel welcome. I adored Paris.

Really, Mum has had a fascinating life. I think she's probably developed her brain even more since Dad died. She's really become her own person now. She was very much the wife and mother and Dad's support and hostess rather than herself ... I think I can still remember dinner parties where Dad did most of the talking rather than Mum. I think she really believed that the man of the house was the boss.

To me, what my mother has done with her life has been so wonderful. She's always been so warmly enthusiastic about things and so profoundly interested. She really listens if someone tells her something is a good cause and, if she is interested, she really gets behind it. She loves to drive, although we've got her to use a driver now to take her up and down to Melbourne when she is coming home late. If she can, she will drive to town for a luncheon, drive the fifty kilometres back to Cruden Farm, and then drive back again for an engagement at night.

My mother is a very strong person. She's totally fearless. She's had a very public life and done a lot for the community. Everyone asks after her wherever you go. She's a great people person. When *The Herald* had to cease publication as an evening broadsheet newspaper, Rupert was dreading having to tell her. It was so sad for her but she knew all along: 'We'll just put it behind us and look forward to the new round-the-clock tabloid *Herald Sun*.'

My mother is totally unextravagant, particularly when it comes to herself, but she is so unbelievably generous. The Murdoch charitable trust really does give her so much pleasure. Rupert tells me my office at *The Herald* was Dad's office but I think someone else has that now. Still I always remember coming to visit Dad in one of these offices. Mum comes to visit me now but she never stays long. Her favourite portrait of Dad is on the wall.

She certainly gave us a happy, happy home. She has always been the centre of the family, although she dislikes the term, 'The Matriarch'. The thing I remember Mum and Dad being so strong about was that there was never to be any publicity at all about our family. Well, we've tried to keep it that way. You see, Mum's so conscientious. She has always had this desire to serve the less fortunate. It's really second nature to her. She must help lame dogs with her time if not her money. People write to her – and she's always got time for people. It must be exhausting.

One of her great loves is Cruden Farm, of course. It was Dad's wedding gift to her. She still gets a kick out of people saying how lovely Cruden Farm is, and, of course, she has made her garden quite outstanding.

ACKNOWLEDGEMENTS

I am indebted to Dame Elisabeth Murdoch for the many entries made in her crowded little red diaries over the past four years which indicated the time she could spare me to relate the story of her two busy lives.

The Murdoch children – Helen, Rupert, Anne and Janet – also found the time to provide chapters and suggestions for this book.

Letters, family records and photographs were made available by Dame Elisabeth and members of her family.

Dame Elisabeth's kinsman, Captain Nevill de Rouen Forth, has in his possession family papers and documents going back hundreds of years and these have been used in his book, *The Fighting Colonel of the Camel Corps*, as well as Marion Ward's books, *Forth* and *The Du Barry Inheritance*. These three books, as well as papers in the Murdoch family files, have been used in research for early chapters of this book.

Acknowledgements

A valuable guide to Sir Keith Murdoch's career and marriage to Elisabeth Greene has been provided by *In Search of Keith Murdoch*, written by my old friend and colleague, Desmond Zwar.

Many books have now been written about Sir Keith and his famous son, but few make more than passing reference to Elisabeth and the upbringing of her family. However, *Rupert Murdoch – A Paper Prince*, by the late George Munster, was a valuable reference for the earlier days.

Frank Shaw, a former News Ltd Group General Manager and Director, who is now engaged in the monumental task of writing the history of the firm, was kind enough to let me see his informative chapter on the Murdoch Family – and the work he had completed on the Murdoch family tree.

Dr Howard Williams, a former Executive Chairman of the Royal Children's Hospital's Research Foundation, who for many years worked closely with Dame Elisabeth at the hospital and wrote *From Charity to Teaching Hospital*, gave me much valuable information about Dame Elisabeth's hospital years and allowed me to sit in on a long interview with Dame Elisabeth for a new book he is writing.

Then there was the excellent La Trobe Library in Melbourne, the well-organised libraries of *The Herald Sun* and *The Australian* in Melbourne, all of which had extensive files on members of the Murdoch family.

Photographs of Cruden Farm and more public moments in Dame Elisabeth's life were provided by *New Idea* and *The Australian Women's Weekly*. Jutta Malnic of Sydney provided some of the stunning colour photographs she took at Cruden Farm, while Ian Cook of the Leader Newspaper Group spent many hours copying old – in some cases one-hundred-year-old – photographs so they could be reproduced. To Dame Elisabeth's grandson, Martin Kantor, go our thanks for the front cover photograph.

I also thank the many friends and admirers of Elisabeth Murdoch who gave me information about the many unsung activities of this remarkable woman.

Jack Kennedy, Dame Elisabeth's friend and long-time financial advisor, provided me with many documents and much sound advice as he read the manuscript.

I will long remember the interview with Dame Elisabeth and her sister, Mrs Sylvia Ritchie, at Delatite, which provided a deep insight into the upbringing of the Greene girls at Pemberley.

In researching the early days of Dame Elisabeth's kinsmen in Victoria and Tasmania, extensive use was made of the Melbourne Club's excellent reference library.

The National Library of Australia, which owns the copyright, kindly allowed the reproduction of a charming passage from Joan Lindsay's book, *Time Without Clocks*.

My sincere thanks also go to Michael Morrison, Cruden Farm's master gardener, who broadened my knowledge of the role played by Dame Elisabeth in creating one of Australia's finest gardens and set me straight on the names of the plants, shrubs and trees that flourish there.

I wish to thank my brother-in-law, historian Michael Cannon, for his expert guidance.

Our journalist daughter, Suzanne, transcribed many taped interviews and did valuable research.

Finally, without the tireless support of my wife, Dina, who corrected proofs and kept me on track, this book would not have been possible.

JOHN MONKS

INDEX

Advertiser 194
Advisory Council for Children with Impaired Hearing 237
Age 78, 79
Albany Road 155, 186–7, 193
Alexandra Club 45, 235
Anderson, Charlotte 225
Anderson, Colin 272
Andrew, Carl 238
Annear, Harold Desbrowe 101, 107–8, 116
Argus 78, 89
Australian Garden History Society 276
Australian 228–9

Baillieu family 10, 104, 113, 115, 160
Bancks, Jimmy 100
Beaverbrook, Lord 1, 174, 175, 182
Bitcon, Barney 205
Blackwood, Margaret 258
Blanch, John 246, 247
Bohemian Club 21, 25–6
Bolte, Sir Henry 209, 211, 218, 229, 233, 234
Booker, Patricia 199
Boonoke 253
Booromba 176–7, 188, 193
Bowles, Leslie 272
Brass, Douglas 194, 285
Brass, Joan 194
Bray, Theodore 151
Bredbo 143

Brennan, Archie 246, 247
Brett, General George (US) 151
Brockhoff, Sir Jack 263
Brown, Reverend George 75
Brown, Mary Smith (nee Shepherd) 75

Calvert-Jones, James 237
Calvert-Jones, Janet (nee Murdoch) 39, 100, 127, 148, 212–14, 222, 237; life with Elisabeth 324–31
Calvert-Jones, John 213–14, 222
Camberwell Grammar School 78
Caro, George 123
Cavan 254
Chair of Landscape Architecture (Melb. Uni.) 254–6
Chance, Peter 278
Chauvel family 55
Cheek, Dr Donald 225
Chirnside, Elsa (nee Andrews) 63
Churchill, Sir Winston 65, 81, 103–4
Clark, Manning 167
Clarke, Ernestine (nee Govett) 38–9
Climie, Reverend James 77
Cliveden 87, 95
Clyde 43–58 *passim*, 61, 149, 162

Coates, Lady 241
Cocks, Annie 124
Colebatch, Dr John 224–5
Collins, Vice-Admiral Sir John 63
Collins, Vernon 204–5, 215
Como 232–3
Companion of the Order of Australia 284
Coronation 179, 180, 196, 197–8
Courier Mail 95, 189
Cruden Farm 35, 39, 74–5, 94, 97, 100, 113, 122, 123, 125, 126, 138–9, 143–5, 147–8, 152, 159–60, 194–5, 255, 280–1, 291–2; alterations 101, 107–9, 111; fire 161–4; garden 115–17, 179, 267–78, 296
Cruden Investments 74, 170, 177–8, 194

Daily Express (UK) 175, 198
Danks, Dr David 223, 224, 263–5
Darling, Sir James 43–4
Davenport, Mrs Wally 63
Davey's Bay Yacht Club 148
DBE Royal Investiture 218–19
de Crespigny, Geoff 60
de Neeve, Anton 169

335

de Pury, Ted 134
Delacombe, Lady 244, 245, 246, 278
Delacombe, Sir Rohan 278
Delatite 26–7, 268
Dennis, Miss (governess) 34–5, 42
Derham, David 257
Derham, Frances 237
Doctor of Laws honorary degree 257–61
Downing, Dick 232
Duell, Mr (gardener) 116, 269
Dumbrell, Merrill 248
Durnford, Vice-Admiral John 134, 197, 239–40
Durnford, Marie (nee Greene) 16, 20–1, 26, 32, 33, 37, 44, 45, 62–4, 91–2, 93, 133–4, 197–8, 239–40, 222, 280
Dwaroon 11, 14
Dyson, Will 100

Elisabeth Murdoch Californian Garden 278
Elisabeth Murdoch Sculpture Foundation 239, 284
Elizabeth II, Queen 216–17, 218

Fairbairn, Mrs Fred 87
Fairfax family 211–12
Feint, Mr (RCH manager) 217
Felton Bequest 140–1
Ferguson, Donald 205
Fink, Theodore 86–7, 123
Fisher, Andrew 80
Fisher, Patricia 245
Fitts, Sir Clive 229
Fletcher, Marion 245
Fogarty, Mrs (RCH) 126–7
Forell, Annetine 240
Forth forebears 1–17
Forth, Grannie (nee Anne Ware) 11, 16, 17, 27, 40, 62, 104, 133, 172
Forth, Marie (Bairnie) de Lancey see Greene, Bairnie
Fraser, Malcolm 119, 241–2
Fraser, Neville 119, 120
Fraser, Una 119, 251–2
Free Kindergarten 111
Friends of the Gallery Art Library 241

Geelong Grammar School 43, 47, 58, 149, 157, 160, 167
Giddy, Harry 187, 188, 191, 193–4
Glue, Nancy 240
Good Friday Appeal 203–4, 206
governor-generalship 241–3
Graham, Mr and Mrs Jim 238
Greene, Bairnie (Marie de Lancey, nee Forth) 3, 11, 13, 14, 15, 16–17, 18, 22–45 passim, 91, 96, 99, 137, 156, 169–70, 214–15, 232, 237, 239
Greene, Ethel 16
Greene, Fanny (nee Govett) 15
Greene, Marie see Durnford, Marie
Greene, Olive 16
Greene, Rupert (Pop) 3, 14–38 passim, 100, 111, 112, 119, 167, 169–70
Greene, Sylvia see Ritchie, Sylvia
Greene, William 15
Greenhalf, Vi 204
Grimwade, Sir Andrew 232
Grimwade, Russell 117, 163, 164
Grounds, Roy 230, 247
Gullett, Henry 67, 100, 139
Gullett, Penny 67, 68, 97, 100, 139

Hamer, April 245, 247
Hamilton, General Sir Ian 81–3, 84
Handbury, Geoffrey 155–7
Handbury, Helen (nee Murdoch) 39, 72, 100–1, 102, 111, 114, 122, 129–30, 131, 132–3, 136, 147, 149, 155–7, 179; life with Elisabeth 301–9
Handbury, Matt 292
Harris, Max 195–6
Harrison, William 238
Hay, Bobbie 52
Heathfield 113–15, 117, 120, 130, 136, 137, 151, 152, 154–5, 208
Henderson, Miss (teacher) 54
Herald and Weekly Times 86–7, 100, 109, 110, 119, 123–4, 138, 170, 184, 237, 254
Herald 65, 66, 86, 87, 110, 118, 119, 122, 123–4, 127, 138, 172, 175–6, 177, 183, 184, 187, 194, 254
Higgins, Mrs (RCH) 126–7
Home Beautiful 116
Howson, Peter 233
Hughes, Billy 80, 85, 139–40

John, Nancy 237
Johns, Peter 205
Kantor, Anne (nee Murdoch) 39, 100, 130–1, 132, 142, 148–9, 152, 200; life with Elisabeth 317–23
Kantor, Milan 200
Keith and Elisabeth

Index

Murdoch Travelling Scholarship (art) 231
Kennedy, Jack 170, 187–8, 193, 194
Kimpton, Joan (Kimpo) 134–5, 136, 147, 149, 152–3, 158, 163
King, Miss (Kingo) 35
King, Whitney 237
Kline, Mr (gardener) 115, 129–30
Klose, Simon 285
Koort-Koort-Nong 11

Lady Northcote Kindergarten 62
Lambert, Eduard 124
Lambert, George 94–5
Langley, Miss (headmistress) 44–5, 46
Langwarrin Reserve 233, 278
Latham, Ella (Lady) 118, 126, 203, 204–5, 209, 210, 212, 223
Latham, Sir John 118, 209
Leslie, Jim 262–3
Lindsay, Daryl 101, 108, 129, 144, 146, 163, 237–8
Lindsay, Joan (Lady) 53, 101, 129, 145, 146
Lindsay, Lionel 146
Lindsay, Norman 145

Macdonald, Claude 143
Macdonald, Ethel 104–5
Macdonald, Hamish 142
Macdonald, Nancy (nee Syme) 142–3
Macfarlan, Peggy 52
Mackinnon, Dame Patricia (Patsy) 205–6, 226, 263
Manifold, Peter 59
Manion, Professor Margaret 232
Maroochydore 94, 95
Maud Gibson Garden 233, 234–5
McCarthy, Michael 255

McCaughey, Patrick 231–2
McClelland Gallery 237–9, 241, 284–5
McClelland, Annie 237
McClelland, Dr Margaret 205
Melba, Dame Nellie 66, 90, 93, 106
Melbourne 61, 76–7, 89, 112
Melbourne Club 21, 26, 90
Menzies, Dame Pattie 131
Menzies, Sir Robert 131, 138
Miller, Keith 156
Mills, Peggy 88
Mirror (Sydney) 212
Morrison, David 20–1
Morrison, Michael 268, 272, 273, 274, 277, 278, 296
Morrison, Dr Reginald 20, 34, 44
Murdoch Courtyard (NGV) 230–1
Murdoch Institute for Research into Birth Defects 224–5, 263–6
Murdoch Magazines 292
Murdoch, Alan 184
Murdoch, Anna (nee Torv) 229, 277, 298, 299
Murdoch, Anne *see* Kantor, Anne
Murdoch, Annie Brown (nee Shepherd) 75–7
Murdoch, Elisabeth (granddaughter) *see* Pianim, Elisabeth
Murdoch, Frank 121, 191
Murdoch, Helen *see* Handbury, Helen
Murdoch, Helen (sister-in-law) 149, 318
Murdoch, Ivon 184
Murdoch, Janet *see* Calvert-Jones, Janet

Murdoch, Keith 86, 109, 138; *Age* 78–80; childhood 77–9; courtship 65–73; funeral 182–5; Gallipoli letter 31, 32, 81–4; *Herald* 65, 86–7, 175–6, 177; ill health 119–20, 122–3, 166, 167–8, 176–80; knighthood 117–18; National Gallery 161, 163; newsprint industry 125–6, 166; properties 142, 143, 176–7; World War 2 149–51, 159, 165–6
Murdoch, Patricia 199, 229
Murdoch, Reverend Patrick 1, 75, 76–7, 78, 84–5, 92, 93
Murdoch, Prudence 199
Murdoch, Rupert 24, 39, 61, 77, 112, 118, 127, 175, 182, 184, 249–50, 253, 254, 279–80, 298–9; *Australian* 228–9; childhood 122, 129–30, 131, 132–3, 135, 136, 147, 149, 157, 160–1, 167; life with Elisabeth 310–16; media empire 124, 138, 166–7, 170, 172, 178, 185–6, 188, 191–4, 198–9, 202, 211–12, 251, 280–1, 288–91, 293–4; Oxford 170–81 *passim*, 189, 198
Murdoch, Sir Walter 76
Murray, Sir Hubert 44, 45
Murray-Smith, Stephen 167
Myer, Baillieu 232, 245, 248

National Gallery of Victoria 128, 140, 161, 163, 238, 228–35

337

New Idea 175
News Corporation 74
News Limited 194, 252
News of the World
  (UK) 251
News (Adelaide) 188, 196,
  198–9, 202
Noah's Ark Toy
  Library 240
Noall, Mrs (teacher) 50
Northcliffe, Lord 82, 85–6

Osborn-Fairbairn,
  Mrs 156

Papal audience 171–2,
  173–4
Parr, Lenton 232, 239, 248
Pemberley 17, 19–20,
  24–5, 27, 28, 44, 57, 93,
  137, 239
Pentecost, Mr
  (chauffeur) 171, 185–6
Pianim, Elisabeth (nee
  Murdoch) 297–300
Pianim, Elkin 297–9
Pillars, Winifred 45, 50

Queensland
  Newspapers 138, 191–4

Ramsay family 52
Ramson, Belinda 247
Rankin, Peter 245, 248
Riddoch, John 51, 71–2,
  91
Ritchie, Robert 63, 91
Ritchie, Sylvia (nee
  Greene) 16, 20–1, 24,
  26–7, 30, 32, 33, 37, 40,
  44, 63, 68, 72, 91, 198,
  268
Rivett, Rohan 172, 198
Robbie (gardener) 28
Robertson, Professor 245

Royal Children's
  Hospital 56, 111–12,
  122, 128, 155, 168–9, 203;
  man. cmtee 22, 118–19,
  126–7, 136, 152, 153, 259;
  President 149, 204–19,
  225–7; rebuilding 168–9,
  202, 208–11, 212,
  215–16; research 223–5,
  227
Royal Society for
  Prevention of Cruelty to
  Children 111
Russell, Sarah (Nanny
  Murdoch) 101, 107, 111,
  114–15, 131, 132, 133,
  135, 160, 162

Sechiari, Lucy 169
Seddon, Dick 232
Seddon, George 254–5,
  267
Shepherd, James 75
Simmons, Bob 115
Smith, Geoffrey 216
Smith, Victoria Alexandra
  (Queenie) 299–300
Southdown Press 175, 176,
  188, 193, 199
SPELD 240
Spowers, Mrs Allan 66,
  89–90
St Catherine's 41, 42–3,
  45–6, 52, 149
St Ives 55
Staley, Tony 241–2
Stephens, Douglas 223,
  225
Stevenson, Sir Arthur 210,
  212
Stevenson, Dame
  Hilda 225
Stonnington 63
Sun (UK) 251

Sun News Pictorial 119,
  124
Sun (Sydney) 80
Sunday Times (WA) 199
Syme, David 78

Table Talk 66, 88
Taralye 237
Toorak 18–19, 20, 28, 57
Truth 176
Tucker, Dorothea 50, 53,
  90

Uncle Bob's Club 204
United Cable Service 85

Victorian Tapestry
  Workshop 244–50

Walker, Sue 244, 248
Walling, Edna 116, 268,
  269–71, 273
Walsh Street 87–8, 90,
  96–7, 99, 111, 112, 113,
  114
Walsh, Matron Hilda 205
Wantabadgery 142, 152,
  159, 188, 193
Ware forebears 10–14
Watts, Peter 276–7
Wentcher, Tina 220–1,
  237
Westbrook, Eric 245
Whitehead, June 52
Whiting, Ruth 89–90, 95,
  101
Whitlam, Gough 230
Williams, Dr Howard 207,
  223–4
Williams, Sir John 151,
  252
Windeyer, Phil 54
Winter, Carmen 207
Woomargama 38–40
Wren, John 95–6

Yencken, David 255

Rev. Patrick John Murdoch **m** Anne Brown Shepherd
(eldest of 14, youngest being Walter Logie
Forbes: Foundation Professor of English,
University of Western Australia)

Keith Arthur Murd...

Helen Murdoch **m** Geoffrey Norman Handbury

Patricia Booker **m** Rupert Murdoch **m** Anna M...

- Matthew Keith Handbury **m** Fiona Mary Ferguson Campbell
  - Campbell Keith
  - Jessie Helen

- Paul Richmond Handbury **m** Robyn Irwin

- Patrick Geoffrey Handbury **m** Helen Patricia Godfrey
  - Robert James
  - Deborah Patricia
  - Christina Claire

- Judith Handbury **m** Rowland Woolcock Paterson
  - Sarah Elisabeth
  - Helen Fleur